Entrepreneur® MAGAZINE'S

startup

Start Your Own

RESTAURANT AND FIVE OTHER FOOD BUSINESSES

Your Step-by-Step Guide to Success

Jacquelyn Lynn

EP
Entrepreneur. Press

▲

Editorial Director: Jere L. Calmes
Cover Design: Beth Hansen-Winter
Production: Eliot House Productions

This publication is designed to provide accurate and authoritative information in regard to the subject matter covered. It is sold with the understanding that the publisher is not engaged in rendering legal, accounting, or other professional services. If legal advice or other expert assistance is required, the services of a competent professional person should be sought.

Library of Congress Cataloging-in-Publication Data

Lynn, Jacquelyn.

    Entrepreneur magazine's restaurant and five other food businesses / [Jacquelyn Lynn].

      p. cm. —(Start-up series)

    Includes index.

    ISBN 1-891984-26-8

    I. Title: Restaurant and five other businesses. II. Entrepreneur (Santa Monica, Calif.) III. Title. IV. Series.

2001023650

Printed in Canada

10 09 08 07 06 05 04   10 9 8 7

Contents

▲

Preface

Food is a basic need. Though tastes and trends will change, technology will advance, and demographics will shift, people will always need to eat.

Now that doesn't mean that starting and running a profitable food-service business will be a proverbial piece of cake.

Quite the contrary: This will probably be the hardest work you've ever done. But it has the potential to be tremendously rewarding, both financially and emotionally—and it can be lots of fun.

There are many ways you can enter the food-service industry, from buying a small coffee cart to building a high-end restaurant from the ground up. In this book, we examine six basic food-service businesses: a generic restaurant, a pizzeria, a sandwich shop/delicatessen, a coffeehouse, a bakery, and a catering business. It's important to remember that these are not mutually exclusive businesses; they can be customized and combined to create the specific business you have in mind.

Perhaps you know exactly what type of food-service business you want to start, or perhaps you haven't made a final decision yet; either way, it's a good idea to read all the chapters in this book—even those that pertain to businesses you think you aren't interested in. If you read with an open mind, you may get ideas from one type of operation that you can apply to another.

This book will give you the basic information you need to start a food-service business. You'll learn how to develop a business plan; what the day-to-day operation is like; how to set up your kitchen and dining area; how to buy and maintain equipment and inventory; how to deal with administrative, financial, personnel and regulatory issues; and how to market your venture.

Because the best information about business comes from the people who are already in the trenches, we interviewed successful food-service business owners who were happy to share their stories. Their experience spans all types of food-service operations, and several of them are illustrating in practice that you can blend more than one type of operation in a successful business. Throughout the book, you'll read about what works—and doesn't work—for these folks, and how you can use their techniques in your own business.

You'll also learn what the food-service business is *really* like. The hours can be flexible, but they're usually long. The profit margins are good, but only if you're paying attention to detail. The market is tremendous, but you'll have a substantial amount of competition, which means you need a plan to set yourself apart. The opportunity to express yourself creatively is virtually limitless, but sometimes you have to do what the market demands—even if it's not your preference.

Like anything else, there's no magic formula, no quick path to success. Thriving in the food-service business takes hard work, dedication and commitment. But it can be well worth the investment of your time, energy and resources. After all, everybody's got to eat—including you.

1

Introduction

As increasing numbers of consumers want to either dine out or take prepared food home, the number of food-service operations has skyrocketed from 155,000 about 25 years ago to nearly 800,000 today. But there's still room in the market for your food-service business.

▲

Shifting demographics and changing lifestyles are driving the surge in food-service businesses. Busy consumers don't have the time or inclination to cook. They want the flavor of fresh bread without the hassle of baking. They want tasty, nutritious meals without dishes to wash. In fact, the rise in popularity of to-go operations underscores some clear trends in the food-service industry. More and more singles, working parents, and elderly are demanding greater convenience in buying their meals and are turning to operations that provide that convenience.

Though the future looks bright for the food-service industry overall, there are no guarantees in this business. Even the most successful operators will tell you this isn't a "get rich quick" industry. It's more like a "work hard and make a living" industry.

A hard reality is that many restaurants fail during their first year in business, frequently due to a lack of planning. Does this mean your food-service business must be an extremely complex operation? Not at all—in fact, the more streamlined you can make it, the better your chances for success. Robert O., owner of a casual seafood restaurant in Nags Head, North Carolina, observes, "The restaurant business is a simple business that people make complicated." His formula for success is quality food, good service, and great people—an approach that's worked for him for nearly two decades.

Who Are the Diners?

Stat Fact
Almost 50 billion meals are eaten in restaurants and school and work cafeterias each year.

No single food-service operation has universal appeal. This is a fact that many newer entrepreneurs have trouble accepting, but the reality is that you will never capture 100 percent of the market. When you try to please everyone, you end up pleasing no one. So focus on the 5 or 10 percent of the market that you can get, and forget about the rest.

With that said, who is eating at restaurants? Let's take a look at the main market categories of food-service business customers:

Generation X

Generation X is a label applied to young adults who were born between 1965 and 1977. While members of this group have lower incomes than the typical baby boomer, they definitely have a desire to eat out. In fact, young adults eat a greater percentage of their dinners out than any other age group. They enjoy Mexican food, pizza, hamburgers, Asian food, and sandwiches. Generation X consumers appear to prefer casual, convenient establishments to formal, upscale restaurants. They are also concerned with value, and they favor quick-service restaurants and midscale operations that offer all-you-can-eat salad and food bars. To appeal to this age group, offer a comfortable atmosphere that focuses on value and ambience.

Baby Boomers

Born between the years of 1946 and 1964, baby boomers make up the largest segment of the U.S. population. Prominent in this generation are affluent professionals who can afford to visit upscale restaurants and spend money freely. During the 1980s, they were the main customer group for upscale, trendy restaurants that offered expensive meals. A decade ago, value was not the main goal for baby boomers who dined out, but as they have children and expand their families, value may become a greater concern. In the 1990s, many baby boomer families included two incomes and children. By 1995, 80 percent of baby boomers had children living with them. To appeal to this market, restaurants may want to offer a family-friendly atmosphere or, as a different option, an upscale, formal atmosphere where boomers can visit or entertain without the children.

Stat Fact

During a recent year, households with annual incomes of $90,000 or more allocated just over 11 percent of their total expenditures on food and 51 percent of that on food away from home, according to the U.S. Department of Labor's Bureau of Labor Statistics.

Behind the Angel-Hair Curtain

The typical American food-service business owner began his or her career in an entry-level position such as a busperson, dishwasher, or cook; works long hours; is energetic and entrepreneurial; and is usually more involved in charitable, civic, and political activities than the average American.

Although these traits are characteristic of restaurateurs, they are not required attributes. For example, some food-service business owners have entered their fields without any previous experience. They hire employees who have the experience they lack and who can help guide their operation to success. There is, however, no substitute for energy and a desire to succeed. Successful restaurateurs know they've chosen an industry where hard work is the norm, and they're willing to do what it takes to turn their dreams into reality.

▲

Beware!

The three primary reasons food-service businesses fail are:

- undercapitalization
- poor inventory control
- poor payroll management

Empty Nesters

This group consists of people in the age range between baby boomers and seniors (people in their early 50s to about age 64). They typically have grown children who no longer live at home, and their ranks will continue to increase as the baby boomers grow older and their children leave home. With the most discretionary income and the highest per-capita income of all the generations, this group typically visits upscale restaurants. They are less concerned with value and are more focused on excellent service and outstanding food. Appeal to this group with elegant surroundings and a sophisticated ambience.

Seniors

The senior market covers the large age group of 65 and older. It's a market that will continue to grow in both numbers and economic diversity as empty nesters and baby boomers age. Generally, the majority of seniors are on fixed incomes and may not be able to afford upscale restaurants often, and they tend to visit family-style restaurants that offer good service and reasonable prices. "Younger" seniors are likely to be more active and have more disposable income than "older" seniors, whose health may be declining. Seniors typically appreciate restaurants that offer early-bird specials and senior menus with lower prices and smaller portions, since their appetites are less hearty than those of younger people.

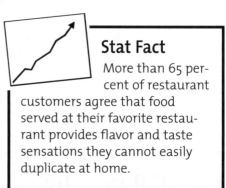

Stat Fact

More than 65 percent of restaurant customers agree that food served at their favorite restaurant provides flavor and taste sensations they cannot easily duplicate at home.

Industry Trends

In the 1980s—the decade of greed—new restaurants were typically upscale establishments that centered on unique and creative dishes by famous chefs. Young, professional baby boomers, often on liberal expense accounts, supported these concepts. The 1990s brought a trend to the restaurant industry that is expected to continue well into the new century. Generation Xers and family-minded baby boomers are concentrating on stretching their dollars, and the trend is value-oriented.

Some other industry trends include:

- *Carts and kiosks.* Eating establishments no longer require customers to come to them; in many cases, the restaurant goes to the customer in the form of a cart or kiosk. Many limited-service mobile facilities are operating at locations that attract large numbers of people. Malls, universities, airports, sports stadiums, and arenas now allow customers to choose from a variety of restaurants operating from kiosks on their premises. These restaurants typically offer very limited menus but attract customers with their recognizable names.

- *Dual-branded operations.* A relatively new but popular trend is the dual-branded restaurant, where two well-known restaurants, typically quick-service operations, combine their menus in one location to offer customers a wider selection of items.

- *Nutrition-conscious customers.* The importance consumers place on nutrition appears to be on the decline. This trend can be largely attributed to the value-minded Generation X market group, whose members tend to frequent quick-service establishments, which are not known for their nutritious fare.

- *Popular menu items.* Barbecued foods and appetizers are two of the most popular menu items. Barbecue appears to satisfy customers seeking spicy foods and regional cuisines. Appetizer orders are also growing, a trend led by customers who omit entrees and choose appetizers instead.

- *Catering to children.* Catering to families is a recurring trend for restaurants. Because many baby boomers have children still living at home, the majority of their dining-out experiences are family-oriented. Restaurants wanting to reach this market are offering children's menus and children's value meals with child-size portions. Some even offer child-friendly environments with booster seats, toys, balloons, crayons, menus featuring games on them, and free table-side entertainment in the form of magicians and clowns.

> Catering to families is a recurring trend for restaurants.

Menu Trends

As you put together a plan for your food-service business, be aware of some of the trends in terms of menu content and design: these factors could—and, in fact, should—influence the type of food-service business you open.

Restaurant operators report that items gaining popularity include vegetarian items, tortillas, locally grown produce, organic items, fusion dishes (combining two or more ethnic cuisines in one dish or on one plate), and microbrewed/local beers. Pita dishes and wraps continue to be in high demand, particularly as an easy-to-consume alternative to sandwiches. You'll also see a strong demand for bagels, espresso/specialty coffees, and "real meals," which are typically an entree with a side order. Consumers are also eating more chicken, seafood, and beef entrees than they have in recent years. At the same time, they expect to see meatless alternatives on the menu.

Bright Idea

To satisfy diners in a hurry, consider offering wraps, a handheld item consisting of a tortilla or flatbread filled with a mix of marinated meats, seasoned rice, baked vegetables, and sauces.

Customers also are demanding "comfort food"—the dishes that take them back to their childhoods, when mothers baked from scratch, and meat and potatoes were at the center of each plate. Creative chefs are looking for ways to redefine and reinvigorate comfort-food favorites. Instead of the traditional shepherd's pie, for example, you might see one made with mushrooms, spinach, carrots, and lobster sauce.

Menus are also showing a number of ethnic dishes and spice-infused offerings. It's not surprising to find Thai, Vietnamese, Creole, Tuscan, and even classic French cuisines on the same menu, and even the same plate.

Stat Fact

Low-fat cooking methods such as grilling are gaining popularity, with more than seven out of ten menus including grilled entrees.

Though menu variety has increased over the years, menus themselves are growing shorter. Busy consumers don't want to read a lengthy menu before dinner; dining out is a recreational activity, and they're in the restaurant to relax. Keep your number of items in check and menu descriptions simple and straightforward, providing customers with a variety of choices in a concise format.

Your menu should also indicate what dishes can be prepared to meet special dietary requirements. Items low in fat, sodium, and cholesterol should be marked as such.

Understanding Take-Out Customers

Research conducted by the National Restaurant Association is a strong indicator of the popularity of off-premises consumption of restaurant food. Of respondents to a National Restaurant Association survey, 21 percent who use off-premises restaurant service purchase one or more such meals a day; 26 percent purchase off-premises meals every other day; 22 percent purchase meals for off-premises consumption about twice a week; and 31 percent make purchases for off-premises consumption less than once a week.

Fast-food restaurants capture the largest share of off-premises dining occasions (52 percent) and dollars (41 percent). Carryout restaurants capture 10 percent of off-premises dining patronage and 15 percent of sales. Full-service restaurants account for six percent of off-premises dining patronage and 11 percent of sales.

What motivates consumers to buy prepared food to consume elsewhere? They're in a hurry and want easy access, fast service, and reasonable prices. Another reason is that they're just too tired to shop for and prepare food themselves.

Stat Fact
During any given month, 70 percent of U.S. households make at least one carryout purchase; 33 percent order meals to be delivered; and 25 percent make both carry-out and delivery purchases, according to a National Restaurant Association survey.

Often, consumers looking for a special treat are inclined to buy take-out food, particularly ice cream, snacks, and gourmet coffees. Another strong motivator of take-out customers is the desire to eat "something that is good for me." These customers tend to patronize full-service restaurants, grocery stores and cafeterias/buffets for tasty, fresh foods.

Where Is the Competition?

Competition in the food-service industry is widespread, varied, and significant. When you open a restaurant, you'll be competing not only with other similarly themed restaurants, but every restaurant in the area you serve. In addition, your customers themselves are a form of competition, because they can make their own meals at home if they choose. Let's take a look at the primary categories of competition:

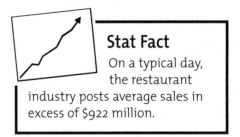

Stat Fact
On a typical day, the restaurant industry posts average sales in excess of $922 million.

Chains

Chain restaurants may be the biggest threat to independent operators. Chains are growing as private companies and franchises take over a greater portion of the market. With well-known names and large advertising budgets, chains enjoy significant consumer recognition.

What these restaurants do not offer is the personalized attention that many small, independent operations provide—so this is where independent restaurants have an advantage. Many restaurateurs become acquainted with their regular customers and build relationships with them. This is not to say that chains do not offer personalized service—indeed, many of them excel in this area—but there is a difference when customers know they are dealing directly with the owner.

Independent restaurants have several other competitive advantages over chains. Independently owned fine-dining restaurants are usually willing to take reservations, while chains often do not. Independents may also offer live music, experienced chefs (rather than just basic cooks), and creative foods and beverages. While chains have the advantage of a well-known name, many independents offer the atmosphere customers prefer.

> ### Bright Idea
>
> Combine two or more types of food-service businesses for maximum profitability. For example, caterer Maxine T.'s Salt Lake City operation is a combination upscale catering business and delicatessen. The businesses complement each other; deli customers often use the catering service, and catering customers visit the deli.

Supermarkets and Convenience Stores

Supermarkets and convenience stores are fairly recent competitors for restaurants. They offer customers food that is freshly prepared and ready to go; their menus typically include fried chicken, sandwiches, side dishes, salads, and desserts. The primary concern of customers who visit these establishments is convenience, so supermarkets and convenience stores offer serious competition to quick-service restaurants that compete on the basis of convenience and value.

Eating at Home

Dining out is not a necessity for most people. Restaurants, like other service businesses, sell convenience: they perform a task that consumers could otherwise handle themselves. Some consumers perceive dining out as something to do only on special occasions, which may be the attitude of a larger portion of upscale restaurant customers. Quick-service and midscale restaurants must appeal to value-conscious and time-conscious consumers. They must stress how eating out can save customers the time and trouble of cooking, and how customers can relax while they eat and not worry about cleaning up afterward.

Operations

wning a food-service business may seem like an entrepreneurial dream. Even the smallest operations have an element of glamour—on the surface, it looks like the owners make their living greeting guests and serving meals while becoming recognizable figures in the community. And as more and more celebrities enter the food-service dd to the restaurant business's image as an exciting, lucrative oppor-

raciously with customers and playing the role of elegant host is only rateur's many duties. Food-service business operators spend most of developing menus; ordering inventory and supplies; managing personnel; creating and implementing marketing campaigns; making sure their operation is in compliance with a myriad of local, state, and federal regulations; completing a wide range of paperwork; and other administrative chores. Certainly the financial opportunities are there—as are the fun aspects of the business—but starting, running, and growing a food-service business is also hard work.

Regardless of the type of food-service business you intend to start, the best way to learn is to work for a similar operation for a while before striking out on your own. Doing so will give you significant insight into the realities and logistics of the business.

Jim A. started working in bakeries when he was 15. "I worked my way up from washing pots and pans to frying doughnuts to doing the basic American-type retail bakery stuff," he recalls. Today, he owns a bakery specializing in sourdough breads that does $2 million a year in both wholesale and retail business out of three locations in Maine.

Michael G. was also 15 when he got his first restaurant job, washing dishes on Friday nights. He then attended Cornell and worked in all aspects of restaurants and private clubs before opening his own operation in Haverhill, Massachusetts.

Ann C. worked for an Irvine, California, caterer for 15 years. When the owner passed away, she bought the company from his heirs.

Phyllis J. took a slightly different route to the coffeehouse business. She originally opened a retail store selling coffee beans, coffee makers, and related supplies. Then she realized her location was better suited to a coffeehouse rather than simply a retail store, and she shifted into the food-service business. Prior to getting into the coffee business, she was a social worker—an experience, she says, that has helped her tremendously in dealing with people in a retail and food-service environment.

Rebecca S. started out partnering with her mother in a small retail gourmet pasta shop in West Des Moines, Iowa. The business has grown to include a restaurant, cooking school, catering operation, private-label foods, gift baskets, and wholesale distribution in addition to the retail shop.

Tip...

Smart Tip

Be sure each square foot in your restaurant generates income. You'll pay the same rent for the kitchen and the closets as you do for the dining area, so be sure you have absolutely no wasted space, and that every part of your operation is contributing to revenue generation.

Anthony A. didn't have any food-service experience when he opened his first pizzeria—a small, 300-square-foot take-out shop—and he now says some practical experience would have helped tremendously. "Even though I was just doing pizza, and it was a very narrow menu, there were many things I needed to learn along the way, from making the dough to figuring out what it took to get the type of dough I wanted. It took us [several months] to achieve the dough I felt comfortable with. Not having any background in that area was definitely a liability." But he didn't go into the business blind; he did some serious research. He went to Rome, where he observed and interviewed pizza-makers. When he returned to the United States, he visited numerous pizza parlors to watch what they did and how they operated and talked at length with equipment sellers. "I put together what I thought was reasonable," he says.

There are several ways to get started in the food-service business. You can purchase a franchise, build an independent operation from the ground up, buy an existing operation or lease space in an existing structure. Each has its advantages and disadvantages, which you need to consider carefully before making a final decision. Chapter 12 discusses these options in greater detail, but regardless of how you get started, there are a number of operations issues common to virtually all types of food-service businesses.

Setting Hours of Operation

Your hours of operation will vary depending on the particular type of food-service business you have. Ultimately, it is up to you to determine the hours for your business.

Most quick-service restaurants are open for lunch, dinner, and the post-dinner crowd. Typically, they open at 10:30 or 11 A.M. and close anywhere between 9 and 11 P.M. Some national fast-food franchises and chains also serve breakfast and open as early as 6 A.M. Still others stay open until well past midnight on weekends, and some are open 24 hours a day.

The hours of midscale and upscale restaurants vary by the concept. A restaurant offering only a buffet will most likely not serve breakfast and may open from 11 A.M. to 9 P.M. Many family-style restaurants, on the other hand, specialize in serving breakfast and typically open at 6 A.M. and continue serving meals until after dinner, closing at around 9 P.M.

Casual-dining restaurants tend to cater to the lunch and dinner crowds. They open around 11 A.M. but stay open later, especially on weekends, to appeal to the post-dinner crowd. During the week, they tend to close at 10 or 11 P.M. On Fridays and Saturdays, they may stay open until midnight or 1 A.M.

Often, upscale restaurants that just serve dinner are only open from 4:30 or 5 P.M. to 9 or 10 P.M. They are able to survive on dinner sales only because they have found

Stat Fact

Lunch is the most popular meal for people to eat away from home. Popular lunch items include hamburgers, wraps, salads, soups, and ethnic foods.

a concept that works, and they're sticking with it. Most full-service restaurants, however, are open for both lunch and dinner, six or seven days a week. Those that are only open six days a week close on either Sunday or Monday.

Hours vary somewhat among full-service restaurants. If you open such a restaurant and do not plan on offering cocktail service, start off with a split-shift operation: Open for lunch from 11 A.M. to 2 P.M., and then for dinner from 4:30 to 9 P.M. each day. If you decide to serve cocktails, you could keep the same dinner hours but serve appetizers and drinks at all hours, say from 11 A.M. to 11 P.M. If you have just a beer-and-wine bar, the split-shift system can work well.

Sandwich shops, delicatessens, and pizzerias are typically open for lunch and dinner six or seven days a week. Hours vary depending on location and market, but most

Closed for Business

If you have a retail food-service business, you may find you don't have time to spruce up your facility during the year. For this reason, many independent restaurants close for one to two weeks every year, during which owners look over their facilities and make any necessary changes. They may add a fresh coat of paint, repair ripped upholstery, and inspect all the equipment. Since there are no customers or employees in the facility, repair people can work quickly and without interruptions. This annual closing also allows employees to take vacations. Paid time off is an attractive benefit for employees.

To maintain good relations with your customers, give them advance notice of your upcoming closure. Post a sign on your door stating the dates during which you will be closed and the date you will reopen. Record a message on your answering machine or voice mail with the same information. While you're closed, check your answering machine or voice mail regularly in case a supplier or anyone else needs to get in touch with you or someone on your staff.

Generally, restaurants close during the slowest time of the year, when the closing will have the least impact on revenue and customers. Of course, if you're a seasonal operation, such as a restaurant in a resort area as Robert O.'s Nags Head, North Carolina, seafood operation is, you can take care of major maintenance and updates when you're closed during the off-season.

open from 10 or 11 A.M. to 6 or 8 P.M. (for sandwich shops) or as late as 11 P.M. or midnight (for pizzerias and full-service delis).

Commercial bakeries begin baking the day's products as early as 2 or 3 A.M.; some even operate 24 hours a day. Retail bakeries and coffeehouses tend to open early enough to capture the breakfast crowd.

Caterers typically have an office staffed during normal business hours, perhaps 8 or 9 A.M. to 5 P.M. The actual hours people work depend, of course, on the particular jobs they have and span all hours of the day and days of the week.

Scheduling Employees

When you'll need employees to report to work depends a great deal on the type of food-service business you have. As a general guide for restaurants, the first person to arrive in the morning should be your chief cook or chef. This person will be responsible for the kitchen. He or she should arrive a few hours before opening to begin preparing the side dishes that you will serve throughout the day. These can include soups, vegetables, sauces, batter, homemade breads or biscuits, rice, and generally anything else you might serve in large quantities over a span of hours. This person can also accept and inspect deliveries. If you prefer, your manager or assistant manager can arrive at the same time to take care of paperwork and deliveries.

The preparation of side dishes should be completed 30 minutes before the doors open for business. If your chief cook comes in before opening, he or she will be able to leave after the lunch crowd or evening dinner has been served, with the second cook carrying on until closing. The second cook will be responsible for cleaning the kitchen so it is ready for the next morning.

Your dining room manager, maitre d', or chief host or hostess should arrive 30 minutes to an hour before opening to make sure that everything in the front of the house is in order. This will allow time to check the dining room table settings, napkins, salt and pepper shakers, and any other elements that will make the front room more presentable to the public.

The person in charge of these front-of-the-house pre-opening chores can continue through the lunch hour and dinner hour, if you serve both meals, or from the dinner hour through closing if you only serve dinner. This employee can also close out the cash register.

> **Tip...**
>
> **Smart Tip**
> To build a profitable food-service business, you need systems. Approach your operation with the understanding that regardless of how creative or fun it might be, it is a business, and successful businesses are built on systems that produce consistent, reliable results.

Tip...

Smart Tip

Be around and visible. Of course, large chain restaurants are run by managers, and you may want to hire managers to help you run your operation. But most successful independent food-service businesses have an owner who works in the business every day. They're in touch with their customers and their employees, they know what's going on in the day-to-day operation, and they're available to make decisions as needed.

The bar manager should come in 30 minutes before the restaurant opens for business. He or she will be responsible for the appearance of the lounge area, stocking the liquor inventory of the bar, making sure that appetizers are out for the lunch and dinner crowds, and preparing the bar to open.

The bar manager will also be your chief bartender. This person will continue working through the early-evening shift, and your second bartender will usually handle the late-evening crowds. Because weekend evenings are the busiest for both bars and restaurants, schedule your bar manager to work Tuesday through Saturday, covering the busy weekend. In addition to the bar manager, one or two part-time bartenders can assist with the weekend crowd.

Service Policies

Regardless of how formal or casual your operation is, your goal should be to treat customers like royalty, and you can meet this goal with strong, professional service from the moment your customers walk in the door. Your team of employees will determine how well your customers are treated, and they will reflect the policies you've established as the owner.

Uniforms will help develop a sense of identity and pride, as well as project a professional image. Each employee at the same level should wear an identical uniform. For example, all buspersons should wear the same uniform, and everyone on your wait staff should wear the same uniform.

Set standards for your business's appearance. Everything from the toilet paper in the restrooms to your plates and utensils should receive the same careful consideration. If you find spots on your glassware or plates, then you have failed to meet your standards. If the restrooms have toilet paper and towels strewn about and writing on the walls, then you have failed to meet your standards. If you are trying to create a dining experience, make it a good one.

The actual service should range from polite to almost ingratiating. The host or hostess should greet customers with a cheerful hello and ask for the number of persons in the party and a smoking preference (unless you're located in an area that prohibits smoking in public places). If a line forms, or if all the tables are full, the host or hostess should take customers' names and let them know how long they should expect to wait. Unless you take reservations, customers should be seated on a first-come, first-served basis. If you have a bar, give customers the option of waiting there. Make menus available to people who are waiting so they can be thinking ahead of time about what they'd like to order.

Once customers are seated, promptly present them with a menu and inform them that their server will be with them in a moment. The busperson should fill their water glasses immediately unless you are in an area with water restrictions. When the server arrives, the first thing he or she should do is inquire if the customers would like anything before ordering their meals, such as a beverage or appetizer.

After giving the customers time to review the menu, the server should come back to answer any questions and take meal orders. The server should be thoroughly familiar with the menu and any specials so he or she can answer any questions. All orders should be recorded on a check and should be repeated back to customers to make sure they are correct.

Servers should remove food from the left and beverages from the right, and should never reach in front of a customer to serve or remove anything.

The wait staff and buspersons should always be in their stations checking to make sure that customers have everything they need for a satisfying meal. They should refill water glasses regularly, supply the necessary condiments to customers, and ask if the food is satisfactory after customers have had time to start eating. After customers have finished their entrees, servers should ask if they would like dessert or coffee. Only when the server is sure the customer is finished with the meal should the check be presented.

If a customer complains about a particular dish, offer to replace the item at no charge. If there has been an unavoidable service failure of any sort, do your best to make amends, perhaps with a free dessert or after-dinner drink. Above all, never argue with a customer; even if you win, you lose, because chances are that customer will never return, and you will have created negative word-of-mouth advertising that might prevent other customers from visiting your establishment.

Cleaning Your Facility

At the end of every working day, regardless of what time that is, you must clean your facility. Either your staff or an outside commercial cleaning service can handle this task. Your cooks can clean the grill and mop the floor after closing. The wait staff and buspersons can refill condiments and clean the tables, booths and floors in the dining area. The dishwasher will finish the day's dishes and restock dishes for the cooks and wait staff.

If you cannot afford to pay your employees to complete these duties or would simply prefer not to, a commercial cleaning service can take care of this. For a set fee, a cleaning service will visit your restaurant every night after the employees have left. They clean the entire restaurant, including the kitchen, wait stations, dining area, and restrooms. If you decide to use a cleaning service, ask for references and check the company out before making a final decision. It's also a good idea to find out what cleaning products they use; you wouldn't want someone to use the same product to clean the grills as they do for the restrooms. A growing number of janitorial and commercial cleaning services are expanding to target the restaurant market. Ask other restaurant owners for recommendations, or check your telephone directory for companies.

Details on operational issues relating to specific types of food-service businesses will be explained in later chapters.

Developing
Your Plan

Whether you've got years of food-serv-
ice experience behind you, or you're a novice in the industry,
you need a plan for your business. This chapter will focus on a
few issues particular to planning food-service businesses, but
they are by no means all you need to consider when writing
your business plan.

> ## Tip...
> ### Tip
> ...ou think your business plan is complete, look at it with a fresh eye. Is it a true and honest representation of the facts? Is it realistic? Does it consider all the possible variables that could affect your operation? After you're satisfied, show the plan to two or three professional associates whose input you value and trust. Ask them to be brutally honest with their evaluation; you need to know now if there are any glaring problems with your plan so you can correct them before they cost you time and money.

Many entrepreneurs view writing a business plan with even less enthusiasm than they had for homework when they were in school. But if you're excited about your business, creating a business plan should be an exciting process. It will help you define and evaluate the overall feasibility of your concept, clarify your goals, and determine what you'll need for start-up and long-term operations.

This is a living, breathing document that will provide you with a road map for your company. You'll use it as a guide, referring to it regularly as you work through the start-up process and then during the operation of your business. And if you're going to be seeking outside financing, either in the form of loans or investors, your business plan will be the tool that convinces funding sources of the worthiness of your venture.

Putting together a business plan is not a linear process, although the final product may look that way. As you work through it, you'll likely find yourself jumping from menu development to cash flow forecasts to staffing, then back to cash flow, on to marketing, and back to menu development. Take your time developing your plan; whether you want to start a coffee-and-snack cart or an upscale gourmet restaurant, you're making a serious commitment, and you shouldn't rush into it. And again, for a breakdown of the specific elements you'll need to include in your business plan, see *Business Plans Made Easy* (Entrepreneur) by Mark Henricks and John Riddle.

Carving Your Niche

Before you can begin any serious business planning, you must first decide what specific segment of the food-service industry you want to enter. While there are many commonalities among the vari-

> ### Bright Idea
> Your business plan should include worst-case scenarios, both for your own benefit and for your funding sources. You'll benefit from thinking ahead about what you'll do if things don't go as you want them to. You'll also increase the comfort level of your lenders/investors by demonstrating your ability to deal with the unexpected and potentially negative situations.

> **Beware!**
> When you make a change to one part of your business plan, be sure you think through how that change will affect the rest of your operation. For example, if you decide to add more items to your menu, do you need to change your kitchen setup to accommodate it? Or if your original plan was to offer limited service where customers ordered and picked up their food at a counter, but you've decided to take the food to the tables, how will that affect your staffing plans?

ous types of food-service businesses, there are also many differences. And while there is much overlap in the knowledge and skills necessary to be successful, your own personality and preferences will dictate whether you choose to open a commercial bakery, a coffee cart, a fine-dining restaurant, or other type of operation. Then, once you've decided what business best suits you, you must figure out the niche you'll occupy in the marketplace.

Chances are you already have a pretty good idea of the type of food-service business that appeals to you. Before you take the actual plunge, read through the chapters that describe the various operations and see how they suit your particular working style.

For example, are you an early riser or do you prefer to stay up late and sleep late? If you like—or at least don't mind—getting up before dawn, your niche may be a bakery or a casual breakfast-and-lunch operation. Night owls are going to be drawn to the hours required for bar-and-grill types of restaurants, fine-dining establishments, and even pizzerias.

Do you like dealing with the public, or are you happier in the kitchen? If you're a people person, choose a food-service business that gives you plenty of opportunity to connect with your customers. If you're not especially gregarious, you'll probably lean more toward a commercial type of business, perhaps a bakery or even a catering service, where you can deal more with operational issues than with people.

Do you have a passion for a particular type of cuisine? Do you enjoy a predictable routine, or do you prefer something different every day? Are you willing to deal with the additional responsibilities and liabilities that come with serving alcoholic beverages?

As you do this self-analysis, think about your ideal day. If you could be

> **Bright Idea**
> Update your business plan every year. Choose an annual date when you sit down with your plan, compare how closely your actual operation and results followed your forecasts, and decide if your plans for the coming year need adjusting. You will also need to take your financial forecasts out for another year, based on current and expected market conditions.

doing exactly what you wanted to do, what would it be? Now compare your preferences to the requirements of each type of food-service business (as described in Chapters 5 through 10) and come up with the best match for you.

Once you have decided on the best niche for you as an individual, it's time to determine if you can develop a niche in the market for your food-service business.

Researching Your Market

You must do an in-depth examination of your market. Market research will provide you with data that allows you to identify and reach particular market segments and to solve or avoid marketing problems. A thorough market survey forms the foundation of any successful business. It would be impossible to develop marketing strategies or an effective product line without market research.

A primary goal of market research is for you to identify your market, find out where it is, and develop a strategy to communicate with prospective customers in a way that will convince them to patronize your business.

Market research will also give you information you need about your competitors. You need to find out what they're doing and how that meets—or doesn't meet—the needs of the market.

One of the most basic elements of effective marketing is differentiating yourself from the competition. One marketing consultant calls it "eliminating the competition" because if you set yourself apart by doing something no one else does, then you essentially have no competition. However, before you can differentiate yourself, you first need to understand who your competitors are and why your customers might patronize them.

Are You On a Mission?

Your mission statement is the foundation of your business plan. At any given moment, most food-service business owners have a reasonably clear understanding of the mission of their company. They know what they are doing, how and where it's being done, and who their customers are. Problems can arise, however, when that mission is not clearly articulated into a statement, written down, and communicated to others.

"A mission statement defines what an organization is, why it exists, its reason for being," says Gerald Graham, dean of the W. Frank Barton School of Business at Wichita State University. "Writing it down and communicating it to others

creates a sense of commonality and a more coherent approach to v
ing to do."

Even in a very small company, a written mission statement
involved see the big picture and keeps them focused on the true
ness. According to Graham, at a minimum your mission statement sn...

who your primary customers are; identify the
products and services you offer; and describe
the geographical location in which you operate. For example, a caterer's mission statement
might read "Our mission is to provide businesses and individuals in the Raleigh area with
delicious food delivered to their location and
set up and served according to their instructions." A coffeehouse's mission statement
might read "Our mission is to serve the downtown business community by providing the
highest-quality coffees, espresso, baked goods,
and sandwiches in an atmosphere that meets the needs of customers who are in a
hurry as well as those who want a place to relax and enjoy their beverages and
food."

> # E
> ven in a very small company, a written mission statement helps everyone involved see the big picture and keeps them focused on the true goals of the business.

A mission statement should be short—usually just one sentence and certainly no
more than two. A good idea is to cap it at 100 words. Anything longer than that isn't
a mission statement and will probably confuse your employees.

Once you have articulated your message, communicate it as often as possible to
everyone in the company, along with customers and suppliers. "Post it on the wall,
hold meetings to talk about it, and include a reminder of the statement in employee
correspondence," says Graham.

Graham says it is more important to adequately communicate the mission statement to employees than to customers. "Sometimes an organization will try to use a
mission statement primarily for promotion, and then as an aside use it to help the
employees identify what business they're in," he says. "That doesn't work very well.
The most effective mission statements are developed strictly for internal communication and discussion, and then if something promotional comes out of it, fine." In
other words, your mission statement doesn't have to be clever or catchy—just moti-
vating and accurate.

Although your mission statement may never win an advertising or creativity
award, it can still be a very effective customer-relations tool. One idea is to print your
mission statement on a poster-sized panel, have every employee sign it, and hang it in
a prominent place so customers can see it. You can even include it on your brochures
and invoices.

Finally, make sure your suppliers know what your mission statement is; if they understand what you're all about, it will help them serve you better.

A critical part of your plan to open a food-service establishment will involve setting up your facility. In the next chapter, we'll take a look at the fundamentals of setting up a kitchen and dining area.

Kitchen and
Dining Room
Basics

The two key parts of your facility are the production area, where the food is prepared, and the public area, where you customers either dine or make their carryout purchases. How you design and equip these areas depends, of course, on the particular type of operation you want to have. This chapter will take a look at the basics that apply to most

▲

operations, and the following six chapters will go into more detail regarding specific types of food-service business.

As you begin planning your facility, you might want to consider hiring an experienced, reputable consultant to assist with the layouts of your dining and production areas. Consultants can help with your facility design and also help you link all the elements—menu content and design, pricing, décor, kitchen layout, staffing, training, and other support services. "All of the components have to work together," pizzeria owner Anthony A. says. "If you have one weak link, it breaks up the whole system." To find a good consultant, network with other restaurateurs who have businesses similar to the one you want to open, read trade publications, talk with equipment dealers, and perhaps even ask restaurant brokers for referrals.

The Dining Room and Waiting Area

Much of your dining room design will depend on your concept. It will help you to know that studies indicate that 40 to 50 percent of all sit-down customers arrive in pairs; 30 percent come alone or in parties of three; and 20 percent come in groups of four or more.

To accommodate these different groups of customers, use tables for two that can be pushed together in areas where there is ample floor space. This gives you flexibility in accommodating both small and large parties. Place booths for four to six people along the walls.

Develop a uniform decorating concept that will establish a single atmosphere throughout your restaurant. That means whatever décor or theme you choose for the dining area should also be reflected in the waiting area. Also, be sure your waiting area is welcoming and comfortable; whether your customers are seated immediately or have to wait any length of time for their tables, they will gain their first impression of your operation from the entrance/waiting area, and you want that impression to be a positive one.

> **Tip...**
>
> **Smart Tip**
>
> All restrooms should be supplied with hand soap; sanitary paper towels or a hand-drying device providing heated air; toilet tissue; and easily cleanable waste receptacles.

Production Area

Generally, you'll need to allow approximately 35 percent of your total space for your production area. Include space for food preparation, cooking, dishwashing, trash

Furniture and Fixtures

The specific furniture and fixtures you'll need depend, of course, on the specific type of food-service business you start. Your shopping list may include all or part of the following:

- ❏ Bar(s)
- ❏ Benches
- ❏ Chairs
- ❏ Hat/coat racks
- ❏ Host stand
- ❏ Merchandise display cases
- ❏ Planters
- ❏ Room dividers
- ❏ Stools
- ❏ Tables

disposal, receiving, inventory storage, employee facilities, and an area for a small office where daily management duties can be performed.

Allow about 12 percent of your total space for the actual food preparation and cooking areas. If you want to entertain your customers with "exhibition cooking," then expand the area behind your counter to include the food preparation area.

Allow about 12 percent of your total space for the actual food preparation and cooking areas.

Set up the dishwashing area so the washer can develop a production line. The person responsible for washing dishes should rinse them in a double sink, then place them into racks on a small landing area next to the sink. From the landing, the racks full of dishes are put through the commercial dishwasher, then placed on a table for drying. The size and capacity of your dishwasher will depend on the needs of your particular operation.

Receiving and inventory storage will take up to about 8 percent of your total space. These areas should be located so they are accessible to shipping vans. Use double doors at your receiving port, and keep a dolly or hand truck available at all times. Locate your dry storage area and walk-in refrigerator/freezer adjacent to the receiving area.

Because most food-service businesses require employees, you should have a private area for them. The employee room should include a table, a few chairs, a closet or garment rack (for them to hang coats and street clothes after they've changed into their work clothes), lockers for safe storage of personal belongings and valuables, and a restroom. The staff facility should not take up more than 5 percent of your total space.

▲

These Mats Were Made for Standin'

An important piece of equipment in every food-service operation is matting. Rubber mats help reduce employee fatigue and prevent falls from spills. Place quality mats in all areas where employees such as cooks, dishwashers, and all preparation staff will be standing for long periods of time. Also place mats wherever spills may occur, such as wait stations, storage areas, and walk-in refrigerators and freezers. A good 3-by-5-foot mat will range in price from $42 to $60.

You'll also need a small space where you or your manager can perform administrative tasks, such as general paperwork, bank deposits, and counting out cash drawers. This space is essential even if you have an office at home where you do the majority of your administrative work.

To make your production area as efficient as possible, keep the following tips in mind:

- Plan the shortest route from entrance to exit for ingredients and baked goods.
- Minimize handling by having as many duties as possible performed at each stop.
- Eliminate bottlenecks in the production process caused by delays of processes at strategic locations. This depends on both the adequacy and care of your equipment, as well as its location.
- Recognize that the misuse of space is as damaging to your operation as the misuse of machinery and labor.
- Eliminate backtracking, overlapping of work, and unnecessary inspection by constantly considering possibilities for new sequences and combinations of steps in food preparation.

Ventilation

Pollution control across the country is tightening, and new regulations are being introduced every year. This has had a significant impact on ventilation requirements. New, more efficient systems that meet the more stringent requirements have increased the cost of starting a food-service business. Expect to pay $100 to $350 per linear foot for the hood and grease filter, and $18 to $48 per linear foot for the ductwork. While ventilation systems are expensive to install, they offer a tremendous opportunity for energy conservation. The more efficient systems are worth their extra cost because they contribute to substantially lower monthly utility expenses. Check with prominent HVAC (heating, ventilation, air conditioning) system manufacturers and installers to find the best options for your particular facility.

You have three basic ventilation system options. The first is reducing the quantity of exhaust air, which will decrease the exhaust fan size and ultimately your purchasing and operating costs. In conjunction with this option, you can also reduce the amount of make-up (fresh) air you have to introduce to compensate for the amount of exhaust air you release. This, in turn, will reduce the size of the make-up air fan you need, along with its purchasing and operating cost. Finally, you can change the method of introducing make-up air so it need not be conditioned; this will significantly reduce the air-handling cost.

One of the best ways to achieve a reduction in exhaust air and make-up air is to install a high-velocity, low-volume system, which reduces the exhaust air output by 40 percent. This directly affects the make-up air quantities, since make-up and exhaust must balance, which results in savings from processing the make-up air. A key benefit of such a system is the introduction of raw, unconditioned air directly to the exhaust ventilator, a process that eliminates the cost of heating or cooling a portion of the make-up air.

Merchandising

How you present your food and beverages is as important to sales as how they taste. You can have the most delicious sirloin steak in your area, but if you don't present it to the customer properly, it won't be as enjoyable as it could be. Presenting food

Shedding Light on the Subject

Throughout your facility, be sure you have adequate and appropriate lighting. The kitchen and work areas should be brightly lit to assure productivity, accuracy, and safety. Your dining, waiting, and other customer areas should be lit in a way that is compatible with your theme and overall décor. Keep safety in mind at all times. A candlelight dinner is certainly romantic, but not if your patrons trip and fall on their way in or out because they couldn't see where they were going.

in an attractive manner is called merchandising, and it is a powerful marketing tool that successful restaurateurs take advantage of to improve sales.

Merchandising is an art that requires a creative mind that can anticipate public likes and dislikes. Your concept, for instance, is a form of merchandising. So is how you present the dishes on your menu and the drinks in your bar. Arrange each of your dishes so the food looks appealing. Doing so will not only please the customer who ordered the dish, but it will also attract the attention of other customers.

> **Bright Idea**
>
> Food doesn't have to be served on traditional plates. A California barbecue chain serves a full meal family-style in a wooden wagon—it's different, memorable, fun, and keeps the customers coming back.

Many restaurants use parsley as a basic garnish, but an increasing number of restaurateurs are turning to more creative options ranging from fresh fruits and herbs to little ornaments and even edible flowers.

Just as important as garnishing is selecting the right plate or glass for your food and beverages. For instance, you can serve a regular cut of prime rib on one type of plate, and the deluxe cut on a completely different plate. This also applies to drinks. Have one type of glass for regular beer and a better glass for premium beer and imported classics. You might, for example, serve a German beer in a stein.

Merchandising properly is a good way to increase your sales. It is also a good way to enhance your image and develop that all-important word-of-mouth advertising.

Pricing Menu Items

In pricing each item, you must first account for the actual cost to purchase the ingredients. Next, you incorporate the labor cost for preparing and serving the food, as well as your overhead costs, into the price of each item. Finally, you add your profit. The net profit restaurants expect on food ranges from 8 to 20 percent. In many cases, the menu price is about three times the food cost. But Anthony A. points out that this is just a general guideline; there will be many situations when the market will allow you to charge more. For example, the first few years his first pizzeria was in operation, he priced based on food costs, but he was delivering a product of significantly higher quality that people would have been willing to pay more for.

> **Bright Idea**
>
> Check the dirty dishes when they are returned to the kitchen to evaluate waste and determine whether you're serving too much. You may be able to increase profits by reducing portion size.

Finally, a friend persuaded him to increase prices beyond the basic cost-times-three formula; sales stayed steady, and profits increased. "[I had] two or three years of lost revenue from not doing more scientific research on pricing," he says.

Bright Idea
Produce a concise paper version of your menu that your customers can take with them to make placing to-go or delivery orders easier.

Your net profit before taxes on drinks can be quite high, as much as 60 percent—or even more—of your total selling price. You will generally charge anywhere from 1,500 to 4,000 percent of your cost for drinks, depending on the particular drink and your location.

Setting prices can be tedious and time-consuming, especially if you don't have a knack for juggling numbers. Make it your business to learn how to estimate labor time accurately and how to calculate your overhead properly so that when you price your menu, you can be competitive and still make the profit you require.

Restaurant

The mainstay of the food-service industry is the general category restaurant. The popularity of restaurants stems primarily from the fact that people have to eat. But there's more to it than just that. The rise in single-parent families, dual-income couples, and individuals working more than one job are all factors driving customers who don't have the time or desire to cook for themselves into restaurants. Of course, time issues aren't the only reason people dine out. Restaurant customers also benefit from the relatively low inflation of menu prices; competition in the industry has kept menu prices at fairly reasonable levels in recent years.

Bright Idea

Choose a site for your restaurant that is near a well-known landmark. It will be easier for customers to find you if they can use a local landmark as a reference point.

Restaurants are also great places to entertain or conduct business. Going to a restaurant with friends or associates takes the pressure off people who want to concentrate on issues other than preparing a meal. Many restaurants offer private rooms, large tables, and banquet facilities for these customers.

Restaurants also cater to customers who want a certain dish but for whatever reason—perhaps a lack of culinary skill or the inability to find ingredients—are unable to prepare it for themselves. Ethnic restaurants or restaurants that serve exotic desserts often attract customers with such strong cravings.

Finally, beyond the food itself, many customers want to enjoy the atmosphere of the restaurants they visit. Ethic restaurants and specialty-themed restaurants are examples of operations that meet this particular market need.

Before starting any type of restaurant, you must know who your customers are and where they are located. With that information, you can decide on the best site and move forward with your plans. However, restaurateurs don't always agree on the best approach to concept development and site selection.

Some restaurateurs believe you must determine your concept and market before choosing a location. For example, you may want to start an Italian restaurant, so you research the market for this type of cuisine, and then, based on what you find out, choose a general area and then a precise location for the restaurant.

Others believe that finding the location is the most important task and place secondary emphasis on concept and market. For example, an entrepreneur may find a great building in a downtown business district, decide that it is perfect for a restaurant, and then determine the best concept for the location.

Smart Tip

Dine out often. You need to know what other restaurants are doing—it will help you maintain your own competitive position, as well as give you ideas to improve your operation.

When it comes to restaurants, it doesn't really matter whether you research your market or your location first; what's critical is that you take the time to research both thoroughly.

Choosing Your Concept

Restaurant patrons want to be *delighted* with their dining experience, but not necessarily *surprised*. If you're anticipating a family-style steakhouse but you find yourself in a more formal environment with a bewildering gourmet menu, the surprise alone may keep you from enjoying the restaurant. Concepts give restaurateurs a way to let patrons know in advance what to expect and also provide some structure for their operation. Here are some of the more popular restaurant concepts:

Seafood

Seafood restaurants offer a wide array of fish and shellfish prepared in a variety of ways. Quick-service seafood restaurants generally offer a limited range of choices, often restricted to fried fish and shrimp. Midscale and upscale restaurants offer a wider selection of seafood items, prepared in ways other than fried, including baked, broiled, and grilled. Most seafood restaurants also offer a limited number of additional menu items, such as steak and chicken.

Seafood can be a risky item on which to focus. Seafood prices are always changing, and many kinds of seafood are seasonal. Prices change rapidly, and quality can vary tremendously. When shopping for seafood, make sure that the items are fresh and meet your standards of quality. If you are not happy with what a distributor offers, you can be sure your customers won't be, either.

The décor of a typical casual seafood restaurant consists of sea-related items, such as fishing nets and aquariums. Finer seafood restaurants will have minimal sea-related furnishings. Seafood restaurants are often located on a waterfront, which adds to the nautical ambience.

Beware!
Consider your options carefully before deciding to open a theme restaurant. Some theme operations—especially those owned by celebrities—have enjoyed popularity, but the allure of theme operations appears to be on the wane. One restaurant analyst says the problem with theme restaurants is that most people visit them once, twice, or maybe three times but don't go back. It doesn't matter how good the food is if you can't pull in repeat customers because they take a "been there, done that" attitude toward your operation.

Steakhouses

Steakhouses are part of the midscale and upscale markets. Midscale steakhouses are typically family-oriented, offering a casual environment with meals perceived as

The Three Food Groups

Restaurants are classified into three primary categories: quick-service, midscale and upscale. Quick-service restaurants are also known as fast-food restaurants. These establishments offer limited menus of items that are prepared quickly and sold for a relatively low price. In addition to very casual dining areas, they typically offer drive-thru windows and take-out service.

When people think of fast-food restaurants, they often think of hamburgers and french fries, but establishments in this category also serve chicken, hot dogs, sandwiches, pizza, seafood, and ethnic foods.

Midscale restaurants, as the name implies, occupy the middle ground between quick-service and upscale restaurants. They offer full meals but charge prices that customers perceive as providing good value. Midscale restaurants offer a range of limited- and full-service options. In a full-service restaurant, patrons place and receive their orders at their tables; in a limited-service operation, patrons order their food at a counter and then receive their meals at their tables. Many limited-service restaurants offer salad bars and buffets.

Midscale restaurants embrace a variety of concepts, including steakhouses, casual dining, family dining, and ethnic restaurants such as Italian, Mexican, Asian, Mediterranean, and others. Even in full-service midscale operations, the ambience tends to be casual.

Upscale restaurants offer full table service and do not necessarily promote their meals as offering great value; instead, they focus on the quality of their cuisine and the ambience of their facilities. Fine-dining establishments are at the highest end of the upscale restaurant category and charge the highest prices.

good values. In décor, comfort is emphasized, and Western themes are popular.

Upscale steakhouses offer a more formal atmosphere and may serve larger cuts of meat that are of better quality than those served in midscale restaurants. Upscale establishments also charge higher prices, and their décor mimics that of other fine-dining establishments, offering guests more privacy and focusing more on adult patrons than families.

Although red meat is the primary focus, many steakhouses offer additional items, such as poultry, seafood, and pasta selections. Salad bars are popular at midscale steakhouses.

Family-Style Restaurants

As the name implies, these establishments are geared toward families. Since they charge reasonable prices, they also appeal to seniors. They offer speedy service that falls somewhere between that of quick-service and most full-service restaurants. Their menus offer a variety of selections to appeal to the interests of a broad range of customers, from children to seniors. Family-style restaurant prices are just higher than those at fast-food restaurants, yet these establishments still provide table service.

The décor of family-style restaurants is generally comfortable, with muted tones, unremarkable artwork, and plenty of booths and wide chairs. Booster seats and high-chairs for children are readily available.

Casual-Dining Restaurants

Casual-dining restaurants appeal to a wide audience, ranging from Gen Xers to baby boomers with families to seniors, and they provide a variety of food items, from appetizers and salads to main dishes and desserts. These establishments offer comfortable atmospheres with mid-range prices. Many successful casual-dining restaurants center on a theme that is incorporated into their menus and décor.

Ethnic Restaurants

Ethnic restaurants enjoy a significant share of the U.S. restaurant market. They range from quick-service to upscale, with a comparable range of menu items and décor. Their menus typically include "Americanized" versions of ethnic dishes, as well as more authentic food prepared as it is in the country of origin. Most ethnic restaurants also include a few dishes representative of American cuisine.

The three most popular kinds of ethnic restaurants are Chinese, Italian, and Mexican. Other popular ethnic restaurant types include Caribbean, English, French, German, Indian, Japanese, Korean, Mediterranean, Thai, and Vietnamese. An even wider variety of ethnic restaurants can thrive in areas with a culturally diverse population, such as large metropolitan areas.

Setting Up Your Facility

The major factors to include in a restaurant's design are the size and layout of the dining room, kitchen space, storage space, and office (see sample layout, page 39). Dining space will occupy more of your facility than any other kind of space, followed by the kitchen and preparation area, then by storage. If you have an office on the premises—and you should—that will most likely take up the smallest percentage of your space.

What's On the Menu?

Your restaurant's menu is an important sales and communication tool. It must portray your restaurant's theme clearly and consistently. It also must clearly describe the dishes you offer and their prices. Some restaurant owners also use the menu to describe the history of their operation or to provide other information that customers may find interesting. Make it attractive and easy to read.

If you run an upscale, fine-dining establishment, use a paper menu with a cloth binder. Midscale and other upscale restaurants use paper or laminated menus. If you plan to make changes to your menu throughout the year, a cost-effective method is to use plastic menu covers and insert paper menus that can be changed whenever necessary. The plastic menu covers are easy to clean and preserve paper menus for extended use.

If you offer take-out service or delivery, consider a smaller version of your standard menu printed on inexpensive paper for customers to take with them.

You may want to hire a food-service consultant or designer to help plan your layout, or you could do it yourself. Restaurant owner Anthony A. has done it both ways, and he recommends using a consultant. "I'd recommend using a consultant for dining room design, kitchen design, menu design," he says. "All those components—and there seem to be a thousand of them—all have to work together. If you have one weak link, it can break up your whole system."

Typically, restaurants allocate 40 to 60 percent of their space to the dining area, approximately 30 percent to the kitchen and prep area, and the remainder to storage and office space. The design of your restaurant should promote an efficient operation. The kitchen should be close to the dining room so that the wait staff can serve meals promptly, while they are still hot—or cold, as the case may be. The office is the least important factor in the design. You can locate it in the back of the restaurant, or even in the basement, along with the storage area. Consider which personnel will need access to which items, then try to locate these items as conveniently as possible to the appropriate workstations.

Beware!

Before hiring a consultant, determine exactly what you want the consultant to do, then get a complete proposal in writing, including the scope of the work, a timetable, and fee schedule.

Customer Service Area

The customer service area is important because it determines the first impression your restaurant will make on your guests. It must accurately convey the atmosphere of the restaurant in a way that takes advantage of the space available. Your customer service area should include a waiting area for customers, a cashier's station, public restrooms, and a bar, if you choose to have one.

The waiting area and cashier's station should be located near the entrance. The cashier's station can be designed as a small counter with a cash register, or you can use more space to display merchandise or any baked goods you might sell.

If you decide to set up a small retail center, your cashier's station will take up a little more room, and you'll have to invest in a counter with a glass casing. This is a small investment, however, when you consider the potential return.

You can also use your cashier's station as the host or hostess station, or set up a separate station at the threshold between the customer service area and the dining area. A host or hostess stand usually consists of a small wooden podium with a ledger in which to record the names of waiting guests.

> ## Bright Idea
>
> A popular and effective marketing technique used by quick-service restaurants is offering value meals. These meals typically include a main item, side dish, and beverage, all packaged at a price lower than a customer would pay to buy each item separately. For example, a hamburger restaurant may offer a value meal of a burger, fries, and soft drink. A Mexican restaurant might offer a burrito, side salad, and beverage. Like fast food in general, value meals offer convenience and savings to the customer.

The waiting area itself should have a few bench seats lining its walls. Don't skimp on these seats. They should be cushioned, unless your theme dictates otherwise, so your customers are comfortable during their wait. If the wait is usually long, and if your seats are hard and uncomfortable, chances are you will lose customers and generate some bad word-of-mouth.

In some restaurants, a bar will generate a good portion of the operation's revenue. Profit margins on beverage sales are much higher than they are on food sales, so a bar will improve your bottom line. Generally speaking, have one bar seat for every three dining seats. For example, if you have 150 dining seats, your bar should have about 50 seats, including bar stools and seats at tables. Allow about two square feet of floor space per stool. Your tables should have about 10 to 12 square feet per customer.

A bar also provides an additional waiting area for your restaurant. It's a good place for your waiting customers to relax and enjoy themselves while their table is being prepared.

The Dining Area

This is where you'll be making the bulk of your money, so don't cut corners when designing and decorating your dining room.

Visit restaurants in your area and analyze the décor. Watch the diners; do they react positively to the décor? Is it comfortable, or do people appear to be shifting in their seats throughout their meals? Make notes of what works well and what doesn't, and apply this to your own décor.

The space required per seat varies according to the type of restaurant. For a small casual-dining restaurant, you'll need to provide about 15 to 18 square feet per seat to assure comfortable seating and enough aisle space so servers have room to move between the tables.

The Production Area

Too often, the production area in a restaurant is inefficiently designed, and the result is a poorly organized kitchen and less-than-top-notch service. Your floor plan should be streamlined to provide the most efficient delivery of food to the dining area.

Keep your menu in mind as you determine each element in the production area. You'll need to include space for receiving, storage, food preparation, cooking, baking, dishwashing, production aisles, trash storage, employee facilities, and an area for a small office where you can perform daily management duties.

The food preparation, cooking, and baking areas are where the actual production of food will take place. Allow about 12 percent of your total space for food production. You'll need room for prep and steam tables, fryers, a cooking range with griddle top, small refrigerators that you will place under the prep and steam tables, a freezer for storing perishable goods, soft drink and milk dispensers, an ice bin, a broiler, exhaust fans for the ventilation system, and other items necessary to your particular operation.

Stat Fact
Nearly four out of five adults say they have a larger selection of restaurants available today compared with several years ago, according to a National Restaurant Association consumer survey.

Arrange this area so everything is only a couple of steps away from the cook. You should also design it in such a way that two or more cooks can work side-by-side during your busiest hours.

The dishwashing and trash areas usually create a lot of confusion. You want to devote about 4 percent of your total space to these areas. Place your dishwashing area toward the rear of the kitchen. You can usually set this up

Sample Restaurant Layout

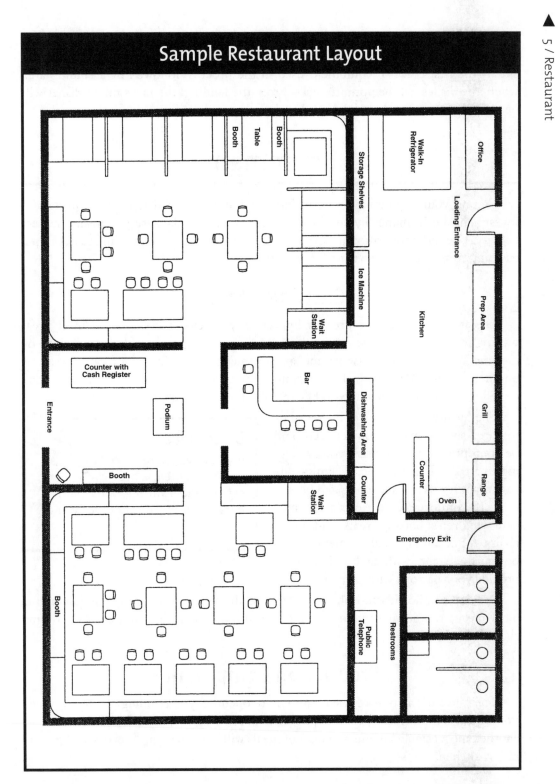

in a corner so it doesn't get in the way of the cooks and servers. Set up the dishwashing area so the washer can develop a production line. A two- or three-compartment sink is the first piece of equipment used in the process, followed by a landing area where the dishes will be put into racks. From the landing, the racks full of dishes will be put through the dishwasher and then left on a table for drying.

Equipment

Getting your restaurant properly furnished and equipped requires a substantial investment, both financially and in taking the time to make sure you make the best choices. Use the information in this section as a guide, but take the time to develop a customized plan for your particular operation.

Customer Areas

The areas that have the greatest impact on your customers are the dining area, waiting area, and restrooms. Essential items for your dining area include your china or dishware, plates, glasses, flatware, and an assortment of containers for foods not served on dinner plates. Make sure all your dinnerware is compatible with your overall concept. Figure on paying about $2,000 to $3,500 for a complete set of dinnerware.

The furniture and fixtures in your dining area should match your concept and be appropriate to the market you are trying to attract. For example, a family-style restaurant needs to have tables and booths that are comfortable and can accommodate children's booster seats and highchairs. A fine-dining establishment should be more elegant, with tables situated to provide your patrons with privacy.

> **Bright Idea**
> If you have a large facility, consider wireless headsets to allow various staff members to communicate quickly and efficiently.

Develop a uniform atmosphere throughout all the public areas of your restaurant. That means the décor of your waiting area, dining room, bar, and even restrooms should match.

Production Equipment

Regardless of the type of restaurant you're opening, you're going to need production equipment. While specific equipment needs will vary from one restaurant to another, most establishments serving hot meals will have to equip a service and preparation kitchen.

Restaurant Major Equipment and Fixtures Checklist

- ❏ Bakers' bins and tables
- ❏ Bar
- ❏ Beverage dispensing system
- ❏ Blender
- ❏ Broiler
- ❏ Can openers
- ❏ Cash register
- ❏ Cheese melter
- ❏ Coffee maker
- ❏ Convection oven
- ❏ Dishwasher
- ❏ Food cutter
- ❏ Freezer
- ❏ Fryer
- ❏ Garbage disposal
- ❏ Griddle-top range with an oven
- ❏ Hand truck (dolly)
- ❏ Heat lamps
- ❏ Ice machine
- ❏ Ice cream cabinet
- ❏ Ladles
- ❏ Meat grinder
- ❏ Microwave oven
- ❏ Mixer
- ❏ Pans
- ❏ Portion scale
- ❏ Pot holders
- ❏ Prep and steam table
- ❏ Preparation sinks
- ❏ Pressureless steamer
- ❏ Refrigerator
- ❏ Roll warmer
- ❏ Sandwich table
- ❏ Security system
- ❏ Signage
- ❏ Slicer
- ❏ Soap dispensers
- ❏ Soda system
- ❏ Spatulas
- ❏ Spoons
- ❏ Steam kettle
- ❏ Storage shelves
- ❏ Three-compartment sink
- ❏ Toaster
- ❏ Tongs
- ❏ Utensil rack
- ❏ Ventilation system

If you're entering a facility that already has a kitchen, it may already have much of the equipment you need. You can modify what's already there to meet your needs and add any additional pieces. Just be sure you have all the equipment necessary to perform the functions you need to.

Outfitting your preparation kitchen requires a substantial amount of equipment. Plan on budgeting anywhere from $27,000 to $40,000 for your heavy production equipment. Before you buy anything, study all the developments that have taken place in the industry, and look for versatile, cost-effective equipment.

Most full-service restaurants will have a mixer, a slicer, preparation sinks, a portion scale, a food cutter, baker's bins and tables, a meat grinder, a blender, a griddle-top range with an oven, a convection oven, a fryer, a cheese melter, a broiler, a pressure-less steamer, a steam kettle, and a refrigerator and freezer in their preparation kitchens.

Figure on spending another $1,000 to $2,500 for small production items like ladles, tongs, spoons, pans, pot holders, spatulas, can openers, and other miscellaneous items.

The service area of the kitchen is typically where the final touches are put on the plate and where side orders like salad, soup, sandwiches, and so forth are prepared. A kitchen helper or the server will generally be responsible for food preparation in the service kitchen.

A complete service kitchen will consist of a prep and steam table, a toaster, heat lamps, a microwave oven, a utensil rack, a roll warmer, and a sandwich table. You'll also want to place your beverage center in or near your service kitchen. You'll need a coffee maker, an ice machine, a beverage stand, a soda system, an ice cream cabinet, and a water station. You'll end up spending from about $10,000 to $18,000 to equip this area.

Dishwashing

A three-stage dishwashing machine is probably the best way to tackle your dishwashing chore. The machine itself will cost from $3,000 to $9,000. Installing the equipment, complete with landing area, dish table, garbage disposal, and three-compartment sink, will run you anywhere from $4,000 to $20,000.

Receiving and Storage

The largest and most costly piece of equipment in your receiving and storage area will be your walk-in refrigerator/freezer; you'll spend about $2,000 to $6,000 on it. This will be your main storage area, and one of your most important pieces of equipment, because it will preserve your food and keep it fresh. Don't cut corners here.

Your receiving area will also need a scale, a breakdown table, and shelving for the walk-in refrigerator/freezer. You should be able to pick these items up for $1,500 to $3,000.

Bar Equipment

Outfitting a lounge area in a restaurant can be almost as taxing as buying equipment for the restaurant. The first piece of equipment you'll need, of course, is the bar itself. You can buy a standard bar with a refrigerator underneath from an equipment dealer, or you can have one custom-made. Either way, plan to spend about $4,000 to $7,000 for the bar.

Equipping the bar will require a cash register, a three-compartment sink with a drain board, an ice bin, an ice machine, a beverage dispensing system, a beer dispensing system, glasses, mixers, blenders, ice crushers, bottle openers, and other miscellaneous tools. Altogether, the bar equipment will cost between $10,000 and $18,000.

Perhaps the most important piece of equipment for your bar is your beverage dispensing system. You want one that performs a variety of functions. Two types of automatic beverage dispensers are available: one for mixes and one for liquor. A seven-valve dispensing system that can calibrate the amounts of mix served will be sufficient when you start out. You can lease this piece of equipment for $150 to $300 per month, and leasing makes it easier to upgrade if demand warrants.

You can also pour liquor by hand. To help with portion control, you can attach pre-pour plastic spouts to each open bottle. They prevent over-pouring by dispensing a measured amount of liquor into a drink. Bar equipment manufacturers usually sell these spouts for $28 and up apiece.

Tableware and Miscellaneous Supplies

Purchase your tableware, dishes, and glasses based on the seating capacity of your operation. (See "How Much Do You Need?" below for quantity guidelines.) In addition, you need salt, pepper, and sugar containers for each table, plus one dozen sets as a backup. You'll also need a dozen sets of tongs and a dozen large pans.

You'll need paper products such as napkins, doggie bags, to-go containers with covers, place mats, towels, and tissues. Suppliers can advise you on how large an order you should place based on your seating capacity and anticipated volume.

You'll also need ashtrays, pot holders, spatulas, a wire whisk, a can opener, towel dispensers, garbage cans, a first-aid kit, a mop, a bucket, a broom, a dustpan, and bus boxes.

How Much Do You Need?

Use the following chart to determine how much tableware and how many dishes and glasses to buy for your restaurant. Simply multiply the quantity needed by your restaurant's seating capacity.

- 2 spoons and knives
- 1 iced-tea spoon
- 1 soup spoon
- 3 forks

- 2 salad plates
- 2 cups, saucers, and plates
- 1 12-oz. soda and iced-tea glass
- 1 ice cream/salsa dish

Uniforms

Most restaurants require their staffs to wear uniforms, which gives the employees and the restaurant a more professional appearance. Your cooking staff will need aprons, chef's hats, hairnets, etc. Uniforms for serving personnel are available in a wide range of styles and colors. Choose attractive uniforms and, if possible, uniforms that reflect the theme of your establishment.

Inventory

A restaurant's inventory consists of those items used in the preparation of meals and other restaurant fare. This includes fresh food items such as milk, produce, and meat, and preserved items such as canned vegetables and frozen sauces. Nonfood items, which also make up part of a restaurant's inventory, include garnishes that accompany the food items, miniature umbrellas for drinks, and disposable bibs for customers who order dishes like ribs or lobster. Restaurant supplies such as napkins, paper towels, cups, plates, and silvers are considered equipment rather than inventory because they are not actually part of the food served.

Your basic stock must fulfill two functions: First, it should provide customers with a reasonable assortment of food products. Second, it should cover the normal sales demands of your business. To calculate basic stock accurately, you must review actual sales during an appropriate time period, such as a full year of business. Of course, during your start-up, you will have no previous sales and stocking figures to guide you, so you'll project your first year's stock requirements based on your business plan.

Depending on the size and type of your restaurant, during your first year you can expect to spend anywhere from $8,000 to $60,000 on food, $2,000 to $15,000 on beverages, and $300 to $1,000 on paper products.

Staffing

There are several categories of personnel in the restaurant business: manager, cooks, servers, buspersons, dishwashers, hosts, and bartenders. Each has a specific function and contributes to the operation of the restaurant. When your restaurant is still new, you may find that some of the duties will cross over from one category to another. For example, the manager may double as the host, and servers may also bus tables. Because of this, be sure to hire people who express a willingness to be flexible in their duties.

Your payroll costs, including your own salary and that of your managers, should be about 24 to 35 percent of your total gross sales. If payroll costs are more than 35 percent of gross sales, you should look for ways to either cut those costs or increase sales.

Most restaurant workers typically work shifts from 10 A.M. to 4 P.M. or 4 P.M. to closing. One lead cook may need to arrive at your restaurant early in the morning to begin preparing soups, bread, and other items to be served that day.

Manager

The most important employee in most restaurants is the manager. A manager can help you with your duties or handle them entirely if you plan to be an absentee owner.

Your best candidate will have already managed a restaurant in your area and will be familiar with local buying sources, suppliers, and methods. A manager should be able to open and close the restaurant; purchase food and beverage inventory; open the cash register(s); track inventory; train and manage the staff; deal with suppliers; develop and implement a marketing strategy; and handle other miscellaneous duties. Beyond these responsibilities, the manager must reflect the style and character of your restaurant.

A good manager should have at least three years of nonmanagement restaurant experience in addition to two years of managerial experience. It's often best to hire a manager with a background in small restaurants because this type of person will know how to run a noncorporate eatery. As a rule, restaurant chains buy in mass quantities from central suppliers, which means chain managers probably won't have the buying experience your type of operation requires.

You also want a manager with leadership skills and the ability to supervise personnel in the kitchen, the service area, the hospitality entrance, the front state, the bar, the lounge, and the restrooms—and at the same time be able to make customers feel welcome and comfortable.

Restaurant managers typically work long hours—as many as 50 to 60 hours a week—which can contribute to a high burnout rate. To combat the potential of burnout and reduce turnover, be careful not to overwork your manager(s), and be sure they have adequate time off to relax.

To get the quality of manager you want, you'll have to pay well. Depending on your location, expect to pay a seasoned manager

Smart Tip

If you want your food prepared according to basic recipes you have developed, hire a cook rather than a chef. Cooks will follow your instructions, whereas chefs typically want to create their own dishes in addition to preparing standard fare. Chefs generally have more extensive training and command significantly higher salaries than cooks.

$30,000 to $40,000 a year, plus a percentage of sales. An entry-level manager will earn $22,000 to $26,000 but will not have the skills of a more experienced candidate. If you can't offer a high salary, work out a profit-sharing arrangement; this is an excellent way to hire good people and to motivate them to help you build a successful restaurant.

Hire your manager a month before you open so that person can help you set up your restaurant. Once the business is up and running, the manager will be able to anticipate slower times of the day or week and schedule his or her off-hours during these periods. Depending on your level of hands-on work and the size of your operation, the manager should hire and train one or two assistant managers so the restaurant will run smoothly in his or her—and your—absence.

> **Smart Tip**
>
> Be sure your entire wait staff is familiar with everything on the menu. They should know how items are prepared, how they taste, and if special requests can be accommodated. Spend at least 15 minutes with your entire crew every day before the restaurant opens, going over the menu, the specials, and any events that will be occurring that day. "Everybody must be aware of what the game plan is," says restaurateur Michael G., "and the plan can change on any given day."

A good manager can make you, and a poor manager *will* break you, so take your time finding the right person for the job.

Cooks

When you start out, you'll probably need three cooks—two full time and one part time. One of the full-time cooks should work days, and the other evenings. The part-time cook will help during peak hours, such as weekend rushes, and can work as a line cook during slower periods, doing simple preparation. The full-time cooks can also take care of food preparation before the restaurant opens, during slow times, and after the restaurant closes.

Hire your cooks according to the type of restaurant you want. If your goal is a four-star, fine-dining establishment, you'll want to hire a chef instead of a short-order cook. If you plan to have an exciting and extensive dessert menu, you may want to hire a pastry chef. Cooking schools can usually provide you with the best in the business, but look around and place ads in the paper before you hire. Customers will become regulars only if they know they can expect the best every time they dine at your restaurant—and to provide that, you need top-notch cooks and chefs.

Salaries for cooks vary according to their experience and your menu. If you have a fairly complex menu that requires a cook with a great deal of experience, you may have to pay anywhere from $400 to $500 a week. You can pay part-time cooks on an

How Many Servers Does It Take . . .

The number of servers you need depends on the type of service you want to offer, your table turn rate, the size of your restaurant, and the type of technology you're using. Massachusetts restaurateur Michael G. recalls, "When everything was done by hand, you had two forms of service. In the first, the server worked alone with maybe 15 seats to handle. A single server took the order, got the drinks, served the food, wrote the check—did everything with just the help of a busboy. The other was more elaborate, with a captain, a front and back waiter, and a busboy for each station. A team could handle 25 to 30 seats that way."

But technology is changing the way many restaurants approach staffing and service. Computers are streamlining the ordering and serving processes, with one server taking the order and entering it into the computer, where it is transferred to the kitchen, and then, when the food is ready, it's delivered by a runner who may have no further contact with the guests. A restaurant may have one or two runners whose sole job is to deliver food as it comes out of the kitchen.

Michael advises designing a floor plan that will let you create flexible stations that can be adjusted based on your volume and staffing. If you're using runners to support the servers, and the server is doing everything else except delivering the food and busing the tables, limit each server to 25 seats, or "covers." If you're not using runners, Michael suggests no more than 15 seats per server.

hourly basis; check around to see what the going rate in your area is. Remember, college students can make good part-time cooks.

Chefs

At some restaurants, the star attraction is the chef. A chef creates his or her own culinary masterpieces for you to serve. Chefs command salaries significantly higher than cooks, averaging $600 to $700 a week, and often more. You may also find chefs willing to work under profit-sharing plans.

Dishwashers

As the job title implies, dishwashers keep clean dishes available in your restaurant. You can probably get by with two part-time dishwashers, one working the lunch shift and the second covering the dinner shift. If you're open for breakfast, you can go with either one full-time and one part-time, or three part-time dishwashers. Expect to pay minimum wage to minimum wage plus $1.50 an hour.

Serving Staff

Finding the right serving staff is just as important as finding the right manager. The individual the customer will have the most interaction with while in your restaurant is the server, so servers must make a favorable impression to keep customers coming back. Servers must be able to work well under pressure, meeting the demands of customers at several tables while maintaining a positive and pleasant demeanor.

There are only two times of day for wait staff: very slow and very busy. Schedule your employees accordingly. The lunch rush, for example, starts around 11:30 A.M. and continues until 1:30 or 2 P.M. Restaurants are often slow again until the dinner crowd begins arriving around 5:30 to 6 P.M. Volume will typically begin to slow about 8 P.M. This is why some restaurants are only open for lunch and dinner peak times. During slow times, your wait staff can take care of other duties, such as refilling condiment containers.

Because servers in most types of establishments earn a good portion of their income from tips, they are usually paid minimum wage or slightly above. It's also customary for the wait staff to share their tips with the buspersons who clean the tables at their stations; some restaurants require their servers to pay the buspersons assigned to the same section 10 percent of their tips.

Bright Idea

When training servers, give them an opportunity to work in every department of your operation. Let them take reservations, greet and seat guests, bus tables, and even work in the kitchen. They'll not only be able to provide superior service once they're out on the floor waiting tables, but they'll be better team players because they'll have a first-hand understanding of everyone else's role in the process of satisfying the customer.

When your restaurant is new, you may want to hire only experienced servers so you don't have to provide extensive training. But as you become established, you should develop a training program to help your employees understand your philosophy and the image you want to project.

As part of your serving staff, you may want to hire runners who are responsible only for delivering food from the kitchen, freeing up the servers to focus on the customers.

Host Staff

Depending on the size and style of your restaurant, you may need someone to seat guests, take reservations and act as cashier. You may want to hire someone part time to cover the busy periods and have the wait staff or manager handle these duties during less busy times. Hire people-oriented, organized individuals for host positions; after all, they will determine the first impression your customers form of your service staff. Students often make great hosts. Pay for this position typically ranges from minimum wage to minimum wage plus $1.50 an hour.

Buspersons

Buspersons are responsible for setting up and clearing tables, and filling water glasses after customers are seated. Your buspersons will have stations to serve, just as your wait staff will; in fact, they should work together as a team. They should be trained to pay attention to their stations, refilling water glasses as necessary, making sure condiment containers are clean and full when the table is turned, and generally supporting the server.

Typically, your buspersons will be part-timers who work during peak periods. Servers can handle these tasks during slow times. Consider high school and college students for buspersons; they usually earn minimum wage plus a portion—generally 10 percent—of the tips the servers they assist receive.

Bartenders

If you have a small bar in your restaurant and it is only open at night, one bartender will probably be sufficient. Of course, if you expect to earn a good portion of your business from the bar, you'll need two bartenders—one full time and one part time to assist during peak periods. If your bar attracts customers both at lunch and dinner periods, you'll need two or three bartenders, or you might try a combination of a full-time bartender or bar manager, plus two or three part-time helpers.

The bartender begins his or her day by prepping the bar, which includes preparing the condiments and mixers for the entire day as well as ordering supplies. The bartender needs to check the liquor requisition sheet and the liquor inventory, and restock the bar. If you use a computerized beverage dispensing and inventory management system, the bartender will check the meters and hook up the necessary bottles.

The night bartender will close the bar. Last call for drinks occurs 30 minutes before the legally required closing time. The closing process includes packaging the garnishes and placing them in the refrigerator, and wiping down the bar area and stools.

For qualifications, look for a bartender who knows how to pour regular drinks well and prepare special requests. Experienced bartenders can make small talk and relate to people individually while juggling several drink orders in their heads. They also know when to stop pouring drinks for intoxicated customers and call a taxi or other transportation to take the customer home. Bartenders are usually paid an hourly wage—often $5 to $6 an hour—plus tips.

Pizzeria

The first pizza restaurants appeared in the United States during the 1930s. In the following decades, pizza went from novelty to fad to habit: Originally an Italian dish, pizza is now one of the most popular American fast foods. It's enjoyed as lunch, dinner, and even snacks by consumers of all age groups and socioeconomic backgrounds. People flock to try new varieties, such as Chicago- or Sicilian-style, stuffed crusts, double crusts, and creative topping combinations. But as popular as pizza is, the competition is intense—and a successful pizzeria is much more than a great pie.

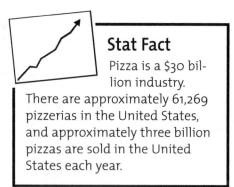

Stat Fact
Pizza is a $30 billion industry. There are approximately 61,269 pizzerias in the United States, and approximately three billion pizzas are sold in the United States each year.

You have two primary choices when starting a pizzeria. One is a to-go restaurant in a modest facility with a specialized menu highlighted by pizza and beer, limited seating, and a self-service atmosphere. The other is a full-service pizza restaurant with a menu that features not only a variety of pizzas, beer, and wine, but also Italian entrees like spaghetti, ravioli, and lasagna, side dishes such as salads (or even a salad bar), and a few desserts.

Within these generalities, specialization is the key to success for any pizzeria. A to-go pizzeria will specialize in pizza and beverages, perhaps with a limited selection of salads and simple sandwiches. Of course, even a full-service pizzeria will specialize in pizza, though you may offer a wider range of sandwiches, pasta dishes, garlic bread, and either salads or a salad bar. If your goal is a pizzeria, don't try to grow your operation into a full-service Italian restaurant; this will detract from your image as a pizzeria and will probably reduce your profits.

An operation that would work well by itself and could easily be multiplied into a chain is the to-go concept, with anywhere from 30 to 55 seats for a small section of sit-down customer dining, but without any table service.

If you don't have the extra money necessary for the sit-down portion of the business when you start, you'll be able to grow into it after things are rolling. Just be sure to plan for that growth, and be sure your facility has the space to accommodate it.

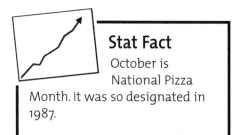

Stat Fact
October is National Pizza Month. It was so designated in 1987.

Many to-go pizza stores also deliver and find the revenue from this portion of their market substantial. With a little advertising and two or three licensed drivers from the local high school or college, you, too, can offer the convenience and reap the profits of home and/or office delivery.

The Pizza

The foundation of a pizzeria is, of course, the pizza. If you don't know how to make a good pizza, hire a good pizza cook who does. Without a good product, it doesn't

The Art of the Pie

Roll out the dough about two inches larger than the pan. Press it into the curves of the pan, then pull some slack dough into the center for shrinkage, and trim the edges around the pan. Spread sauce with a ladle over the entire surface to the edges. Use more cheese on the plain cheese pizzas and less on those with other toppings. Add the toppings chosen by the customer, spreading them evenly. Never overload the pie, because it will take so long to cook through to the middle that the bottom will burn.

The oven should be set from 500 to 550 degrees Fahrenheit—hotter if you are busy and opening the oven door often. If you are using fresh dough, cook the pizza in the pan until the top is golden brown; then slide the pie off the pan to brown the bottom.

Remove the pizza from the oven with the peel, slide it onto a cool pizza pan, cut, and serve.

matter what else you do; you will fail. Invest in top-quality ingredients and preparation methods, and make every pizza as if you are going to eat it yourself. Do that, and your customers will keep coming back.

Should you offer thick or thin crust? It depends on your market. People who hail from the eastern United States seem to like a thick, doughy crust, while Westerners generally prefer a thin, crisp one. But in our mobile, homogenized society, you may be wise to offer both. For thinner crusts, use pre-formed shells, and make the thick ones yourself.

You might also want to offer a choice of crust flavors. Do that by sprinkling special toppings or spices—such as garlic, Parmesan cheese, or poppy seeds—on the crust before baking. The market response to these "specialty" crusts has been tremendous, and you can offer them for free or a nominal extra charge, because they cost you practically nothing extra, yet they make the pizza much more flavorful. If you offer a variety of crusts, be sure to promote them on your menus and other marketing materials.

Stat Fact

Thin pizza crust is still the most popular crust, preferred by 61 percent of the population. Thick crust and deep dish tied for second place, at 14 percent. Only 11 percent of the population prefers extra-thin crust.

Beyond the basic crust is the style of pizza. Sicilian- and Chicago-style pizzas are varieties

And to Top It Off . . .

What do Americans want on their pizzas? Their favorite topping is pepperoni. Other popular toppings are mushrooms, extra cheese, sausage, green peppers, and onions. Anchovies rank last on the list of favorite toppings.

In some parts of the country, gourmet toppings are gaining popularity. Pizza lovers are experimenting with such toppings as chicken, oysters, crayfish, dandelions, sprouts, eggplant, shrimp, artichoke hearts, and tuna. Approximately two-thirds of Americans prefer meat toppings; one-third prefer vegetarian toppings.

with thick, chewy crusts. Chicago-style is baked in a deep dish, while Sicilian is baked on a flat pan. But the ingredients are essentially the same, so you can try experimenting with both traditional and other styles to see what sells best in your market. But don't get carried away with variety—you don't want to overburden your cook with too many shapes and sizes that have different cooking times, require customized pans, or need special dough-rolling procedures.

Setting Up Your Facility

A to-go pizzeria has minimal space requirements. Most range in size from small takeout and home-delivery operations of only 800 square feet to larger limited-seating-capacity operations of 1,500 square feet. For a full-service pizzeria, you'll need a facility between 2,500 and 4,000 square feet. Depending on the type of facility you want to open and your own resources, expect to spend $70,000 to $1.5 million to get your pizzeria ready for your grand opening.

There are no textbook ratios for distribution of space in a pizzeria, but a good formula is to allocate 20 percent for your customer service area (25 percent in a strictly to-go/home-delivery operation); 45 percent for the dining area; and 35 percent for your production area (see sample layouts on pages 57–58). Of course, if you do not provide a dining area, your production area will be adjusted upward to 75 percent.

For dine-in pizzerias, allotting 60 to 65 percent of the space for dining and customer service allows adequate room for quality food production. If you let the production area fall below 35 percent, you run the risk of limiting yourself in a way that could result in poor-quality food.

Customer Service Area

Your customer service area determines the first impression your customers will have of your pizzeria's atmosphere. Use this space to create an appropriate ambience that takes maximum advantage of available space. The customer service area should include a waiting area for customers, a cashier's station, and public restrooms.

The exact layout will depend on whether your operation is a to-go or full-service pizzeria. In both types, the waiting area and cashier's station will be located directly at the entrance to the facility, but this is where the similarities end.

Stat Fact

Kids between the ages of 3 and 11 prefer pizza for lunch and dinner over all other food groups.

In addition to the waiting area and cashier's station, a to-go pizzeria will have an order/pick-up counter that serves both the take-out and sit-down customers. This counter will usually stretch wall-to-wall across the facility to separate the production area from the customer service and dining areas. The cashier's station should be incorporated into the order/pick-up counter so customers can pay when they order.

Location Is Everything

Most pizzerias are located near business sections of cities and towns. The industry leaders—Domino's, Pizza Hut, and Papa John's—are looking for strong lunch business, as well as early dinner, dinner, and post-dinner-crowd business. Pizzerias are typically located in areas where the disposable income is high. Your best location choice is one with a strong day and nighttime population, easy access for both cars and pedestrians, and a consistent traffic flow.

Most pizzerias used to be in free-standing buildings, but that trend has shifted. Pizzerias are springing up in all sorts of locations, including shopping centers and mall food courts. You may find it profitable to locate either in a mall or in a free-standing building next to a mall, which lets you share the mall's traffic. Another good location would be one that is convenient to commercial office developments. You can turn almost any space into a thriving pizzeria if you have the customer base, the knowledge, and the capital to make it happen. Just be sure your market research supports your final location decision.

Line the walls of the waiting area for take-out customers with bench seats. Don't skimp on quality here; this should be cushioned seating so your customers are comfortable during their wait. Face it: Even a short wait will seem like a long time when someone needs to get back to the office at lunchtime or is tired, hungry, and in a hurry to get home in the evening. Hard seats or no seats in an uncomfortable waiting area can generate unfavorable word-of-mouth advertising and will send customers to your competition.

In a full-service pizzeria, make the cashier's station a small counter that parallels one wall at the entrance. To conserve space, the cashier's station can double as the host stand, or you can set up a separate host stand at the threshold between the customer service area and the dining area. A small wooden lectern with a ledger-type book to record the names of waiting guests, and perhaps a storage area underneath for menus, is usually sufficient for a host stand. As in a to-go pizzeria, the waiting area should have a few bench-style seats lining its walls.

Locate your beverage center behind the customer service counter toward its end. If you choose to have customers serve themselves beverages, as many fast-food and self-service restaurants are doing these days, place the dispenser near the front counter so your employees can keep an eye on it. You need to make sure it is clean and functioning properly at all times.

If you have sit-down customers, you will need to provide public restrooms, which are usually located close to the dining area.

Dining Area

Whether your pizzeria is self-service or full-service, a sit-down dining area increases your profit potential. That's why it's imperative that you don't cut corners when designing and decorating your dining room. This is, after all, the area that has the most impact on your customers.

The space required per seat will vary depending on your type of operation. In a to-go, self-service pizzeria, the amount of space per seat should range between 12 and 15 square feet. A full-service pizzeria will need between 15 and 18 square feet per seat; this ensures comfortable seating and enough aisle space so servers have room to move between tables.

Essential service items for your dining area include dishware, plates, glasses, flatware, and an assortment of containers to hold foods not served on dinner plates. Salt and pepper shakers and napkin holders for each table are optional; if you prefer to present them on request, be sure you have enough for at least half the tables at any given time. If your menu includes bread with most meals, you'll need as many bread baskets as you have tables.

Keep your overall concept in mind when choosing your dinnerware. Many to-go pizzerias place paper plates and plastic forks, spoons, and knives on a self-service table

Sample To-Go Pizzeria Layout

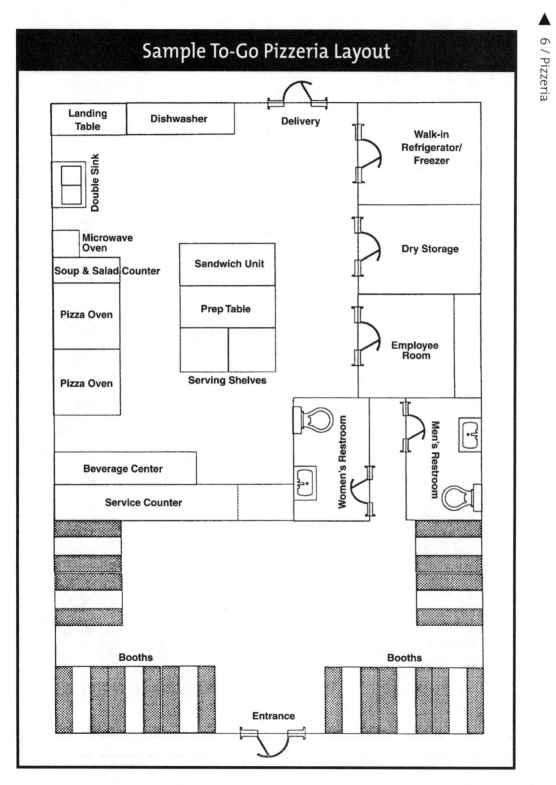

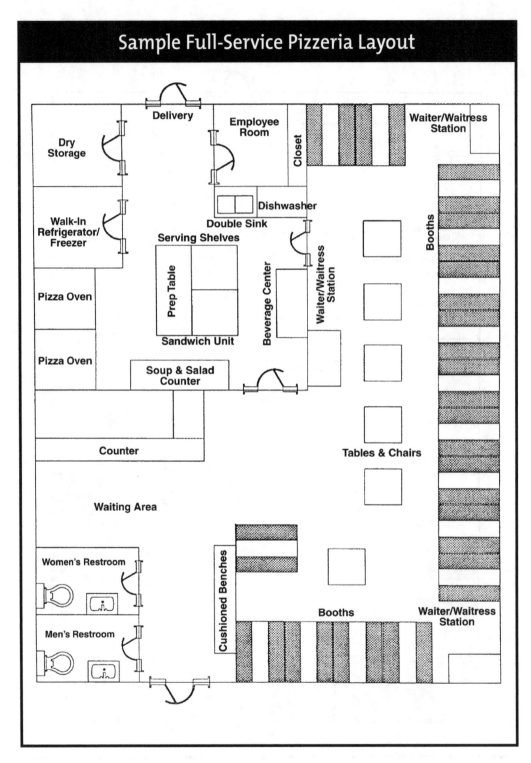

Sample Full-Service Pizzeria Layout

and serve the beverages in mugs. A full-service pizzeria can't get away with this cost-cutting approach. Plan to spend about $2,000 to $3,500 for a complete set of dinnerware for a full-service pizzeria.

Production Area

You need enough room in the food preparation area to accommodate prep tables, pizza oven(s), range, microwave oven(s), a small refrigerator/freezer, an exhaust fan for the ventilation system, utensils and smallware, and other food production equipment you need. To-go pizzerias might need less food prep space than full-service operations, depending on menu offerings and specific equipment needs. In any case, arrange this area so everything is positioned within a few steps of the cook. It should also be designed so that two or more cooks can work side by side during rush periods.

Dishwashing and trash areas should be located toward the rear of your operation, near the receiving port. Allow about 4 percent of your total space for these areas. Dishwashing equipment can usually be situated in a corner so it doesn't get in the way of food-service personnel. A to-go pizzeria may not need a commercial dishwasher, but you will need adequate facilities—a three-compartment sink and adjacent counter space and racks—for washing cooking utensils and the small amount of dishware and tableware you use.

Your production area will also need receiving and inventory storage facilities, an employee room, and a small office or administrative area. See Chapter 4 for more on setting up your facility.

Equipment

Aside from building preparation, equipment will be one of your biggest start-up expenses. New equipment to run your pizzeria will cost from $50,000 to $100,000, depending on the type of operation you choose. The good news is that you don't have to buy everything new. This section will explain the process of deciding what you need, how and where to find it, and how to acquire it for as little as possible.

Equipment selection for a pizzeria is a complex process and will require some time and research beyond the scope of this guide. For example, some ovens can perform a multitude of cooking procedures, from baking pizza and cooking meats to reheating entrees and melting cheese on appetizers. Ice machines, on the other hand, have only one use: they make ice. Some equipment is basic to every food-service operation; other items are unique to pizzerias. The prerequisite to purchasing equipment is knowing exactly what you need to prepare the foods on your menu. It will also help you to know how other pizzerias are equipped. Before Anthony A. started his pizza

▲

Where the Ovens Are

You have three choices when it comes to pizza ovens: electric, gas, and wood-fired. Electric is the least desirable, because it doesn't generate enough heat to properly cook the pizza crust. Anthony A. says gas generates a good hot, dry heat, which can produce a consistently good product. But, he adds, "Wood-fire beats gas and electric hands down because you can get the temperature almost twice as hot as you can with a gas oven. In my opinion, the rate of that heat is what really makes the dough—deliciously crunchy on the outside and chewy on the inside. Wood-fire heat is the way to go." He insists that even the nonconnoisseur who routinely orders pizza from take-out chains can tell the difference between a conventionally cooked pizza and a wood-fired pizza.

Though wood-fired ovens may be best, they're not cheap. Anthony and his current business partner, Michael G., installed two wood-fired ovens imported from Italy in their current restaurant at approximately $12,000 each. "They give us a superior product," he says.

---

parlor, he visited other pizzerias, observed as much as he could, and asked as many questions as he could. "I tried to find people to interview, people who worked in pizza places, and people who sold the equipment," he says. "I found out as much as I could, then put together what I thought was reasonable."

You may want to spend some time talking with a restaurant consultant before making your final purchase decisions. Don't rush into choosing your furniture, fixtures, and equipment—especially if you're not sure exactly what you want or require, or how it will all blend together.

Food Production Equipment

While the equipment needs of a to-go pizzeria and a full-service facility will vary, one piece of equipment essential to both is a pizza oven. Your oven should be able to heat to 650 degrees Fahrenheit and have a minimum deck space of 32 inches deep and 42 inches wide, with a seven-inch mouth. A new single-deck oven can be purchased for $2,000 to $3,000. If you anticipate a sales volume of $1,500 or more per week, buy a double unit for $3,000 to $7,000. Because gas ovens heat more intensely than electric, most pizza chefs prefer them.

In addition to the oven, you'll need a range or hot plate for cooking sauces and pastas. You can buy a used household range for about $125 or a used commercial gas

Pizzeria Major Equipment and Fixtures Checklist

- ❑ 45-gallon bakers' bins on wheels (2)
- ❑ Beer/wine serving equipment
- ❑ Breakdown table
- ❑ Cash register
- ❑ Coffee maker
- ❑ Company vehicle
- ❑ Dinnerware
- ❑ Dishwasher
- ❑ Dolly/hand truck
- ❑ Dough mixer/blender
- ❑ Dough roller
- ❑ Dry storage shelving
- ❑ Fixtures (booths/tables)
- ❑ Gas hot plate/range
- ❑ Grinder
- ❑ Hand slicer/electric slicer
- ❑ Hot boxes
- ❑ Ice machine
- ❑ Microwave oven

- ❑ Office equipment
- ❑ Office furniture
- ❑ Pasta machine
- ❑ Pizza oven(s)
- ❑ Portion scale
- ❑ Prep table
- ❑ Production area refrigeration units
- ❑ Scale for receiving area
- ❑ Security system
- ❑ Service counter
- ❑ Signage
- ❑ Soft drink system
- ❑ Stainless-steel shelving for walk-in
- ❑ Three-compartment sink
- ❑ Toaster
- ❑ Utensils and production tableware
- ❑ Ventilation system
- ❑ Walk-in refrigerator/freezer

hot plate for about $100. Whichever you choose, set it up next to the pizza oven for the cook's convenience. Other necessary items include a toaster oven for preparing garlic bread and a microwave oven for reheating pasta.

The service area of the kitchen is typically where the pizza will be made and side orders (such as salads and bread sticks) prepared. The cook should be in charge of preparing the pizza, and a kitchen helper or the servers can handle side orders.

A complete service area for a pizzeria kitchen usually contains these basic components: a prep table, a slicer or grinder, a portion scale, a dough mixer/blender, a dough roller, production hardware, and a utensil rack.

Your health department may require a stainless-steel top on the prep table. If so, a six-foot table will cost about $100 used and up to $400 new. If not, you can buy a Formica top or work counter for about $50 used. It's a good idea to have an inexpensive second table to use for cutting and boxing orders.

Some pizzerias grind their toppings; others slice. It doesn't seem to make a lot of difference to customers, so the choice is yours. A slicer is a must, however, if your menu will include Italian sandwiches. A new electric slicer will cost $800 to $3,000 and should last for several years. You may consider a hand slicer with various attachments for smaller jobs; expect to pay $250 to $650 for that.

You'll need a small grinder or cheese grater to grate the cheese for your pizzas. Invest in a good professional grinder; they range in price from $3,000 to $4,000. Don't try to "make do" by grating cheese by hand; you'll wear yourself out and probably won't be able to keep up with the demand.

To maintain consistency in quality and give your inventory control procedures a fighting chance, you'll need a portion scale. It's not enough to buy the scale; make sure your employees use it. It will let you estimate the amount of each ingredient you need to prepare

Smart Tip

Budget between $27,000 and $40,000 for the heavy production equipment in your pizzeria kitchen. Before you buy, study all the new developments in the industry—new technologies and methods are being developed constantly, and you need to know what's out there so you can make the best choice for your operation. Read trade magazines and industry newspapers to keep up on the latest equipment advances and facility design innovations.

each dish efficiently and with a strong degree of accuracy. If your chefs are "guesstimating" on portions, they'll probably use too much inventory and you'll be serving your profits rather than taking them to the bank. Dollar for dollar, the $30 to $150 you'll spend on a portion scale may well be the wisest investment you make in your pizzeria.

Assuming you're going to make your own pizza dough but don't want the upperbody workout mixing dough by hand provides, you'll need a dough mixer/blender. This is not a necessity when starting, but will probably become crucial as your business grows. A new heavy-duty dough mixer/blender will cost about $1,200; used ones can be found for as low as $350.

For rolling out your pizza shells, you can either do it by hand or purchase a mechanical roller. The speed and efficiency of a mechanical roller lets you prepare shells as you need them; if you're going to do it by hand, you can roll the shells in advance and refrigerate them until you're ready to use them. Don't roll more than you can use in two or three hours, though, as shells get tough and gummy if left sitting around too long.

If you're planning on a full-service restaurant and your menu will include a variety of pasta dishes in addition to pizzas, consider a pasta machine. This is a purely optional investment that lets you make your own noodles from scratch rather than buying pre-made pasta from grocery wholesalers. Because your main menu focus is pizza, a home-kitchen-style pasta machine should be sufficient; expect to pay about $200 for a high-quality machine.

Bakers' bins are especially useful in a full-service operation. They will make preparing your pizza crusts, pasta, and other products much easier. Your prep table should have enough space underneath for these large bins. Also, the bins should be on rollers so they can be easily moved around. You'll spend $175 to $350 for bakers' bins.

Utensils and Miscellaneous Equipment

The cost of the small stuff can add up, so pay close attention to what you really need in this area. In a typical pizzeria, you'll need 12 plastic or stainless-steel bins (about $2 each) for pizza ingredients; four 12-inch, four 15-inch, and four 18-inch pizza pans (about $4 each, used) for baking pizzas and sorting dough; one *peel*, which is the large, long-handled wooden spatula that is used to lift the pizzas from the oven ($7 used to $35 new); a large pot (20- to 40-gallon variety) in which to cook sauces; two four-quart pots (for weighing dough ingredients, etc.); one rolling pin; one can opener; one pizza cutter; one large ladle (for spooning sauce); and knives. Plan to spend $800 to $1,200 on these items.

You may or may not want to insist on uniforms for your cooking staff, but they will at least need aprons, chef's hats, and hairnets. Uniforms for servers are available in a variety of styles, colors, and price ranges.

Beverage Center

Your beverage center can be located completely in the service kitchen or split between the service kitchen and the customer service area if you offer self-service drink machines. The typical beverage center will include a coffee machine, an ice machine, a water station, and a soft drink dispensing system. If you sell beer, the tap

The Chain Gang

Pizza Hut is the largest pizza seller in the world, with nearly 13,000 restaurants and combination delivery/take-out units in the U.S. and more than 90 other countries. Domino's is the world leader in pizza delivery. Papa John's is considered the fastest-growing pizzeria chain in the United States.

Of the pizza franchise units in the United States, approximately 83 percent offer delivery, 91 percent offer take-out, and 51 percent offer dine-in service.

should be behind the counter under your employees' control. Bottled beer and wine should also be stored in coolers out of the general reach of customers. Expect to spend $6,000 to $11,000 on beverage equipment.

Inventory

Your menu will determine your inventory, but there are some items you must purchase by virtue of the fact that you're running a pizzeria. Here are some of the more typical inventory categories you'll be dealing with:

- *Meats.* You'll need sliced and processed meats as part of your pizza toppings selection. Some of the more common meats are pepperoni, sausage, and Canadian bacon. You may also need ground beef if you will be offering dishes with meatballs or pasta shells filled with meat (such as ravioli).

Stat Fact
Collectively, Americans eat approximately 100 acres of pizza each day, or 350 slices per second. Each man, woman, and child in America eats an average of 46 slices (23 pounds) of pizza a year.

- *Dairy products.* Pizzerias use great quantities of cheese as a primary pizza topping. If you are going to make your own pizza crust, garlic bread, or pasta, you may also be using milk and eggs in large quantities.

The Fight of the Year: Price versus Quality

Pizzerias tend to vacillate between price promotions and focusing on quality in their marketing efforts. Pizza Hut recently decided to conduct a survey to find out what is truly most important to consumers. The survey asked what customers ranked as most and least important when choosing a restaurant. More than half—57 percent—ranked the quality of the food as the most important consideration; 20 percent said cleanliness of the restaurant was most important; 11 percent ranked the price of the food as most important; 4 percent said their chief concern was speed of service; and 3 percent said it was courtesy of employees. Only 4 percent of respondents named quality as their least important concern, and 20 percent said price was least important.

- *Sauces.* You'll need a variety of sauces, both for pizzas and other Italian dishes. Sauces can be purchased by the can in bulk quantities or made from scratch. Most restaurateurs buy canned sauces and add various herbs to spice them to taste and give them a unique flavor.

- *Fresh produce.* You'll use fresh vegetables as pizza toppings, in salads, and as side dishes.

- *Pastas and breads.* If you make your own pizza dough, pastas, and breads, you'll use a great deal of flour. Some of these products are available either pre-made or partially prepared, which can speed up your production process.

Bright Idea

Consider using manufactured pizza shells. While pizza connoisseurs say pre-made crusts don't have the taste of those made with fresh dough, they simplify a pizza operation. Try some and see for yourself; there might be a manufacturer in your area who uses a formula that surpasses the run-of-the-mill recipes. Expect to pay 25 to 30 cents for a 12-inch (small) pizza shell, and more for larger sizes. To find a supplier, look under "Food Products" and "Restaurant Supplies" in the Yellow Pages.

- *Condiments and dressings.* You'll need salt, pepper, cooking oil, garlic, oregano, red pepper flakes, Parmesan cheese, and many other items that help finish off your dishes. If you offer salads, you'll want to stock canned and packaged items like olives, pickles, kidney beans, and garbanzo beans. Unless you are serving only antipasto salads, you'll need a selection of dressings, such as Italian (of course), bleu cheese, French, Thousand Island, and perhaps an herb or honey-mustard flavor. At least one dressing should be low-fat.

- *Beverages.* Soft drinks are considered necessary beverages for a pizzeria. You'll also need to serve coffee, tea, and milk. Beer and wine are very profitable, but state and local licenses may be expensive and are not always easy to obtain.

- *Paper and plastic products.* You will need a variety of paper and plastic products both for your take-out and delivery orders, as well as your dining room service. The list includes: straws, napkins, paper cups, bags, plastic tableware, pizza boxes, spaghetti/pasta cartons, and salad containers. Most of these items are available from paper products distributors; check the Yellow Pages for distributors in your area.

- *Hot food bags.* If you offer delivery, you'll need insulated food bags to keep the pizza and other food warm during transit. Hot food bags run $25 to $35 each, and you'll need three or four for each driver.

▲

Staffing

How you staff your pizzeria will depend, of course, on the size and scope of your operation. You'll definitely need a cook to make the pizzas and other menu items; a cashier; if you offer sit-down dining, you'll need a host or hostess and wait staff; if you offer delivery, you'll need drivers; and possibly buspersons and other cleaning staff.

Pay scales will vary depending on region and whether or not the position is likely to earn tips. A glance through the help-wanted section of your local newspaper will give you a fairly accurate idea of what you can expect to pay.

Sandwich Shop
and Delicatessen

The wide appeal of sandwiches, both nation-
ally and internationally, ensures the stability of sandwich shops
and delicatessens. Sandwiches, after all, have been around for a
long time. In fact, the sandwich is named for the fourth Earl of
Sandwich, John Montagu. This English nobleman of the 1700s is

said to have eaten them while at the gaming table so he didn't have to take time out for a formal meal.

For centuries, sandwich shops have lined the streets of Europe. One cannot walk down a street in Paris, for instance, without passing a sandwich shop or a bakery that sells baguettes (French long bread) and sandwiches. The croque-monsieur (melted ham and cheese on bread) is a popular sandwich in France. Italians, on the other hand, make sandwiches with focaccia (a spiced bread), vegetables, salami, and mozzarella cheese. Sandwiches are no less popular in the U.S. Philadelphia, for example, has become well-known for its "Philly cheese-steak" sandwiches.

One reason sandwich shops are so successful is that they enjoy high profit margins. You can sell a sub sandwich for $1.49 with food costs of just 34 percent. Sandwich shops and delicatessens can also change their menus quickly and easily to adapt to current tastes. For example, with the growing interest in health and nutrition in the United States, sandwich shops and delicatessens have started offering more low-fat, healthy ingredients in their sandwiches, salads, and other menu items. Also, many sandwich shops and delis have been able to keep up with American workers who eat at their workplaces by adding delivery and catering to their sit-down and take-out operations.

Sandwich shops and delicatessens can be differentiated by the foods they serve. Most sandwich shops serve only sandwiches, possibly with some side dishes or desserts. A delicatessen usually serves a more extensive menu, including sandwiches, prepared meats, smoked fish, cheeses, salads, relishes, and various hot entrees. The word "delicatessen" comes from the French *delicatesse*, meaning "delicacy." Delicatessen has now come to mean both the foods themselves and the shops that sell them.

A full-scale delicatessen will usually have a dining area and offer sit-down service as well as take-out, while a sandwich shop may only offer take-out. While this chapter will discuss both types of businesses, you need to decide whether you want to open a sandwich shop, a deli, or a combination.

Factors contributing to the fast growth of sandwich shops and delis are their start-up costs and operating costs, which tend to be lower than those of other fast-food enterprises. Some sandwich shop franchises promise start-up packages as low as $40,000, and many are below $150,000. Low-end independents have started for as little as $36,500. The average start-up cost for a sandwich shop is $91,800.

Competition

Your competition in most locations will consist of other quick-service outlets (fast-food, specialty, and ethnic restaurants, and other sandwich shops and delis), grocery-store deli departments, national sandwich shop chains, and some sit-down restaurants.

> **Bright Idea**
>
> If your sandwich shop/deli will offer party platters or catering as a service, be sure to ask if prospective customers ever buy party platters or use caterers when you conduct your initial market research.

- *Quick-service/fast-food restaurants.* One major advantage a sandwich shop or deli has over many of the fast-food restaurants is the ability to provide both quick service and more healthy food choices. You can promote this as a strong selling point.

You should also be able to compete easily against fast-food restaurant prices. You may not be able to match a 59-cent burger, but you should be able to come close to matching prices for premium sandwiches, such as chicken or steak sandwiches, which usually sell for $2.50 or more. If you offer a pickle or coleslaw with your sandwiches, you can sell a more satisfying meal than some of the fast-food chains, which usually sell just the sandwich.

- *Grocery-store deli departments.* Because they buy in volume and appear to have a captive audience, an in-store deli may seem like strong competition, but don't let it scare you. Many people just don't think of going to the grocery store for lunch and will find your easy-in, easy-out shop preferable to a supermarket.

- *National sandwich shop chains.* National chains may have huge advertising budgets, but you have a number of competitive advantages. You can offer an innovative menu that's customized to local preferences along with high-quality food. Personalized service is another plus for an independent operator; get to know your customers by name, and greet them when they come through the door. Eye contact, good service, and a smile go a long way toward building customer loyalty, whether you're competing against a national chain or another independent.

Setting Up Your Facility

Whether you plan on opening a take-out sandwich shop with a limited menu or a full-scale sit-down delicatessen, you will need enough space for a production area (a kitchen or sandwich preparation area), a customer service area, a receiving and storage area, and at least one employee restroom. You will also need some kind of office, though some sandwich shop and deli owners use a homebased office to keep commercial space requirements to a minimum. A dining area and public restrooms may also be included in your facility. Expect to use a facility with somewhere between 500 and 3,000 square feet (see sample layouts on pages 71–72).

▲

Catering to Their Every Whim

Delivery and small-scale catering can generate additional revenue for your sandwich shop/deli. You can offer delivery of standard menu items to a specified geographic area around your shop for no charge or a small charge, depending on the market demand.

A catering operation could consist of sandwich and party platters or more elaborate menus. Include both of these options in your market research to determine demand. You'll also need to consider whether your start-up budget allows for the equipment you'll need to provide these additional services. You may want to start out with a small shop and expand your service offerings later; however, knowing your eventual goals will help you make better choices on your initial equipment purchases. Maxine T. started with a catering operation and added three delicatessens; each deli has a catering menu prominently displayed.

See Chapter 10 for more information on starting a catering service.

Converting an existing food-service operation (such as a bakery, deli, or small restaurant) can lower your initial investment. In any case, if you will specialize in serving customers on the go, you can probably get by with 500 to 750 square feet, including kitchen space. If you want to offer a more extensive menu and allow space for customer seating, you'll want a facility as large as 3,000 square feet.

In a strictly take-out operation, allow 75 percent for your production area, 15 percent for customer service, and 10 percent for storage, restrooms, and a lounge. If you plan to have a combination take-out/sit-down operation, allow about 35 percent for the production area, 5 percent for customer service, 50 percent for the dining area, and 10 percent for storage, restrooms and the lounge.

Production Area

The production area will include space for sandwich and salad preparation. Depending on your menu, it may require space for preparing hot items as well. If you decide to offer sit-down service and a full menu, you will probably set up both a service and a preparation kitchen. (A service kitchen is simpler than a preparation kitchen. You will use it to

> **Bright Idea**
> Another option for your location is a nontraditional site, such as a mobile kitchen or a cart. With this strategy, you can take your food to where your customers are.

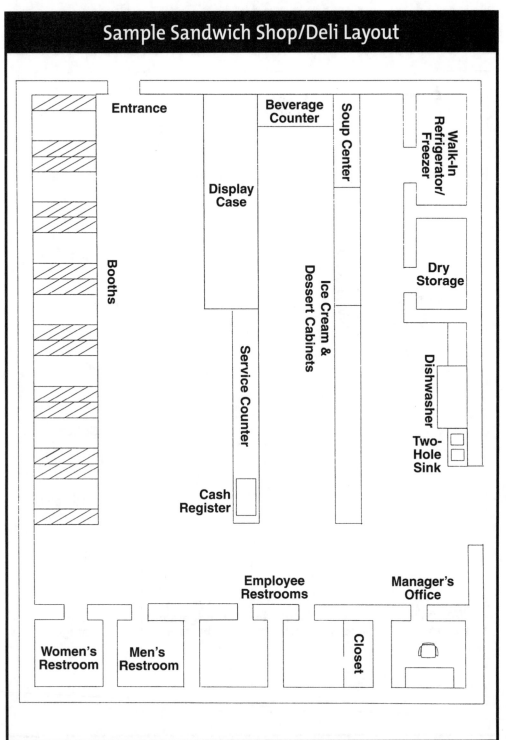

Sample Sandwich Shop/Deli Layout

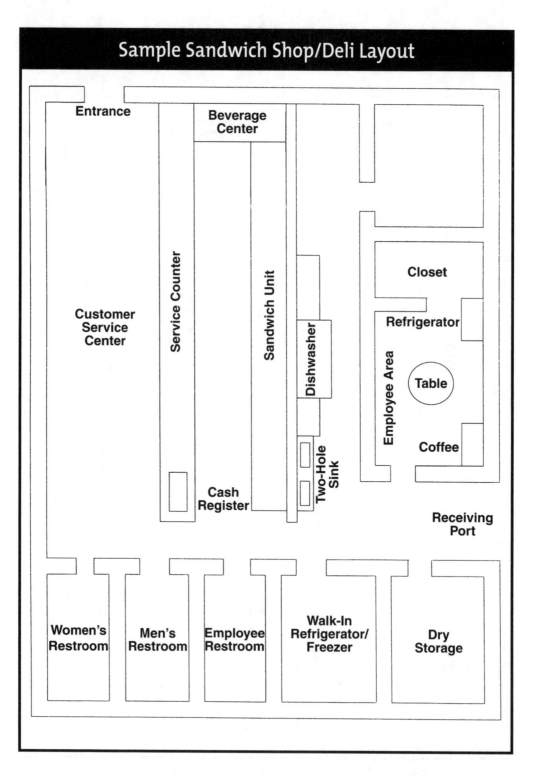

Sample Sandwich Shop/Deli Layout

Entrance

Beverage Center

Customer Service Center

Service Counter

Sandwich Unit

Dishwasher

Closet

Refrigerator

Employee Area

Table

Coffee

Two-Hole Sink

Cash Register

Receiving Port

Women's Restroom

Men's Restroom

Employee Restroom

Walk-In Refrigerator/ Freezer

Dry Storage

prepare sandwiches and basic items such as soups. A preparation kitchen will be more elaborate, allowing you to prepare a wide variety of hot items.) Many sandwich shops/delis can get by with a simple setup such as the following:

In a sandwich shop, the customer service and production areas are usually separated by a simple service counter. A deli will have a three-tiered, refrigerated, glass-fronted case, instead of a counter, to display the wider variety of cheeses, salads, and various types of fish that delis usually offer.

Against the wall behind either the service counter or display case will be the sandwich preparation area. This area will contain bread boards on which sandwiches will be made, a meat slicer, and shelving for frequently used ingredients. Toward the rear of the production area, on the same side of the wall, will be a sandwich warmer, a double sink unit, and a refrigerator. On the other side of the sandwich preparation area, nearest the entrance, will be your soft drink dispensing system and coffee maker.

Whether you use this layout or a more traditional layout with both service and preparation kitchens, your primary concern is to make sure the production area is as streamlined as possible to ensure efficient delivery of food to waiting customers. A poorly designed area reduces the effectiveness of both equipment and personnel.

Customer Service Area

A principal requirement for the customer service area is that it be large enough to accommodate customers, display case(s), or service counter(s) and at least one cashier station. In a strictly take-out operation, you may want to devote as much as 15 percent of your space to this area to accommodate several waiting customers during busy periods. In an operation offering sit-down service, this area should only occupy about 5 percent of your space, which is just enough for take-out customers to place orders and for sit-down customers to wait to be seated (if need be).

In a deli, your refrigerated display cases will be important marketing tools, as they'll be displaying and thus advertising much of your menu. The salads and ingredients should be attractively displayed, and the case should be well-lighted. The glass should be spotless and the chrome shiny and clean.

Likewise, the counter area in a sandwich shop should be spotless. Since the customer service area will be the first thing patrons see upon entering your shop, cleanliness will make a good first impression.

In addition to the display cases or counter, this area will also have a cashier's station. All you need is enough space for the cash register at the end of the counter nearest the entrance.

Dining Area

Dining areas in delis and sandwich shops range from small self-service areas set aside almost as a courtesy to customers (with perhaps three to five tables, each with two to four chairs) to full-scale dining rooms with booths lining the walls, tables, and chairs in the center of the area, and a wait staff to serve patrons. The latter borders on being a full-scale restaurant; if that's your goal, use the information in Chapter 5 to guide you in setting up and managing your operation.

For a typical sandwich shop/deli in a small facility of 500 square feet, consider having six to eight small tables with a total of 12 to 18 chairs. For a larger facility of, say, 1,200 square feet, consider 10 to 12 tables with 20 to 36 chairs. You don't want the chairs to be overly comfortable; look for chairs that discourage lingering. Turnover is key in a business that must capitalize on a few peak periods—or even one period, namely lunch—per day.

How Much Do You Need?

If you're going to offer sit-down dining, use the following guide to determine the amount of dinnerware you'll need:

Item	Times Seating Capacity
Spoons and knives	2.5
Iced-tea spoons	1.5
Soup spoons	1
Forks	3
Cups, saucers and plates	2.5
Salad plates	2
12-oz. soda and iced-tea glasses	1.5
Ice cream/salsa dishes	1

In addition, you'll need salt, pepper, and sugar containers for each table, plus a dozen sets as a backup.

Receiving and Storage, Office, and Restrooms

About 5 to 10 percent of your total space will be used for receiving and storing food. Your receiving area should be accessible to delivery vans. It should have double doors and a dolly for easy transport of goods. Your dry storage facility should be located right next to your receiving area. It might include an additional freezer and an employee restroom. Contact your county or state health department for area regulations that govern how many employee restrooms are required.

For a sit-down facility, you will probably also want to provide at least one, if not two, public restrooms, each fully equipped for handicapped access. Contact your city or county building department for the building and plumbing codes that apply. Your restrooms don't need to be fancy or elegant, but patrons will expect them to be attractive and clean.

A large storage room can double as your back office. You need enough space for a desk, a phone, a small filing cabinet, and shelves. If you have the room, you may also want to provide some lockers in the storage area for your employees.

Image

The image of any food-service operation is important to attracting and keeping customers. Balance professionalism and cleanliness with a comfortable atmosphere.

Research shows that you have less than ten seconds to attract the attention of a passerby, so your signs and the exterior of your facility must have high impact. There are a variety of decorating ideas and thematic treatments you can use to set your operation apart from sterile fast-food restaurants.

In shopping center take-out facilities, operators use eye-catching displays with large, high-quality product photos and unique logos. Be sure to replace photos regularly; a tattered or limp picture of a faded sandwich is not especially appetizing.

A clever attention-getting device used by many sandwich shops is having the production process clearly visible to passersby. Displaying the ingredients and showing the sandwiches being made has proved to be an effective technique for drawing customers.

Inside, create a warm, inviting setting with inexpensive hanging plants (live, not artificial), posters, photographs and so on. Paintings,

Smart Tip

Tip...

If you use plants as part of your decor, be sure they are healthy and well-maintained. Droopy or brown leaves, or plants infested with insects, are not likely to contribute to a positive dining experience.

murals, wall plaques, and pictures can effectively establish a theme, but you don't need to spend too much money on them. Creativity and cleanliness are much more important than thousands of dollars' worth of theme decoration.

Because cleanliness is essential, choose surfaces that are durable and easy to clean, such as washable wall coverings, tile floors, walls covered in enamel-based paints, etc.

Equipment

A key advantage of a simple sandwich shop is that equipment needs are minimal compared to that of a full-scale restaurant. Many sandwich shops serve only cold sandwiches and don't do any on-site cooking, so their equipment costs are comparatively low. A deli or sandwich shop serving hot entrees requires a larger investment.

There is some equipment that all restaurants need, such as preparation tables, slicers, cutlery, pots and pans, ovens, refrigerators, and freezers. Whether you decide to bake your own bread, how extensive a menu you offer, and whether you offer sit-down service will determine what further investment you will need to make in equipment and fixtures. Most likely, it will be somewhat lower than for the typical dine-in restaurant.

Production Equipment

A service kitchen, which you will use for fairly simple tasks such as preparing sandwiches, requires a preparation and steam table, a toaster, heat lamps, a microwave oven, a utensil rack, a roll warmer, and a sandwich table. You'll also need to install your beverage center near your service kitchen. You'll need a coffee maker, an ice machine, a beverage stand, a soda system, an ice cream cabinet, and a water station. You'll end up spending from $10,000 to $18,000 to equip the service kitchen.

Setting up your preparation kitchen will require a lot more equipment and a lot more capital. Budget anywhere from $27,000 to $40,000 for your heavy production equipment. Most sandwich shops and delicatessens have some or all of the following: a slicer, preparation sinks, a portion scale, a food cutter, bakers' bins and tables, a meat grinder, a blender, a griddle top range with oven, a convection oven, a fryer, a cheese melter, a broiler, a pressureless steamer, a kettle, and a refrigerator/freezer. If you're planning to run a sandwich shop/deli, your cooking staff may need aprons, chef's hats, hairnets, etc., and if you have serving personnel, you'll want to provide them with uniforms.

You'll also need a variety of kitchen cookware, such as measuring cups and spoons, ladles of various sizes, tongs, large kitchen spoons, and pots and pans. Other miscellaneous items you will need include ashtrays (if you will allow smoking), pot holders,

Sandwich Shop/Deli
Major Equipment and Fixtures Checklist

- ❑ Bakers' bins and tables
- ❑ Beverage center
- ❑ Blender
- ❑ Breakdown table
- ❑ Broiler
- ❑ Cappuccino maker
- ❑ Cheese melter
- ❑ Coffee maker
- ❑ Convection oven
- ❑ Dinnerware
- ❑ Dishwashing machine
- ❑ Display case(s)/service counters
- ❑ Equipment for dishwashing
- ❑ Fax machine
- ❑ Food cutter
- ❑ Freezer
- ❑ Fryer
- ❑ Griddle top range with oven
- ❑ Heat lamps
- ❑ Hot water machine
- ❑ Ice cream cabinet
- ❑ Ice machine
- ❑ Kettle
- ❑ Lighting
- ❑ Meat grinder
- ❑ Microwave oven
- ❑ Portion scale (for food)
- ❑ Preparation and steam table
- ❑ Preparation sinks
- ❑ Pressureless steamer
- ❑ Refrigerator
- ❑ Roll warmer
- ❑ Sandwich table
- ❑ Scale (for receiving area)
- ❑ Service counter
- ❑ Shelving
- ❑ Slicer
- ❑ Tables and chairs
- ❑ Toaster
- ❑ Utensil racks
- ❑ Ventilation system
- ❑ Water station

spatulas, wire whisks, can openers, towel dispensers, garbage cans, first-aid kits, a mop and bucket, a broom and a dustpan, and dish containers for bussing tables. Plan to spend $1,000 to $2,000 for cookware and miscellaneous items.

Retail/Service Area

The specific equipment you need for this area depends on the type of shop you plan to have. For many sandwich shops, a 6- to 10-foot service counter or display case can also serve as the customer service area. Customers order their sandwiches and pay for them at one end of the counter. Your staff makes the sandwiches and calls customers' numbers when they are ready, and the customers pick up their order at the other end of the counter.

A deli will probably display cheeses, salads, meats, and fish in three-tiered, refrigerated, glass-fronted cases, which can range in cost from about $1,200 (for used equipment) to $8,000 or more (for new equipment). Caterer/deli owner Maxine T. uses two refrigerated delicatessen cases: one for salads, including green salads, fruit salads, specialty pastas and natural grains; and one for what she calls "savory" items, such as chicken tortes, quiches, stuffed manicotti, and lasagna rolls.

Whether you place it on your service counter or have a separate stand for it, you'll also need a cash register in this area.

Dining Area

Preparing your dining area (if you have one) will be another major expense. Expect to spend as little as $300 for tables and chairs for a small sandwich shop and up to $5,000 for tables, chairs, and booths for a larger establishment.

Other necessary items for the dining area include dishware, plates, glasses, flatware, and an assortment of containers to hold foods not served on dinner plates. These items should match your overall theme or image. A very casual sandwich shop or deli may use simple paper or plastic plates and cups. For a more formal establishment, you will need flatware and dishware. Figure on your dinnerware costing up to $2,500.

Dishwashing

If you're going to use disposable plates, cups, and tableware, you'll only need to wash pots, pans, and preparation utensils. A dishwashing machine would be better, but you can make do with a three-compartment sink and do the washing by hand. You'll spend $1,300 to $1,800 for a sink.

If you're going to be using regular dishes, flatware, glasses, etc., you'll need a small, three-stage dishwashing machine. Your dishwashing area, complete with landing area, drying table, garbage disposal, three-compartment sink, and small machine will run anywhere from $6,500 to $20,000.

Receiving and Storage Area

If your volume warrants, you may want a walk-in refrigerator/freezer for your storage area. This will cost between $4,500 and $7,500 and is not necessary for most smaller shops.

Most sandwich shops and delis can get by with just a scale, a breakdown table, and shelving in their receiving and storage area. You can probably equip this area for less than $1,000.

Inventory

Your specific inventory will, of course, depend on your menu. Maxine T. says one of the challenges she faces is offering enough variety to keep nearby business-people returning for lunch on a daily basis while maintaining an efficient inventory system. When starting out, keep your inventory low until you can work out a suitable ordering pattern. You'll probably open with about $8,000 to $10,000 in inventory, and your full food and beverage inventory should turn over about once every two weeks.

Let's take a look at the basic food categories you will probably be dealing with:

- *Bread.* The basic ingredient of every sandwich, the quality of your bread can make or break your sandwich shop/deli. You may be tempted to buy packaged breads and rolls from distributors, but the most successful sandwich shops and delis purchase freshly baked bread daily from a local baker, or bake their own breads on-site. While "home baking" your breads can be an excellent marketing tool, you may not have the budget to invest in the necessary equipment and labor. The equipment alone will cost from $15,000 to $150,000, depending on the quantities of bread you plan to bake each day. The smell of fresh-baked bread can be an excellent marketing tool; however, if you can't afford to do this,

The Paper Chase

In addition to your food and beverage supplies, you'll need a wide array of paper and plastic products, as well as miscellaneous items unique to your type of restaurant.

Paper goods will be a significant monthly expense. Disposable plastic or paper plates, napkins, and cups range from 8 to 16 cents per setting, depending on your business volume. Negotiate with several paper products distributors (they're listed in the Yellow Pages) to get the best prices.

It's not necessary to order paper products with your shop name and logo printed on them. This adds considerably to the cost of these products and doesn't do very much to advertise your business or boost your bottom line. It may work for large chains that order in huge quantities, but it doesn't make sense for the owner of a single shop just starting up.

virtually all cities and towns have bakeries known for their delicious products. Make arrangements with them to buy the bread and rolls you need at wholesale prices.

- *Meats.* Your meats must be of the highest quality—and fresh—so plan to reorder at least every other day. High-volume shop owners use 150 to 300 pounds of roast beef, ham, and salami and 75 to 100 pounds of pastrami, turkey, and other meats each week. Shop carefully for the best quality at the best prices.

Dollar Stretcher

Portion control is a key element in preventing waste and preserving profits. Standardize everything, from the appropriate amount (by weight) of meat and the number of slices of cheese you will use per sandwich to the amount of garnishes, such as pickles, you will serve with each order.

- *Additional deli items.* While sandwich shops may or may not serve the following, delis usually offer a complete selection of salads (potato, three-bean, cole slaw, cucumber, pasta, green); various types of fish (cod, salmon, herring, sturgeon); and a more extensive selection of cheeses.

Sandwich shops and delis may also serve hot entrees, such as soup, chili, stew, quiche, barbecued ribs and chicken, and so on. Dessert items may also be included to round out a sandwich shop or deli's menu. Purchase these extras in limited quantities at first, until you can determine demand.

- *Beverages.* Some delis and sandwich shops offer canned soda, pints of milk, and glasses of iced tea, lemonade, or carbonated drinks. Virtually all serve coffee, and some serve hot chocolate during the winter. You might also want to invest in an espresso or cappuccino machine and provide a variety of hot teas. Some beverage suppliers provide the beverage dispensing systems free or at a reduced cost to high-volume operations. Check with a variety of beverage suppliers and negotiate for the best deal possible.

If you decide to include shakes, malts, floats, and ice cream sodas (or soft-serve ice cream), all the ingredients you'll need should be available from the same distributor who supplies your milk. These ice cream items, as well as frozen yogurt, can dramatically increase your dollar-per-customer sales figures.

Many sandwich shops and delis serve beer by the bottle and wine by the glass or bottle. Most do not serve hard liquor; a limited beer-and-wine license meets their needs and is easier to obtain than a full liquor license.

- *Fresh produce.* It's easiest to order your fruits and vegetables through a fresh produce supplier, although some shop owners like to visit the farmers' market

Know the Locals

Some owners buy for their restaurants the same way their customers buy for themselves—on impulse. This is not necessarily a bad practice, as long as your tastes coincide with a sound knowledge of your patrons' preferences and your estimates closely resemble your actual inventory requirements. In general, a wide array of foods will attract a diversified clientele. With practice and diligent market research, you can identify your strongest menu items and order inventory accordingly.

themselves. Although vegetables are available year-round, they are seasonal and subject to climatic conditions. Be flexible in your buying, and look for items in plentiful supply. Take advantage of price swings by modifying the makeup of your salads or sandwiches according to the season and produce availability. You'll use several cases of lettuce and tomatoes and several pounds of cheese each week.

- *Canned, frozen, and packaged foods:* If you offer soups and salads, you'll need canned and packaged items like soups, olives, pickles, kidney beans, garbanzo beans, and some canned condiments. Purchase these items from a processed-foods distributor, and start with their minimum order, which is usually a case of each.

You'll also need several different dressings for salads, such as bleu cheese, French, Thousand Island, Italian, and honey mustard. Some should be low-fat. Buy them all commercially; homemade dressings generally require too much time and labor. Offer a variety of salad toppings, including chopped vegetables, olives, nuts, bacon bits, grated cheese, soy nuts, raisins, sunflower seeds, etc.

Condiments for sandwiches and other menu items (mustard, ketchup, salt, pepper, cooking oil, relish, etc.) can be purchased through a processed-foods distributor.

If you include french fries on your menu, you can either buy potatoes from a fresh produce supplier and cut them yourself or buy pre-cut, pre-cooked frozen french fries by the pound. You might also want to offer onion rings, which can be purchased pre-cooked and frozen.

▲

Staffing

Your staffing needs will vary depending on the size of your operation. If you're planning to work full time in your sandwich shop/deli, you could probably open with just one additional full-time employee—an experienced sandwich maker. As your business grows, cover busy periods with part-time workers. For security reasons, try to have at least two employees in the shop at all times. Of course, if you're planning a full-service deli with a dining area, you'll need to staff more along the lines of a typical restaurant.

Look for employees who are pleasant, people-oriented, and well-groomed. Food prepared by sloppy employees won't be appealing to your customers.

Most sandwich shop/deli positions do not earn tips. Wage scales vary by region, but expect to pay $.50–$2.00 above minimum wage. A glance through your local newspaper's help wanted section will give you an idea of the going rates in your area.

8

Coffeehouse

Connoisseur or neophyte, aficionado or abstainer, you've probably noticed the tremendous growth in the specialty coffee industry. New incarnations of this previously boring background beverage have taken center stage in restaurants and shops around the world. Once a simple commodity, coffee has become a culture, complete with its own language and accessories, that offers a wide-open retail opportunity.

Coffee is a global industry that employs more than 20 million people and ranks second only to petroleum in terms of dollars traded worldwide. With more than 400 billion cups consumed every year, coffee is the world's most popular beverage.

The first coffeehouses opened in Constantinople nearly 450 years ago and did so well that by the 1630s, European coffeehouses became the center of cultural and social activities. Coffeehouses enjoyed some popularity in colonial New England, but modern-day Americans did not accept the coffeehouse as a place for social or cultural gatherings until well into the second half of the twentieth century. Before the 1970s, Americans either drank their coffee at home or in a restaurant and settled for the canned variety that is brewed in a percolator.

In the 1960s, coffeehouses and folk musicians appeared on the scene. Although they seemed to focus on the counterculture, they managed to create a demand for fresh coffee beans that people could grind and thus brew their own coffee at home. Even so, during the 1960s, '70s, and '80s, the number of people who consumed coffee declined sharply. "In 1962, 75 percent of the population drank coffee on a typical day," says Robert F. Nelson, president of the National Coffee Association (NCA). "In 1997, it was 49 percent." He blames the decline on dwindling social support for coffee, negative publicity about the effects of coffee and caffeine on health, and competition from other beverages, such as soft drinks. He adds, however, that the decline is leveling off. Also, though overall coffee consumption is on the decline, specialty coffee consumption is on the increase.

Smart Tip

Although just about every business guru advises choosing a business where the owner can combine profitability with passion, the requirement to love the product is especially true in the coffee industry. Learn everything you can about the culture of coffee and how to determine and produce quality beverages.

"In the past, coffee was a commodity, and there was very little innovation [in the industry]," Nelson says. "It was seen as an old-fashioned beverage for older folks. In the '90s, the social supports [re-emerged] for coffee. It's seen as a relevant, contemporary beverage." About coffee's impact on health, he observes, "Today, the consumer takes a much more pragmatic approach to healthy eating and living." It's possible and common for a healthy lifestyle to include coffee.

In many situations, coffee is replacing alcohol as the social beverage of choice, with people meeting for coffee instead of cocktails. "Here in Portland, you go to the bigger coffeehouses, and they're real [hot spots]," says Ward Barbee, publisher of *Fresh Cup* magazine, a Portland, Oregon, trade publication for the gourmet coffee and beverage industry.

Beyond the beverage itself, people frequent coffeehouses and espresso bars for a variety of reasons. Some go to meet with friends, socialize, and perhaps enjoy some live music or conversation; some are looking for a quick lunch and a drink that will help them weather the afternoon doldrums; still others simply want a great cup of coffee to start off each morning. Coffeehouse patrons tend to be sophisticated, and they want unusual, exotic coffees that are expertly prepared.

> Beyond the beverage itself, people frequent coffeehouses and espresso bars for a variety of reasons.

Phyllis J., founder of a New Orleans-based coffeehouse chain, says coffeehouses are meeting a strong social need. "Our lives are pretty fragmented, and a coffee shop gives people a place where they belong to some extent, where they see the same faces regularly so they become part of a community," she says. She compares American coffeehouses to European pubs. "The need to have that kind of place is still very strong, but alcohol is not as popular. A lot of people call it the 'third place phenomenon.' You have home, work, and you need a third place to go. It needs to be a place where you can go very regularly so you form relationships with other customers and staff. Coffee and alcohol are probably the only two things—besides food— that you would consume on a daily basis. Most people don't go to their favorite restaurant every single day, but you do go to your coffeehouse almost every day."

Today's coffee cafes cater to a marketplace as varied as the coffee flavors themselves— some targeting the breakfast and lunch on-the-go market, others operating as evening destinations, with food items and perhaps entertainment, and a wide range of styles in between.

"There continues to be innovation, and there continues to be expansion in the whole gourmet and specialty shop area, and that will continue to have a positive impact on the consumption of coffee," the NCA's Nelson says.

Another plus for the industry is the growing sophistication of the American coffee drinker. "As more and more [types of] coffee are introduced to consumers, and more and more coffee beverages are available, the consumer is developing a more educated palate and becoming more educated about the beverage itself," says Nelson. He points out that coffee drinkers are consuming different types of coffee beverages at different times of the day. "You may have one type of coffee at home for breakfast, a different type at lunch, and maybe an espresso after dinner. What the industry has tried to do is respond to consumers by providing them with different varieties so people can choose what they like."

Most successful coffeehouses have heavy foot traffic and high-volume sales. The majority will serve up to 500 customers per day and manage up to five customer turns

Smart Tip

Tip...

Read every book and trade magazine you can find on the subject of coffee and coffeehouses. Become as familiar as you can with the business, the industry and your target markets. Make reading industry magazines and newsletters an important part of your day so you can keep up with the changing commodities market and how it will affect the price of coffee. Most metropolitan newspapers track commodities in their business sections.

during the lunch hour, despite having limited floor space and modest seating capacity. Profit margins for coffee and espresso drinks are extremely high—after all, you're dealing with a product that is more than 95 percent water. At the same time, your average ticket amount is less than $2, so you need volume to reach and maintain profitability.

Though most restaurants try to have either very fast turnover and lower prices or less turnover and higher prices with fancy food, coffeehouses break those rules. People will hang around a coffeehouse for an hour or more, sipping a $1 cup of coffee, but because of the huge profit margins coffee drinks can bring, even relatively low-volume operations can turn a profit if they're run correctly.

Besides specialty roasted coffee by the cup, most coffeehouses also have espresso-based drinks (cappuccinos, lattes, etc.), assorted teas, bottled water, and fruit juices, along with an inviting assortment of baked goods such as biscotti (Italian dipping cookies), bagels, croissants, muffins, and a selection of desserts. Most also sell their beans by the pound so customers can enjoy their favorite brews at home. A hot trend in coffee is flavors—customers are ordering varieties ranging from simple chocolate and vanilla to raspberry and fudge ripple. Flavorings can be roasted into the beans or added in the form of syrups at the time the coffee is served.

Industry Trends

If you're going to operate a coffeehouse, you'll be interested in these trends:

- *Product categories are solidifying their niches.* According to industry experts, straight (unblended) coffees will continue to move toward "estate marks," in which the specific geographic location—not simply the country—of the coffee's origin will play a key role in product marketing. Dark-roast coffees will remain popular for espresso-based beverages, and product quality will improve as the roasting community achieves greater sophistication. Though blends will not demonstrate the same strength as other categories, local roasters will blend coffees that sell well in their marketing area because of regional taste preferences or local water conditions. We can expect a broader range of decaffeinated coffees, and flavored coffees will increase their market share. Finally, we'll see a significant increase in the market for organically grown coffees.

- *Coffee cafes will set the pace for new outlet creation.* The fastest-growing distribution channel will be coffee cafes, including espresso bars and espresso carts. This rapid growth is fueled by three factors: the high gross profit margin of selling coffee by the cup; the fact that espresso-based beverages are difficult for consumers to prepare correctly at home; and existing food-service locations will be slow to upgrade their product quality to the level of specialty coffees.

- *Retail roasters are a driving force in product lines and marketing.* "Micro-roasteries" are growing at an impressive pace, opening at the rate of approximately 100 per year, with the principal limitation being the availability of equipment.

- *Consumers will continue their two-tier system of shopping.* Consumers patronize both establishments that sell bulk items, typically at a discount, and specialty stores, which consumers are visiting with greater frequency. The specialty coffee product category is expanding rapidly.

Setting Up Your Facility

Just as coffeehouses are not restricted to serving a particular market group, neither are they limited to occupying a certain kind of facility to be profitable. Given the markets you are going to target, your hours of operation, the volume of coffee you expect to sell, and the geographical locations under consideration, you can choose from free-standing buildings, downtown or center-of-town storefronts, and mall spaces. A typical coffeehouse is 800 to 3,000 square feet. If coffee and espresso on-the-go will be your specialty, you won't need as large a facility as someone who intends to run a coffeehouse/bookstore. Likewise, starting up in a large facility of 2,500 square feet or more is ideal for an entrepreneur who wants neighborhood regulars to be able to lounge around drinking coffee for hours and not feel rushed or crowded (see sample layouts on pages 90–91).

When allocating space, a good formula to follow is to allow 55 percent of your space for the actual seating area, 25 percent for your production area, and 20 percent for your customer service area, including the bar. If you let the production area fall below 25 percent, you run the risk of problems with service.

Depending on the amount of cash you have to invest, you can spend $20,000 to $200,000—

Tip...

Smart Tip

Coffee experts advocate storing beans so they will be protected from light and air. To let your clients know your beans are properly stored, and therefore of high quality, only display beans that are not going to be sold in transparent containers.

▲

Grab 'Em by the Nose

Since location, high-volume foot traffic, and repeat business are the real keys to success, don't spend more than 5 percent of your advertising budget on conventional advertising. You can do several inexpensive promotions to help get the traffic started and keep it coming to your coffeehouse.

When you walk into a coffeehouse, you are immediately struck by the distinctive aroma of fresh-roasted coffee beans. This is what entices many people to go inside and linger over a hot cup of coffee, a delicious cappuccino, or a shot of espresso. Passing foot traffic can't resist slowing down a bit to see what's brewing inside.

Take a tip from cookie shops and bakeries: Grab customers by the nose. Savvy operators help nature along by having an open-air setup that will push aromas out the door with the help of strategically placed fans and vents. A fan mounted in a door transom is one of your best bets.

The smell of coffee will permeate the store even if you lock the beans in airtight bins. It is crucial that you make sure the smell always stays fresh, which is why it's so important to use the correct display and storage equipment.

or more—on your facility. This depends on whether you are starting from scratch or converting an existing food-service business, and what you plan on for a theme and décor.

Customer Service and Seating Area

This area must convey the atmosphere you have decided on in a manner that takes advantage of the available space. Large coffeehouses use a waiting area and cashier's station located at or near the entrance to avoid causing traffic jams at the service counter. The cashier's station is usually parallel to a wall. You can design it as just a small counter with a cash register or utilize the space to display specialty items, bags of coffee beans, and perhaps some of the baked goods you offer. As an alternative, you can set up your cashier's station at the threshold between the counter and the seating area.

When considering the layout of your service area, keep this in mind: While long lines out the door generally convey the fact that quality goods are inside, they can also deter busy shoppers or commuters who want to pop in and out. Try to leave space to allow for a two- or three-line service approach, with enough room for those who have ordered to stand off slightly to the side if necessary. Also, be sure your coffee production equipment is placed near the service counter, not away from it, so that efficiency in serving beverages is maximized.

Generally, you want to have one bar seat for every three table seats. A coffeehouse with 75 table seats, for example, should have about 25 seats at the bar. For bar stools, allow about two square feet per stool, while tables should have about 10 to 12 square feet per seated customer.

A bar is a good idea because it also serves as an additional waiting area for people looking to grab a table when one opens up. You'll also need to provide public restrooms located close to the dining area.

You don't really need display areas for anything except the coffee and a few pastry or dessert items. Any accessories you sell can go on shelves within customers' reach. More expensive items, such as espresso and cappuccino makers, can go behind and above service counters.

> **Bright Idea**
> Set aside some room for coffee-tasting. This can consist of a simple setup of thermoses of the coffees you sell at the end of a counter. Provide small tasting cups, stirrers, cream, and sugar, and encourage customers to sample coffee before they place their orders.

Production Area

Your coffee and food production area should promote the most efficient delivery of food and coffee to the customer area. Your menu is the prime consideration in the design of your production area. By taking what you serve into consideration, you'll be able to cut down on the amount of space and equipment needed to run an efficient operation. Generally, you'll need to allow approximately 25 to 35 percent of your total space for your production area. This includes space for receiving, storage, food and drink preparation, cooking, baking, dishwashing, trash, employee facilities, and an area for a small office. Receiving and food storage will take up about 8 percent of your total space. These areas should be strategically located as close to the front or rear door as possible. Your dry storage area should be adjacent to the receiving area.

If you have decided to serve food as well as coffee, you'll need about 12 percent of your total space for food preparation, cooking, and baking. Your equipment will include prep tables, fryers, a cooking range with a griddle top, a refrigerator/freezer, soft drink and milk dispensers, an ice bin, a broiler, and exhaust fans for the ventilation system. Arrange this area so everything is positioned within reach and two or more people can comfortably work side by side when you are at maximum production. You can center the prep area in the middle of the kitchen or, for smaller cafes and bars, below or behind the counter. For more on setting up prep or full-service kitchens, study the chapters on sandwich shops/delicatessens, bakeries, and restaurants; then adapt that information to the size and scope of your menu.

Sample Coffeehouse Layout

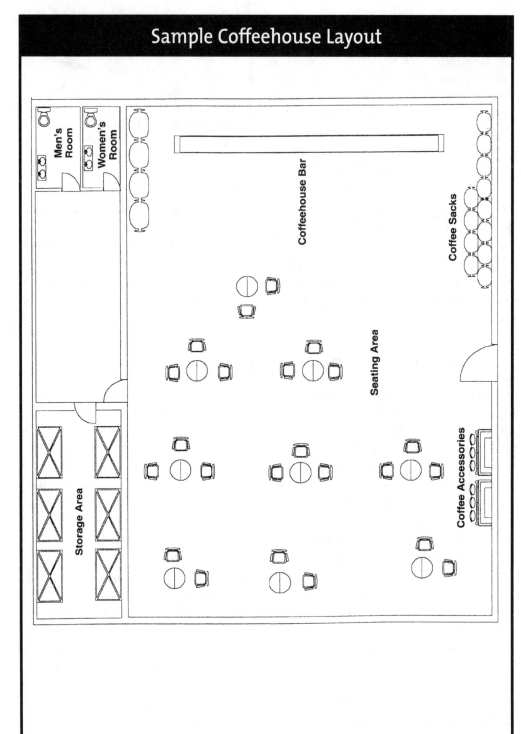

Sample Coffeehouse Layout

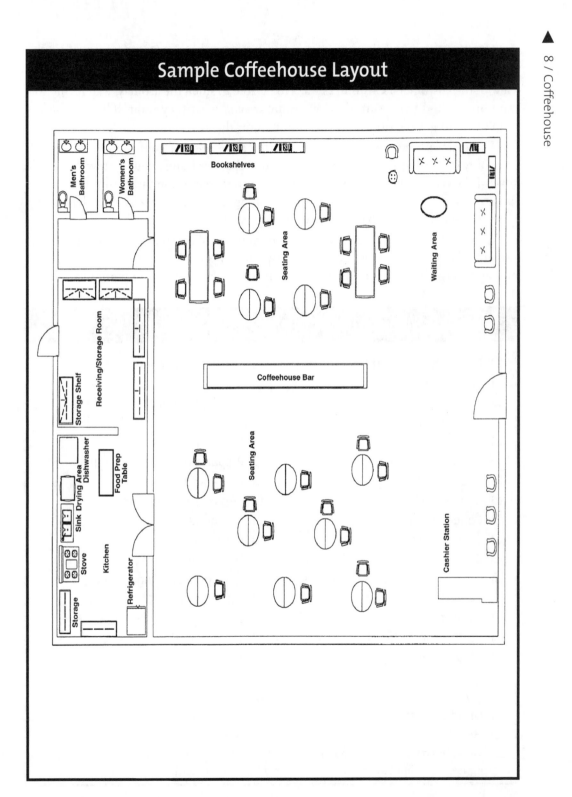

Men's Bathroom

Women's Bathroom

Bookshelves

Seating Area

Waiting Area

Receiving/Storage Room

Storage Shelf

Coffeehouse Bar

Food Prep Table

Dishwasher

Sink Drying Area

Seating Area

Stove

Kitchen

Refrigerator

Storage

Cashier Station

Most coffeehouses use interesting-looking and sometimes ornate espresso machines, so they locate their beverage centers directly behind the counter in full view of the customers. Customers want to be able to smell the aromas, watch you prepare drinks, and make sure they're getting exactly what they want. This also allows employees to get the order to the customer quickly.

The dishwashing and trash areas usually create a lot of confusion, even though they only occupy about 4 percent of your total space. Arrange your dishwashing area toward the rear of the kitchen, perhaps in a corner so it doesn't interrupt the flow of employees in the prep area. Your dishwashing equipment needs will depend on whether you use traditional tableware or disposable products.

Your facility must make serving a large number of customers quickly as easy as possible for you and your employees. By allowing customers to seat themselves and approach the counter when they want to order, you can eliminate most of the

Coffeehouse Major Equipment and Fixtures Checklist

❏ Bakers' bins and tables	❏ Hot water machine
❏ Beverage center	❏ Ice machine
❏ Blender	❏ Ice cream cabinet
❏ Breakdown table	❏ Kettle
❏ Broiler	❏ Lighting
❏ Cappuccino maker	❏ Preparation and steam table
❏ Cheese melter	❏ Preparation sinks
❏ Coffee machines	❏ Pressureless steamer
❏ Coffee grinder(s)	❏ Refrigerator
❏ Convection oven	❏ Roll warmer
❏ Dinnerware	❏ Sandwich table
❏ Display case(s)/service counters	❏ Scale (for receiving area)
❏ Dishwashing machine	❏ Service counter
❏ Equipment for dishwashing	❏ Shelving
❏ Espresso machine(s)	❏ Tables and chairs
❏ Food cutter	❏ Toaster
❏ Freezer	❏ Utensil racks
❏ Fryer	❏ Ventilation system
❏ Griddle top range with oven	❏ Water station
❏ Heat lamps	

Note: This checklist is appropriate for a coffeehouse with a fairly elaborate menu; a coffeehouse with a limited menu will not need all this equipment.

problems faced by traditional restaurants and other labor-intensive food-service operations.

Equipment

For an average-sized coffeehouse, equipment costs range from $10,000 to $60,000, depending on the number of coffee and espresso machines purchased and the extent of food-service operations.

Coffee and Espresso Machines

Coffee and espresso machines are the heart of a coffeehouse. You can operate profitably without a convection oven or a walk-in refrigerator, but good coffee makers and espresso machines are absolutely mandatory.

Coffee makers are used for brewing straight coffee, and espresso machines are used for brewing espresso and making espresso-based drinks requiring steamed or frothed milk. Although they are notoriously expensive and temperamental, industrial espresso machines have come down in price over the years, and their reliability has improved. Still, the most frequent and costly problems faced by coffeehouse and espresso bar owners are with their espresso machines. Sales either stop when the machines go down, or owners have to do what they can with a backup system, which annoys customers who expect prompt service and don't get it. Daily cleaning and regular maintenance of

---

Coffee on Ice

Making delicious iced coffee takes a special knack—it's not enough to just brew coffee and chill it. Phyllis J. uses a cold drip method. She combines the ground coffee with cold water for an extended period of time; the process extracts the flavor and aromatics but not the acidity from the coffee and forms a concentrate, which can then be diluted to make iced coffee drinks.

"Because it has no acidity, it is very creamy and works better as a cold beverage," Phyllis says. "Now, before I give acidity a bad name, keep in mind that acidity is a very important part of the coffee profile. If you were drinking a cup of hot coffee that didn't have acidity, you would call it bland or flat. But we have found that using this cold water process and no acidity for iced coffees makes a much more popular drink."

these machines is a must. Many parts of the machine can be quickly rinsed with hot water and/or wiped down after each drink. In addition, you may want to service your machines completely on a monthly or semimonthly basis.

There are four key features to look for in an espresso machine:

- *Volume.* How much espresso can the machine make each day? Here's how to tell: Espresso machines differ chiefly in the number of "groups" they have. The group is the part of the machine that acts as a stationary lock to fix the removable handle or "head" to the machine. The finely ground coffee is placed in a perforated metal cup known as a "portafilter." The filter is placed into the head and the head locks into the espresso machine at the group. Most of today's machines are single-group or two-group, having one group and one corresponding head that locks into place or two groups and two corresponding heads, respectively. Heated water comes out of the espresso machine's tank at the group and is forced, at ten atmospheres of pressure, through the coffee grounds.

Most coffeehouses and espresso bars that do any volume of business have two-group machines, which range in price from $4,000 to $8,000. You will

Tip...

Smart Tip

High-volume coffee sales help offset the high cost of food preparation. You need to maintain at the very least 30 percent of your total sales in coffee, which has a much lower cost than food and will result in higher profits.

Grinding It Up

A key piece of equipment will be your coffee grinder. Grinding coffee to the right consistency has a lot to do with the quality of the finished product. Electric mills have dials indicating the kind of coffee grind that's right for various coffee makers.

You can buy a new coffee grinder with several grind selections for $700 to $1,200, or you can lease one for $20 to $35 per month. Your coffee supplier will either have them on hand or know where you can get one.

Most shop mills are 24 to 36 inches high. Place the mill on your rear display counter and position it so your clerks can use it easily. When customer traffic increases, add a second grinder. As with your espresso machine, cleaning and maintenance of your grinder is crucial.

probably never need anything larger. Using a single-group machine with a twin head (having two pouts at the bottom of the head instead of one, which doubles your capacity), you can make 100 to 200 espresso-based drinks a day. However, keep in mind that a busy coffeehouse/cafe/espresso bar can sell upwards of 300 espresso drinks a day.

In the beginning, to save on your initial cash outlay, a single-group machine may provide sufficient capacity. After you're established and your business begins to grow, you may find that you need to buy a second single-group machine.

- *Warranty*. Any machine you buy should come with some kind of warranty—at least 90 days and preferably a year. Warranties vary tremendously among espresso-machine manufacturers; if you buy a foreign machine, there's no guarantee that you will be able to find someone who can fix it for you unless you buy it through an American distributor.

- *In-line filters*. When you use an outside water source or line to provide water for your espresso machine, you don't know much about its chemical composition. If the water in your area is high in minerals and other compounds, those substances will begin to collect in your water line much like they do in your reservoir. Espresso machines that come with simple in-line filters will slow the rate at which deposits begin to collect in the machine, allowing the machine to run better and require less maintenance.

- *Reservoir or tank*. Look for machines with reservoirs made of stainless steel rather than copper. Stainless steel is better at retarding the buildup of calcium and other mineral deposits along the tank walls.

Coffee makers are far more widespread than espresso machines in their availability, and their operation is relatively simplistic. With a few exceptions, they all work the same way: Heated water is forced at ten atmospheres of pressure through finely ground coffee beans to infuse them. Regular coffee has about 7 percent soluble solids, while espresso contains roughly 25 percent.

Your expected business volume will determine the number and kind of coffee makers you should purchase. Coffee machines are fairly standard—most use paper filters (some use metal) to hold the coffee grounds as the water filters through, and each pot holds 50 to 70 ounces of coffee. Prices of commercial coffee makers range from $250 to $600. You may want equipment that looks good sitting behind the counter, but reliability and quality output should be the two factors that influence your purchasing decision the most.

> **Bright Idea**
>
> Keep a reasonable supply of tea and hot chocolate on hand at all times so that people who don't drink coffee can still enjoy your coffeehouse.

You've Got to Know Beans about Beans

When it comes to storing and displaying your beans, you may be tempted to go with something attractive instead of practical, such as natural wood cases, barrels, and bins. This is the worst material for coffee bean storage, because wood bins can promote staleness and bad taste. Wood is notorious for absorbing coffee oils, which penetrate the wood grain and then go rancid. When you add fresh coffee beans, they absorb the rancid oils and are ruined.

If you go with a wood décor, get a guarantee that the wood is nonporous or line the bins with heavy-duty nonporous plastic. Replace the plastic routinely to ensure freshness. Remember, coffee is best stored away from light and air.

For displaying limited quantities of beans, your best option is to use nonporous display bins made of acrylic, glass, or plastic. Be sure to wash them on a regular basis.

Inventory

Your initial inventory will depend largely on your amount of available start-up capital. For a 600- to 1,000-square-foot coffeehouse or espresso bar, plan to spend $3,000 to $8,000 on coffee and $1,500 to $5,000 on accessories (if you sell them) to get started.

Your inventory costs will probably fluctuate during the year. If you serve food, you'll likely buy more produce during the summer when you're serving lunches with fresh vegetables. In the winter, coffee sales soar because of the cold weather and gift-giving holidays.

Order coffee beans once or twice a week from local suppliers to ensure freshness. Most roasters do their best to accommodate clients and deliver in whatever quantities are needed. Remember that coffee beans begin to go stale the moment they're roasted and will keep for only one to three weeks if stored properly.

Bright Idea

Coffee-roasting is a complicated process, and it shouldn't be undertaken lightly or without a great deal of study. Roasting is truly an art—it is what transforms the beans into a flavorful brew. Though there are numerous advantages to roasting your own beans (lower cost, quality control, etc.), don't move into this area until you have sufficient industry experience and capital to support the required investment.

Bright Idea

An essential element of success in the coffee business is to remember that the anchor is coffee, but to always explore options that will enhance the primary product, such as pastries and other baked goods, additional beverages, gift baskets, and so on.

Your inventory should include coffees from several countries. To start, offer at least five decaffeinated coffees, plus at least a dozen regular coffees (your wholesaler can give you suggestions about the best-selling varieties). For the sake of variety, do not focus strictly on blended coffees or devote all your inventory budget to select estate-grown beans. Create as much diversity as you can given the amount of start-up capital you have. Begin with a coffee inventory of 400 to 700 pounds.

The following is a list of the coffee, decaffeinated coffee, tea, and accessory items that can be used to stock your coffeehouse:

- *Coffee.* House blend (your choice); Espresso Roast; French Roast; Italian Roast; Vienna Roast; Colombian Supremo; Colombian Popayan; Brazilian Santos; Moka Java Blend; Java Estate; Mexican; Guatemalan High-Grown; Costa Rican Terrazu; Royal Hawaiian Kona; El Salvadorian; Kenya Nairobi AA; Antigua; Arabian Moka (Yemen); Arabian Moka Horror (Ethiopia); Yirgacheffe (Ethiopia) Ethiopian Sidamo; Bolivian: Honduran; Nicaraguan; Panamanian; Peruvian; Paraguayan; Venezuelan; Tobago; Celabese; Ecuadorian; Haitian; Madagascar (Malagasy); Indonesian; Jamaica Blue Mountain; Tanzanian; Ugandan; Ivory Coast; Rwanda/Burundi; Sierre Leone; Zaire; Singapore; Philippines; Liberian; Sumatra Mandehling; Sumatra Linton; and Zimbabwe Code 53

- *Decaffeinated coffee.* Espresso; Colombian; Costa Rican; El Salvadorian; Brazilian Santos; Sumatra; Moka Java; Vienna Roast; and French Roast

- *Tea.* Earl Grey; English Breakfast; Oolong (Taiwan Jasmine); Black Jasmine (Mainland China); Lapsang Souchong; Congou; Keemun; Pingsun; Souchong; Darjeeling; Assam; Ceylon; Rose Hip; Russian; Spearmint; Peppermint; Lemon Mist; Lemon Lime; Orange Pekoe; Chamomile; Golden-Tipped Pekoe; True Lemon; Apple Cinnamon; Cherry; Orange Nutmeg; and Cinnamon

Bright Idea

If your coffeehouse is extremely successful and you want to increase your evening and late-night business, consider adding alcoholic beverages to your menu. *Fresh Cup* magazine's Ward Barbee observes, "[You] can make a lot of money selling coffee drinks, desserts, and brandy."

Add It Up

When it comes to extenders and additives, the best route is to sell them, but do so selectively. You might be tempted to have a special spice-roasted coffee available. Many spices go well with coffee—cinnamon, orange, chocolate, and anise, for example—but if you routinely ordered such peculiar coffee, you would probably run into a serious inventory problem. The same holds true of chicory, which is not roasted with coffee, but is added afterward.

Offer spices and coffee extenders (coffee suppliers have them) for consumers to add to their own drink or purchase and take home. Spiced teas are another matter, since many teas are at their best with certain spices. Let a good tea supplier put you on the right track here.

- *Miscellaneous.* Sugar; artificial sweetener; cream; nondairy creamer; ground cinnamon, vanilla, and chocolate; flavored syrups; lemon slices

- *Accessories.* Consumer coffee mills (electric); filter coffee makers (various sizes and styles); tea eggs and filters; coffee filters (various); insulated carafes; tea kettles (include copper); espresso makers (nonelectric); sample espresso machines; mugs, cups, creamers, and sugar bowls; and tea services

Bright Idea
Team up with other food-service businesses to create your menu. Find a bakery that can provide your morning pastries, croissant, sweet breads, bagels, and muffins, as well as your midday sweet snacks, such as cookies and brownies, and even dessert items. Look for a deli or a caterer that will sell you pre-made sandwiches that you can sell from a refrigerated case.

- *Retail and other supplies.* Sealable bags (for selling coffee beans by the pound); labels (for coffee bags); plastic or metal scoops; paper cups and lids; stirrers; napkins

Staffing

It's not enough to have the right equipment and properly roasted coffee. You need people who understand coffee and know how to make the beverages with some skill.

A key member of a coffeehouse staff is the *Barista*, the person who prepares espresso. Baristas are extremely well-versed in the language of coffee, and espresso-based drinks are their specialty.

If you expect to stay open more than 12 hours a day, you'll need two Baristas, one working full time and one part time. The second can help tend the counter during peak hours or work the early-morning or late-evening shifts. Baristas are usually paid an hourly wage and keep whatever tips they generate, which can be substantial if they make exceptionally good espresso. As with a good bartender, you can hire a qualified Barista at a very reasonable $6 to $8 per hour, depending on your location. The best place to find talent is at other coffeehouses, espresso bars, restaurants, and other establishments that sell espresso drinks.

Look for someone who knows how to make all the standard espresso drinks as well as concoct their own creations and fill exotic drink requests of customers. Your espresso expert should be quick-pouring, consistent, and especially personable—more so than any other server in the house. As do good bartenders, experienced Baristas possess the ability to make small talk with people while juggling several drink orders in their heads.

The remainder of your staff will depend on the size and style of your establishment and the range of your menu. The two chapters on sandwich shops/delicatessens and restaurants will also guide you.

The Coffeehouse Market

Even chain coffeehouses will vary in style, design, and menu offerings depending on the particular market they serve. For an independent operator, it's critical that you understand your target market and tailor your operation to meet their needs.

Just about everyone over the age of 15 is a potential coffee/espresso bar patron. But such a vague market description will not help you build a successful coffeehouse. Consider targeting one or more of the following customer groups:

- *Local consumers.* Area residents are clearly a prime market for most coffeehouses. Those who live in the neighborhood are in close proximity for all or part of the day and therefore constitute a substantial group of potential customers. If you plan to set up shop in a rural area, a suburban neighborhood

Stat Fact
Gourmet coffee shop patrons have average household incomes of $48,520, compared to $47,660 for take-out establishment patrons overall.

area, or an urban area with a large residential population nearby, this is the first market to target.

- *Commuters.* A coffeehouse offers precisely what most morning commuters are looking for: a good cup of coffee and a bite to eat. Coffee is the universal breakfast drink, and a muffin, croissant, or pastry is the perfect accompaniment. While competition for the breakfast market among donut shops, fast-food chains, and traditional coffee shops is fierce, a business that specializes in coffee has a competitive advantage over the more generic breakfast places that serve low-grade coffee. The only substitute for good coffee, as far as coffee drinkers are concerned, is better coffee. Coffeehouses can offer quick breakfast foods *and* serve the best coffee in town.

Bright Idea

During peak periods, consider adding an express line to accommodate customers who just want a basic hot or iced coffee and a simple pastry or snack so they can get in and out quickly. The customer who wants the cappuccino, the latte, the double iced mocha, or other more labor-intensive beverage can go through the regular line and get full service.

At the end of the day, coffeehouses in urban areas can target customers who work in the area but live elsewhere and don't have time to go home before meeting up with others for dinner or evening entertainment. Given the choice between battling other drivers on the highway or spending a relaxing hour in your cafe until traffic dies down, many commuters will choose your place. The evening is ideal for promoting "happy hour" coffee specials.

- *Campus folk.* Some of the most profitable coffeehouses in the country are located near schools and universities. High school and college students, as well as faculty members, are a strong market. Despite apparently limited spending power, students have embraced the coffeehouse renaissance and are putting in long hours drinking, studying, and talking within their walls. Coffeehouses near campuses are typically open well into the night, the coffee and foods they serve are inexpensive, and unlike bars, both the atmosphere and the menu are conducive to industrious behavior. Because coffeehouses don't serve alcohol, they don't enforce age limits, and that means students under 21 who cannot go to bars have a place to gather.

- *Entertainment crowd.* Those who travel to shopping districts and commercial centers seeking entertainment are also usually in search of some food or refreshment while there. A coffeehouse located near an entertainment venue is a convenient place for a snack, quick meal, or just a cup of coffee before or after the main event.

- *At-home gourmets.* Most people who call themselves gourmets also enjoy experimenting with new coffee flavors and espresso drinks at home. You can encourage these and other patrons to try different varieties and expand their awareness of unblended or "straight" coffees and espressos. One of the big appeals of a specialty coffee operation is that customers can pick and choose their own coffee beans to take home or to the office.

About Beans

Many coffeehouse patrons are well-heeled in the language of coffee, which means they understand the difference between *arabica* and *robusta* beans, and they know how an espresso, cappuccino, or latte is supposed to taste. This group is acutely aware of

A Matter of Taste

The language of coffee is complex, and you'll need to do some in-depth studying to be able to communicate comfortably with true coffee aficionados. Professional coffee bean tasters use a process called cupping to determine the quality, acidity, and aroma of beans for selection in their blends. Here are some basic tasting terms you'll need to be familiar with:

○ *Acidity.* This is the sensation of dryness that the coffee produces under the edges of your tongue and on the back of your palate. Without sufficient acidity, coffee tends to taste flat, so this is a desirable characteristic. Don't confuse acidity with sour, which is an unpleasant, negative flavor characteristic.

○ *Aroma.* Smell is a very powerful sense, and fragrances contribute to the flavors we discern on our palates. The aroma of brewed coffee has a wide range of subtle nuances.

○ *Body.* The feeling, or the texture, of the coffee in your mouth is its body. An example of body is the difference between the way whole milk and water feel in your mouth. Coffee body is related to the oils and solids extracted during brewing.

○ *Flavor.:* Acidity, aroma, and body combine to create the overall perception of the coffee in your mouth, and that is its flavor. General flavor characteristics are richness, which refers to body and fullness; complexity, which is the perception of multiple flavors; and balance, which is the satisfying presence of all the basic taste characteristics.

the consumer choices it makes, buying food products for prestige, nutritional value, and distinct taste. For instance, they are most likely to buy estate coffee, which is labeled with the name of the estate on which it is grown and carries the same status and appeal of fine wines. Having become accustomed to the taste of high-quality coffee, they no longer consume the low-grade, mass-produced coffee brands that are found in supermarkets.

As a coffeehouse owner, you must at least match, if not surpass, the coffee knowledge of your patrons. While this book will provide you with valuable information on the mechanics of starting and running a successful coffeehouse, you should dedicate yourself to in-depth research on your product before you invest your time, energy, and financial resources in opening a shop of your own. Despite its apparent abundance, only a small amount of the total coffee harvested each year is true gourmet coffee, which is made with premium arabica beans instead of low-grade robusta beans.

You'll need to decide what types of beans you'll offer and use in your beverages. Some people love dark-roasted coffee; others believe it kills the natural taste of the coffee. Will you go one way or the other, or offer the spectrum? How many types of whole beans will you offer?

Starting Each Day

At the beginning of the day, you should inspect your facility to be sure everything is as you or your manager left it the night before. The next step is to make a working plan of the day's events.

By the time your doors open in the morning, all of your preparation work should be done. The better your setup routine, the easier it will be for you and your staff to focus on serving customers and not having to worry about whether they're going to run out of inventory and supplies in the middle of a rush. For heavy coffee and espresso production, you need to be prepared. If you are going to have a slightly different menu each day, all the ingredients that go into the day's menu items—certain coffee beans, milk, sugar, cream, flavorings, toppings, ice, condiments, etc.—must be ready for that day. Give yourself enough time to make sure you have everything you need.

Most coffeehouses have about five different varieties brewed and ready at the bar. You should vary the coffee menu daily; it requires an overhaul, but customers will appreciate the change. Keep the coffee fresh and warm; some shops use the coffee machines and hot pads, keeping it in the brewing pot, and others prefer to take the coffee immediately from the machine and pour it into insulated dispensers or carafes. Warming plates, because of their high temperatures, tend to keep coffees so hot that they lose freshness and develop a burned flavor after 30 minutes or so; don't serve coffee that's been kept on a burner for more than a half-hour.

You will need to grind beans every morning and at intervals throughout the day. To ensure the freshest coffee, you should grind beans for each pot of coffee you make. Espresso is a little different; because it is made a cup at a time, you are better off grinding perhaps half a pound or a pound at a time to accelerate the process. Your customer traffic and your menu will determine what you need to grind and how many pots should be ready for customers.

An over-the-counter coffee bar that seats 35 people may need to keep five varieties of coffee (four regular roasts and one decaf) brewing in five pots at any given time, while operating a single-capacity espresso machine. A popular 100-seat coffeehouse may have 15 different coffees ready to drink throughout the day (perhaps 11 regular and 4 decaf) and have a Barista working a double-capacity espresso machine constantly.

Competition

You may find the competition from large chains such as Starbucks intimidating, but industry experts insist there's a place for everyone in the business. In fact, *Fresh Cup* magazine's Barbee says the independent retailer probably has the potential to be most profitable because he can ride on the marketing coattails of giants like Starbucks, yet his size provides a level of flexibility larger organizations simply don't have.

Phyllis J. agrees. She says she doesn't see the giant chains as a threat, but rather as a marketing engine that can help educate the public about specialty coffee. Each individual shop then competes on its own—and you need to know what the other shops are doing.

Gary B.'s coffeehouse is a kiosk in a mall in Massachusetts. "There's competition everywhere," he says. "But here I am, with a small business that I love. I can't compete with the big companies as far as marketing dollars spent, but I can compete with them with the products, the people, and the presentation. So I let them educate the consumer, and I just keep polishing the apple every day, focusing on people, presentation, and product." Though competition doesn't scare him, he doesn't ignore it. "I'm frequently out comparing my business to other businesses, because that's what the consumer does. They come up, they order something, and they compare you to where they've been before," he says. The only way to make absolutely certain that comparison is favorable is to know what you're up against.

You can get coffee just about anywhere you go—restaurants, bars, nightclubs, department stores, boutiques, gift shops, hair salons, automotive repair shops—even hardware stores. It's a universal drink that appeals to the majority of the population, and it's inexpensive to prepare.

▲

Not all other coffee shops should be considered competitors. Your four primary competitor groups are other coffeehouses, bakery/donut shops, retail coffee and tea stores, and mobile coffee/espresso carts. Study what they're doing; then put together a product, service, and ambience package that your target market will prefer.

Bakery

Bread: Its role in our lives is larger than simple nourishment. Bread has always been a fundamental part of our world. Thousands of years ago, people learned to soak wheat kernels, beat them to a pulp, shape them into cakes, and cook them over a fire. Crushed cereal grains—evidence of an advance to flour—have been found in 8,000-year-old

▲

remains of Swiss lake dwellers. By 1680 B.C., the Egyptians had invented leavened bread as well as the bakery. They established a hierarchy of breads: wheat for the rich, barley for the middle class, and sorghum for the poor. Centuries later, the English parliament enacted a series of laws that limited the profits bakers could make from bread and required that every baker put his mark on his loaves. And that was the beginning of the trademark.

As colonists settled in the New World, their wheat crops flourished and so did bread innovation. The first successful threshing machine was invented, and milling processes were refined, creating better-quality flour. By A.D. 1850, there were more than 2,000 commercial bakeries in the United States.

With the emergence of strip malls and competition from supermarkets that have in-store bakeries, "bread-only" retail bakeries have almost disappeared from the U.S. Bakeries today sell cakes, scones, bagels, cappuccinos, and sometimes even offer full menus, including sandwiches, hot entrees, beer, and wine. Consumers love fresh bakery goods, but the market is extremely competitive. As you develop your particular bakery concept, you'll need something to differentiate yourself from other bakeries in town.

Before you start, survey the market. People strongly prefer some breads over others. The age, income, and ethnic background of your market are important considerations when deciding what breads and other items to bake. Begin by checking area supermarket shelves to see which breads are fast movers and which end up on the day-old rack. Ask grocery-chain buyers what the bestsellers are.

In the West, exotic breads remain popular. In the South, soft white bread is the bestseller, and cakes make up a significant portion of bakery sales. People in the Midwest seem to favor white bread as well, and sales of cakes, muffins, and cookies

---

Easy Bake

Staggering baking schedules throughout the day guarantees fresh product for the customer. To set up your daily baking schedule efficiently, start by baking breads with high yeast levels or shorter proofing times. Get these first batches in the oven while mixing breads with longer proofing times. You'll be ready to take a batch out of the oven at the same time another batch finishes the final proofing stage.

The average batch of bread takes about an hour and 45 minutes to bake. However, you can bake 15 to 20 varieties a day by baking all the whole wheat-based breads together, for example.

are strong in this area. The preferred bread in the Northeast is the traditional Italian loaf; cakes, donuts, and bagels are also popular.

You'll need to decide whether you're going to bake hearth or pan breads, or both. Hearth breads are made directly on a shelf or oven bottom, while pan breads are made in loaf pans. French, rye, and Italian are leaders of the "hearth" breads. Your product mix will depend in part on how much of a purist you want to be and how much your customers like natural foods.

The best location for a bakery is a middle- to upper-middle income area with a population of at least 100,000. In poorer neighborhoods, buyers might not want to pay the extra money for a loaf of specialty raisin bread when they can get plain white bread for substantially less at the supermarket.

Keep in mind that breads are low-margin items. It's possible, but not likely, that you could make a living on bread sales alone with a very high volume. It's better to offer a wide variety of products.

Once you get your system in place, producing volume shouldn't be a problem. After about four months in business, you should be able to easily produce 35,000 loaves of bread a month. Producing thousands of loaves a day is one thing; selling them is another. Set realistic production and sales goals based on customer flow and projected growth. Also, become familiar with your customers' buying patterns; demand for certain products will be different on different days of the week.

You can get formula recipes from suppliers, some flour mills, and, of course, from cookbooks. Many people starting bakeries are avid bakers and spend a lot of time baking at home. Even large multimillion-dollar wholesale bakeries in many cases began with a person baking as a hobby. These tried-and-true home recipes can be adapted for large-scale baking.

Competition

The key to combating your competitors is knowing their business as well as you do your own. Here's where you can expect competition for your bakery to come from:

- *Supermarket bakery.* The supermarket in-store bakery provides a grocery shopper with the convenience of one-stop shopping. What it usually lacks are high-quality baked goods and personal service. Many supermarkets use mixes or even buy ready-to-sell baked products rather than actually baking fresh items. The items they do bake fresh are usually made early in the morning, so the store doesn't have that bakery-fresh aroma throughout the day.

Bright Idea

You can sell more bread and increase profits by selling hot, buttered bread by the slice. This is an attractive concept to customers, especially if you're located in a shopping area and also offer a selection of beverages. The taste of a fresh slice of warm, buttered cinnamon bread will keep shoppers coming back. Most bakers charge at least 50 cents per slice.

Supermarket bakers may not market their services as aggressively as independent bakeries might. While supermarkets may mention these departments in their weekly ads and announce in-store bakery specials over the intercom, they generally do not focus strongly on their bakeries. With aggressive promotion, you should be able to compete successfully with such bakeries.

- *Chain bakeries.* Chain bakeries have the advantage of strong advertising campaigns to promote the chain name so it's recognizable. By purchasing a franchise, the franchisee automatically gets the benefit of the franchisor's marketing skills and ad budget. Chain bakeries also usually sell good-quality food at competitive prices. They should provide good service, but depending on how busy they are, they might not always do so. They don't always get to know their customers as independent bakeries do. Here's where you have the advantage.

- *Party stores.* Party stores have the advantage of a captive audience. If a person goes in to buy party goods, the store can sell them a complete package, providing them with all the decorations and table goods; decorating the cake; and even catering their party. The party store might even offer a package discount.

Many independent retail bakeries have used similar tactics, offering a selection of party items and tableware to go with cakes and other party sweets. Also, the independent bakery has the advantage of offering a wide array of high-quality baked goods. You can ensure that the party won't just look good, but the baked items will taste delicious.

Not by Bread Alone

Bread may be the staff of life, but it is certainly far from the only item produced by bakeries. In addition to, or instead of bread, you may also bake pies, cakes, cheesecakes, cookies, donuts, rolls, pretzels, croissants, bagels, muffins—the list goes on. You may want to offer a range of items, as does Portland, Maine, bakery owner Jim A. Or you may want to specialize in a very narrow product line, which is how Kenny B. built his company in Smyrna, Georgia—he makes key lime pies exclusively, more than 1,500 of them every day.

If you focus on a narrow product line, it needs to be outstanding. "We had people tell us early on, you can't survive on this one product," Kenny B recalls. "But I knew it was so special and so good that we could. Where we were able to excel was that we have something very unique, and something nobody else was doing."

Your product line will be guided by a variety of issues. Jim A., for example, loved sourdough bread, and that's what he started his bakery with. Kenny B. loved key lime pie, and was making them as a hobby when friends urged him to go into business.

In addition to your own personal preferences, consider the demands of your market. Who are your customers, and what type of baked goods do they buy? This information should have been revealed by your initial market research.

Consider your available space and equipment. Be sure it's adequate for the product line you choose. Can your equipment do double or even triple duty? Will you have to spend a lot of time cleaning equipment and work areas to switch from making one product to another—and how will that affect your productivity and profitability?

Think about how your products blend and the collective image they project. For example, if you bake a variety of breads and have only one dessert or sweet item, that product doesn't really fit in with your primary image. Or, if you're promoting your business as a whole grain or natural foods bakery, you don't want to have items that include highly-processed or artificial ingredients.

Setting Up Your Facility

You have several options when selecting your facility. If you will specialize in serving customers on the go, you probably won't need a very large facility; 1,000 to 1,500 square feet, including kitchen space, should suffice. On the other hand, if you choose to offer a full menu and allow space for customer seating, you may want a facility as large as 3,000 square feet. Keep in mind that more square footage doesn't necessarily mean higher sales; you may want to start small and expand or move if business warrants.

Plan on spending anywhere from $20,000 to $200,000 or more on the facility, depending on whether you're converting an existing facility or building from the ground up.

Kitchen/Production Area

The kitchen is usually located in the back of the store and includes all your bread-baking equipment, such as a mixer, divider, roller, proof-box, oven, and walk-in refrigerator or cooler. You will also need counter space for baking and decorating activities, and enough space for your employees to move around comfortably. Arrange production equipment according to the sequence of operations so you eliminate backtracking, reduce materials handling, and streamline the flow of work. Most bakeries allot at least 40 percent of their space to the kitchen.

Front Retail/Display Area

In the front of your operation, you'll have a retail area that includes such things as pastry display cases, a checkout counter, at least one cash register, and maybe a few pieces of equipment behind the counter, such as a cappuccino machine, coffee machine, soft drink dispensers, or other refreshment machines. The presentation of your storefront should draw customers in.

You may also want to provide tables and chairs for customers, either inside or on a patio, so they can eat on the premises. Devote about 35 to 40 percent of your space to this area.

Restrooms

You will need at least one restroom, accessible to employees and possibly customers. You may want to have two—one for men and one for women—especially if you offer a sit-down eating area for customers. Your local health department can advise you on any legal requirements for restrooms that may apply.

Office/Shipping/Receiving Area

See the guidelines in the chapters on sandwich shops/delicatessens and pizzerias for details on setting up this area.

Other Areas

Your bakery may also feature a hot case in the sandwich area for prepared hot foods such as lasagna; a dimmed area with spotlights at each decorator station; and some successful supermarket-style presentations, such as self-service racks for bread and rolls, and half- and even quarter-sized cakes.

Equipment

The only way you'll meet high-volume production goals is with ultramodern automated equipment. To reach this level of automation, figure on a minimum of

$45,000 in total equipment costs. Of course, this equipment can be financed or leased with minimum down payments.

If you're starting on a small budget, you can buy used equipment packages for less than $20,000. Look for ads for bakeries for sale. Also keep an eye out for bankruptcy sales and special equipment auctions where substantial savings on good used equipment can be found. This equipment can get you started, but plan to add the up-to-date items later.

Bright Idea

The commercial bread slicer was perfected in 1928 by Otto Rohwedder—but it was not popular with consumers. Sliced bread grew stale faster than a whole loaf; it took packaging and improved storage techniques for sliced bread to become a truly great thing.

Your main fixtures and equipment will be a refrigerator, sinks, showcases, a mixer, dough divider, molder (rounder), a proofer, a slicer, and a double-rack rotary or revolving oven.

A rounder is a device that shapes the dough and smoothes it into the correct shape for baking. Look for a system with adjustable rounding tracks for more accurate rounding. New rounders range in price from $4,000 to $9,000.

Credit Where Credit Is Due

Most of your retail sales will be paid by cash, check, or credit card. You'll get a deposit or full payment in advance on special orders. But if you are selling wholesale, your customers will likely expect you to extend credit. Accurate record-keeping is critical to maintaining your profitability.

Create a permanent record of credit sales and maintain it separately from your sales slips and invoices. This record should show the date, the invoice number, the amount of any new charges, a running balance of the total amount owed, the date and amount of each payment received, and a record of any invoices, collection letters, and collection phone calls made to this customer.

Make sure your invoices are clear, accurate, and timely. Send them to the right address and correct person. The prices on invoices should agree with the quotes on purchase orders or contracts, and disputes should be handled promptly. Your invoice and contracts should also clearly state the terms of sale (such as "net 30 days").

Dividers cut a large mass of dough, dividing it into individual pieces. Models vary in the pieces of dough per hour they can process. Make certain the divider you purchase is capable of operating at the volume you anticipate for your bakery. Dough dividers can cost as little as $3,000 or as much as $10,000.

Dough is damaged somewhat by the dividing and rounding process, and the proofer gives the dough time to "relax" before the final baking stages. Inside the proofer are pockets where the dough rests. These typically mesh pockets are about the size of half a watermelon. Ranging from $5,000 to $60,000, proofers are available in many models.

Mixers usually come in various sizes, ranging from 40 quarts to about 160 quarts. For high-volume bread baking, use a spiral mixer, which holds from 100 to 200 pounds of flour. A spiral dough mixer is best.

The oven will be one of your most expensive items, at $15,000 to $26,000 or more, depending on its capacity and whether you choose a revolving oven or a more expensive rack oven. In a revolving oven, the bread trays go in a revolving container, and the tray rotates, exposing the bread to all parts of the oven for even baking. Rack ovens work in a similar fashion, vertically. You will be baking many types of breads, cakes, and pastries, so buy an oven with a combustion system that easily converts from direct to indirect heat. This provides flexible control of bottom and top heat,

Going to Sell in a Bread Basket

Your bakery can sell either wholesale, retail, or both. Portland, Maine, bakery owner Jim A. says it's easier for a wholesale baker to transition to the retail side than the other way around. Wholesale bakeries are generally larger and organized differently than retail operations. Wholesalers need to line up their commercial accounts, develop a sales strategy, and be able to service those accounts with fresh, delicious products delivered on a timely basis. Retailers need to be more concerned about generating foot traffic and attracting walk-in customers.

Retailers who try to expand into the wholesale market often find their retail facilities are inadequate in terms of space, capacity, and logistics. Jim A. believes a retailer who understands this issue and is willing to open a separate wholesale location has a better chance of success.

Wholesalers who decide to expand into retail need to take the time to understand merchandising and displays, and create an attractive environment for retail shoppers.

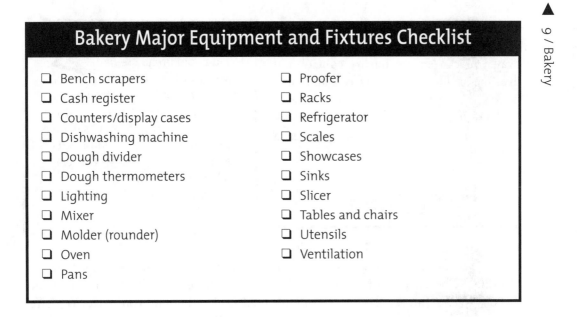

Bakery Major Equipment and Fixtures Checklist

- ❏ Bench scrapers
- ❏ Cash register
- ❏ Counters/display cases
- ❏ Dishwashing machine
- ❏ Dough divider
- ❏ Dough thermometers
- ❏ Lighting
- ❏ Mixer
- ❏ Molder (rounder)
- ❏ Oven
- ❏ Pans

- ❏ Proofer
- ❏ Racks
- ❏ Refrigerator
- ❏ Scales
- ❏ Showcases
- ❏ Sinks
- ❏ Slicer
- ❏ Tables and chairs
- ❏ Utensils
- ❏ Ventilation

allowing you to use different baking methods for different products. For superior-quality hearth breads, the oven should have a steam distribution system. Steam keeps breads like pumpernickel, French, and Italian from drying out and ensures a crisp crust on the outside.

Besides the major pieces of baking equipment, you'll need a wide assortment of small kitchenware like pans, racks, scales, and utensils. Depending on the volume and type of goods you make, you will use as many as 200 pans. A hundred of these will be bread or sandwich pans of different sizes. The remainder may be used for rolls, pastries, and other items baked on a regular basis. One set of five pans can cost $50 or more. Expect to pay from $2,500 to more than $5,000 for pans, depending on whether you buy them used or new.

Inventory

When you're getting started, it's best to order conservatively until you know what will sell best. Your basic larder will include sugar, yeast, salt, dried fruits, shortening, nuts, cheese, and garlic powder. The pre-mixed flours represent the largest single category of ingredient. At least in the beginning, you'll be relying on pre-mixes and won't need many additional ingredients.

You should budget 35 percent of your weekly gross income for inventory, and more than half of this outlay will go toward flour. Your monthly outlay will increase if you use a lot of special flours, like rice flour, which costs considerably more than white flour.

It's best to order flour every week or two from a nearby mill or supplier. This way you can ensure quality control and freshness. These suppliers can also provide the paper goods you need. Polyurethane wrappings and bags represent about 3 percent of gross revenues, a surprising chunk of your business.

Staffing

Bright Idea

Use day-old bread creatively by dicing or grinding it into croutons, stuffing mix, and bread crumbs. You could also set up a thrift counter and sell day-old bread with at least one-third off the price of fresh bread—this way, you'll at least recover the cost of the raw materials on the products you aren't able to sell fresh.

If you're going to be a hands-on owner, you need to be prepared to work long hours and be comfortable working in a routine. "There's a lot of routine to running most bakeries," says Portland, Maine, bakery owner Jim A. "You make onion bread every Tuesday; you make baguettes every day of the week." At the same time, he says, "You need some artistic sense about

Mixing It Up

Ingredient suppliers or flour companies will provide you with bread bases, blended mixes, and plenty of advice. A pre-mix includes ingredients like flour, shortening, milk, and salt. You only add water and yeast. This cuts the number of scalings (ingredient weighing) from seven or eight to three (mix, yeast, water), making it easier to produce a finished loaf quickly.

Bases require flour, yeast, and water. To make bread dough, you add three parts flour to one part base. Once you gain experience, you'll be able to cut back on some expensive mixes and experiment with your own specialties. With mixes for only three types of bread (white, wheat, and rye), you can create an enormous variety of breads by adding ingredients according to quantity recipes (known as formulas) or to your own taste. The difference between your bread and the ordinary loaf will be in these added ingredients.

The type and amount of ingredients you order depends on the products you offer. You'll need molasses to bake a lot of sweet breads. For "health" breads, you'll use wheat flour, honey, and organically grown fruits.

You Don't Have to Bake It at All

Even though you operate a bakery, not every product you sell has to be baked on the premises. You have a range of options when it comes to buying baked goods from wholesale bakers.

You can buy other bakers' goods for your bakery but not advertise their name. Some companies sell fully baked products, which can be put right on the shelf, as well as frozen, fully baked products, and frozen dough that has to be scooped, shaped, proofed, baked, cooled, packaged, and sold. The last choice lets you advertise your products as being "fresh baked."

Another option is to use the wholesaler's products and advertise the name of the supplier. This may require a licensing agreement, so the supplier knows you are presenting their products in a good light. Some suppliers will also require a licensing fee.

Alternatively, you could become a franchisee, operating your business according to an agreement with a franchise operation.

the food you are creating, where it's coming from, and how you are going about making it."

Beware!

Just knowing the mechanics of bread-making is not enough. You and your staff should be able to distinguish a good loaf of bread from a bad or even average one. French bread should have a crisp, golden crust. Italian breads have a denser consistency and a less-crisp crust. A good sourdough has a tough, chewy crust, slightly grayish-white crumbs, and a strong, distinctive flavor.

Unless you have baking experience, you'll need to hire a baker. The most efficient approach is to hire a baker/manager and an assistant baker. Although the equipment does most of the work, machinery isn't entirely reliable. Many things can go wrong that only a baker would know how to correct. Dough can be overmixed, undermixed, overproofed, and so on. It takes experience and practice to develop an intuitive baker's sense.

In addition, bakers know the inventory requirements and are usually well-acquainted with suppliers and manufacturers. Your baker/manager will buy the inventory, deal with suppliers, and supervise production. The assistant baker will work the night or early-morning shift, depending on shop hours and volume requirements.

Experienced bakers demand $400 to $600 or more per week, depending on their background and your local market conditions. Bakers' assistants will sometimes work as apprentices and can be paid less. Depending on your shop hours and volume, it's usually a good idea to have an assistant manager, too.

You'll also need salespeople to work the counter, ring up customer sales, take orders for cakes and other specialty items, and keep the front area clean and orderly. Whether or not you'll need cooks and servers depends, of course, on the scope of your menu. If you sell wholesale, you'll need delivery people.

How much you'll pay in wages will depend on where you're located and the specific skill and experience level of the workers.

Food and
Party Catering

Does working hard in the kitchen while everyone else is eating, drinking, and socializing in the living room sound like your idea of a good time? If your goal is to be in the catering business, the answer should be an emphatic "yes."

Americans' love of dining and entertaining has created a tremendous market for off-premises caterers across the country. A wide range of social and business events are providing the opportunity for caterers to cook up tasty dishes and delicious profits. In fact, growth among social caterers has been one of the strongest in the overall food-service industry in recent years, and that trend is expected to continue.

A successful caterer will be organized, consistent, and creative. They enjoy working in an environment that changes every day. "Most restaurateurs hate catering for the exact reason that I love it: It's different every day," says Ann C., a caterer in Irvine, California. "A restaurateur is happy in a completely confined space where they're in control and they don't have to worry about anything leaving the building. With catering, you can get your inside operations down to the wire, but then you have to put it all in a truck and take it someplace to set it up, and you could lose control." Another appeal of catering, she says, is the strong relationship that tends to develop with clients. "This is something that's really personal. Food is a personal reflection of the host, whether it's in a corporate environment or someone's home."

From a cost-of-entry perspective, catering is probably the most flexible of all food-service businesses. While you need a commercial location, you can start small and build your equipment inventory as you need to. You may even find an existing commercial kitchen that you can rent, as Maxine T. did when she started her Salt Lake City catering operation. She operated in a school cafeteria for ten years before moving into her own commercial facility.

> ## Bright Idea
>
> Catering is a great way to expand an existing food-service operation without investing a significant amount of capital. If you have a restaurant, deli, sandwich shop, pizzeria, or bakery, you can easily add a catering division. For example, Rebecca S.'s pasta shop and restaurant also offers drop-off catering. The food is prepared and arranged on attractive platters and trays that are all disposable. Everything is dropped off, ready to be set up on a buffet, and the containers can be thrown away after the event.

In the beginning, if you need something unusual, such as a champagne fountain for a wedding reception, you can usually rent it rather than buy it. And your food inventory is easy to control, because you know well in advance exactly how many people you're cooking for.

Off-premises caterers—caterers who take the food to the customers, rather than a catering department operating on-site in a hotel or convention center—offer everything from a gourmet breakfast in bed for two to elegant dinners for 20 to charity galas for more than 1,000 people. Some caterers specialize in one kind of food—cakes and breads, for example—while others offer a wide range of services, including floral arrangements, specialized props and costumes for theme parties, and wedding coordination.

Niche Hunt

Before you start your catering business, advises Salt Lake City caterer Maxine T., know your market from both the competition and customer perspectives, and find a niche no other caterer is serving. "Know every catering company and what they do," Maxine says. "Find something someone else is not providing and focus your attention there in the beginning. Start out small. The diversity will happen as your company grows."

She advises targeting areas with corporate parks, because if you do a good job for a company's breakfasts, lunches, and business parties, those people will also hire you to handle their personal social events. Ask businesspeople you know what they look for in a caterer and what they would like to have that they can't find.

You also need to know what every other caterer in town is doing. Call them up and ask for their menus. Find out what services they offer, who works for them, and who their clients are. Use that information to develop your own service package and marketing strategy. "It's much easier to get started," Maxine says, "when you're providing a service people want but that no one else is offering."

The three major markets for off-premises caterers are:

- *Corporate clients.* The primary need of this market is food for breakfast and lunch meetings, although there will be some demand for cocktail parties and dinners. Service can range from simply preparing a platter of food that is picked up by the client to cooking an elaborate meal and arranging it at the site of the meeting.

- *Social events.* Millions of dollars are spent each year on wedding receptions—most of it on food. Other special events that are commonly catered include bar and bat mitzvahs, anniversary dinners, birthday parties, and graduations.

- *Cultural organizations.* Museums, opera houses, symphonies, and other cultural and community organizations frequently have catered events ranging from light hors d'oeuvres to formal dinners, sometimes for as many several thousand people.

You'll see a tremendous amount of crossover between these market groups. Maxine T. started out with a primarily corporate clientele, serving continental breakfasts and boxed lunches. As her business grew, the corporate customers began hiring her to handle their personal social events, such as weddings and parties. And while she still does simple breakfasts and lunches, she's also catered such events as

▲

Don't Try This at Home

Although some successful caterers start their businesses from home, most industry experts caution that the potential risks involved outweigh the economic advantages. Operating without health and fire department approval immediately opens you up to liability risks; most insurance companies won't insure your business without compliance with state regulations and licensing requirements. In addition, you won't get wholesale price breaks from reputable food distributors who refuse to sell to operators without a resale license. Without adequate insurance, licensing, and payment of workers' compensation, some operators have lost their homes in lawsuits filed either by clients or injured workers. Bite the bullet and do it right from the start.

Of course, even when they are properly licensed and located, legitimate caterers often face stiff competition from cooks operating illegally from their homes in violation of health codes. It's difficult for a caterer working out of a commercial kitchen to price competitively against such adversaries who don't have the same overhead expenses. Even so, don't let these illegal operators drive your prices down to an unprofitable level; focus on professional service and quality food, and you'll be around long after the homebased cooks have given up.

the celebration for the 100th episode of the hit television series, *Touched By An Angel*, which is filmed in Salt Lake City.

Of course, there is a wide range of additional markets and specialties. You might cook for very specific dietary restrictions, such as kosher, macrobiotic, or other special food preparation requirements. You might focus on afternoon teas, celebration breakfasts, or even picnic baskets. Another popular niche market is cooking health-conscious meals for dual-career couples who don't have time to cook for themselves. You can either go to their home and prepare the meal there or cook at your own facility and deliver the food ready to be served. Another option is to offer several days' or a week's worth of meals prepared in advance that your customers can simply heat and serve. Let your imagination run wild with possible market ideas; then do some basic market research to see what's likely to work.

First-rate caterers can demand and get top dollar for their services—but the key is that you must perform. You must also keep in mind some general market trends. For the most part, extravagant meals and rich foods are a thing of the past; people are eating less beef and more poultry, drinking less hard liquor and more wine, and are more concerned about the bottom line. Many caterers say these trends have forced them to be more creative chefs, as they work more with spices and ethnic dishes rather than with rich sauces.

Setting Up Your Facility

The foundation of your catering business is your commercial kitchen. Reserve at least 75 percent of the area for food production, 15 percent for receiving and storage, and the remaining 10 percent for the office, where administrative and related activities are performed. If you provide a lot of props and accessories for events, you may need additional storage for those items.

The main thing to keep in mind when laying out your facility is to set up an efficient food preparation area. Organize your appliances, work surfaces, and equipment systematically so you're not trotting ten feet to the sink to wash a handful of vegetables or carrying hot pots across the room to drain the pasta.

Organize your kitchen around the major appliances and work areas for easy accessibility. For example, everything you need for cooking should be in close proximity to the stove, and all necessary peeling and cutting tools should be stored near the vegetable prep counter.

Give yourself plenty of clear work space. Ideally, your counters should be stainless steel for both maintenance and sanitary reasons. Wooden counters are illegal in many areas because they increase the risk of food contamination. "We have a lot of linear table space," says Ann C. "A lot of our business will be 500 box lunches or 20,000 pieces of hors d'oeuvres for a party, and we need a lot of flat counter space, rolling racks, and movable pieces to put them together."

Locate your dishwasher next to the sink so you can pre-rinse dishes and utensils. If you hand-wash your dishes, a triple-sink arrangement (one sink for soaking, one for washing, and one for rinsing) is best. Keep racks on the counter next to the rinsing sink for drying the dishes, and store clean dishtowels near the sink. A garbage disposal is a must for disposing of food scraps. Some municipalities require a separate sink for hand-washing, so check your local health codes to be sure you set up right the first time.

The receiving area should be separate from the food preparation area. It needs to be accessible to delivery vans and ideally should have double doors and a hand truck for easy transport of goods. You should also have a weighing scale set up to ensure that your deliveries are correct.

Your office area does not need to be elaborate; a simple desk, chair, phone, and computer should be sufficient.

If you have room, set up a small area where employees can hang their street clothes and store their personal belongings. You will also want to put your rest-

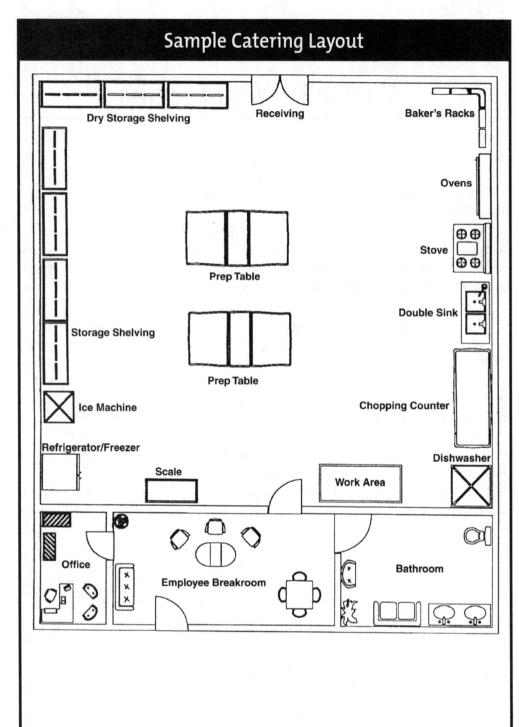

Sample Catering Layout

Dry Storage Shelving

Receiving

Baker's Racks

Ovens

Stove

Double Sink

Prep Table

Storage Shelving

Prep Table

Chopping Counter

Ice Machine

Refrigerator/Freezer

Dishwasher

Scale

Work Area

Office

Bathroom

Employee Breakroom

rooms here. A table and chairs for employees to use while on their breaks is a nice touch.

Kitchen Equipment

As you look at all the possibilities for equipping your commercial kitchen, you may find yourself overwhelmed by the amount and potential cost of what you need. Just keep in mind that you don't need everything listed in this chapter to get started—and you may never need some of the items. It all depends on your volume and the type of food you are interested in preparing. Also, the price estimates listed here are for new equipment; smart shopping for used items can save you a bundle.

Your possible major equipment purchases include:

- Two commercial ovens. One should be a hot-top (an oven with a solid metal top that heats evenly) and one a range-top (an oven with the ringed metal burners you see in consumer kitchens. Expect to pay anywhere from $900 to $2,200 per oven, depending on size and number of burners.
- Two convection ovens that cook by circulating heated air. This type of oven allows for very efficient cooking that uses all the available oven space. A double convection unit, with two ovens stacked on top of each other, will run $4,500 to $5,000.
- Three-door commercial refrigerator for $2,000 to $3,000.
- Two-door commercial freezer that will cost $2,200 to $2,400.
- Single-door commercial dishwasher for about $2,500.

Miss Manners

An extremely valuable piece of "equipment" is a good book of etiquette. Amy Vanderbilt, Charlotte Ford, and others have written informative etiquette guides. You can check out these books from your local library, then purchase the one that best suits your needs. It will help clear up any points of table display, serving protocol, dress, etc., that you may encounter from time to time. Your clients will expect you to know the answers to questions they may have about throwing their party in the most appropriate way, so brush up on your knowledge of etiquette.

▲

- Commercial-grade mixer that can range from $450 to $2,200, depending on capacity.
- 300-pound capacity scale to ensure that items you purchase by weight are delivered in the correct amount: the price of $1,500 to $2,000 is well worth the investment in inventory control.
- Ice machine with a storage capacity ranging from 45 to 400 pounds, depending on your needs: prices increase with capacity; you'll pay $800 to $1,800.
- Food processor for $400 to $850.
- Slicer for meats and cheeses for sandwiches and deli trays; cost is $500 to $2,000.
- Sink, either two- or three-compartments, costing $400 to $700.
- Stainless-steel work tables: you'll pay about $120 each.
- Proofing box (about $1,400) and baker's rack (about $150) if you plan to do your own baking.

Catering Service
Major Equipment and Fixtures Checklist

❑ Baker's rack	❑ Knives
❑ Baking dishes	❑ Linens
❑ Chafing dishes	❑ Meat platters
❑ Chinaware	❑ Mixing bowls
❑ Cocktail accessories	❑ Pizza oven
❑ Coffee makers	❑ Pots and pans
❑ Commercial refrigerator	❑ Proofing box
❑ Commercial ovens	❑ Punch bowls
❑ Commercial freezer	❑ Salad bowls
❑ Commercial dishwasher	❑ Sauce bowls
❑ Commercial-grade mixer	❑ Scale
❑ Convection ovens	❑ Sink
❑ Fiberglass carrying units	❑ Slicer
❑ Flatware	❑ Trays
❑ Food processor	❑ Utensils
❑ Glassware	❑ Vegetable platters
❑ Heat lamps	❑ Ventilation system
❑ Hot boxes	❑ Work tables
❑ Ice machine	

- Pizza oven if you plan to make pizzas: expect to pay $750 to $2,000.
- Two heat lamps for hot hors d'oeuvres at buffets: you'll pay $100 to $250 each.
- Two hot boxes to transport hot food: expect to pay $300 to $600 each.
- Four to six fiberglass carrying units to transport both hot and cold food: these run $100 to $400 each.
- Two to four coffee makers: commercial coffee makers run $200 to $550 each.
- Six stainless-steel chafing dishes for $60 to $120 each.
- Assorted trays, sauce bowls, vegetable platters, meat platters, salad bowls, and punch bowls.

Cooking and Serving Equipment

In addition to major appliances and event accessories, you'll need an assortment of utensils to prepare and serve a variety of hors d'oeuvres and full meals. If you're an experienced cook, chances are you already own most of the cooking equipment you need. "The first mixing bowls I had were from my own kitchen," Maxine T. says. "My first trays were wedding gifts I hadn't used in ten years. My first inventory was my own personal things." Later, she began a wish list of items her chefs said they wanted or needed; when a particular item was repeatedly requested, she would budget the purchase.

It's not necessary to go out and buy everything at once. Get the most frequently used items, of course, but give yourself some time to see what you really need before you buy an assortment of special equipment. And remember, if your rate of use doesn't justify the cost of purchasing, you can always rent.

As you go along, you'll also learn to use whatever the client has for decoration, preparation and serving. Combine your items with theirs, particularly if you are catering an event in someone's home.

You could easily spend $500 to $2,500 or more on miscellaneous cooking utensils such as flatware, spatulas, garlic presses, cutting boards, and so on—but you don't have to. Don't buy needlessly. Use the following list as a guide, and accept or discard the suggestions as seems appropriate for your particular operation.

- *Utensils.* Small and large ladles, tongs, kitchen spoons, measuring spoons (metal and plastic), measuring cups (metal and plastic), carving boards, cutting boards, spatulas, wire whisks, pastry brushes, potato peeler, flour sifter, can opener, knife sharpener, aluminum colander, funnels, cheese grater, radish rose, melon ball maker, garlic press, pastry bag with assorted tips, portion scale, meat and candy thermometers, egg slicer, heavy-duty plastic food warmers, citrus knife, sterno setup(s), wicker bread baskets, wicker cracker baskets, three-prong plug adapters.

- *Knives.* A quality set of kitchen knives (with three brads holding the blade to the handle) can be bought for $200 to $300. The types of knives you need are carving, cheese, bread, paring, boning, and chef's cleaver.

- *Pots and pans.* Frying pans, pots in 1-, 2-, 3-, 4-, 5-, 6-, and 10-quart capacities, double boiler, spaghetti pot, fondue pot with warmer, omelet pans, roasting pans.

- *Mixing bowls.* You'll need an assortment of ceramic, stainless-steel, and glass bowls in varying sizes.

- *Baking dishes.* Depending, of course, on whether you'll be doing your own baking or buying breads and pastries from a bakery, you'll need 9-inch pie pans, 9-inch cake pans, rectangular cakes pans, cookie sheets, muffin pans, angel-food cake pans, bundt cake pans, spring-side pans, loaf pans, tart tins, and quiche dishes.

- *Hors d'oeuvres trays.* Small and large pizza pans, silver serving trays (round, square, and oblong), coffee urn, candle warmer.

- *Chinaware.* Cups and saucers, soup bowls, salad bowls, salad plates, bread plates, dinner plates, base plates, dessert plates. White porcelain is a good choice; it's durable, dishwasher-safe, and goes well with a variety of foods and decorating themes.

- *Glassware.* Water goblets, red wine glasses (10-oz.), white wine glasses (6-oz.), champagne flutes, martini glasses, highball glasses, old-fashioned glasses, cordial glasses, brandy snifters.

- *Flatware.* Dinner knives, butter knives, dinner forks, fish forks, salad forks, soup spoons, teaspoons, iced-tea spoons. High-quality stainless-steel flatware will wear better than silverware and will require much less maintenance (by way of polishing).

- *Linens.* Napkins, round tablecloths, rectangular tablecloths.

- *Cocktail accessories.* Pitchers, serving cart(s), strainers, shakers, stirrers, toothpicks, cocktail napkins, corkscrew(s), ice bucket(s).

- *Miscellaneous.* Sugar and cream sets, ash trays, salt and pepper mills, wheeled serving carts, scissors, candles, ribbons, matches, masking tape, paper napkins, transparent tape, garbage bags, garbage cans, paper doilies, mops, buckets, brooms, dustpans, first-aid kit.

Company Vehicle

For most catered events, you'll be transporting food and equipment. You can either use your personal vehicle if the amount of supplies is small enough, or you'll have to lease or purchase a vehicle that will meet your needs.

It's possible to spend $30,000 or more outfitting a new van with all the inventory and equipment a caterer might need. Some caterers have elaborate vans equipped with virtually everything but running water. Some ideas to consider include propane tanks to cook on-site for outdoor events where electricity is unavailable and mobile warmers and refrigerators for locations where the facility is insufficient. But these are very expensive customizing extras that are not necessary or desirable for someone just starting out. Your best bet is a no-frills approach, such as a good late-model used van. You should be able to find one for $8,000 to $12,000 if you shop carefully.

Inventory

The advantage of catering over other food-service businesses is that you always know how many people you will have to feed. There's no guesswork, no waste, and no inventory needed in the traditional sense—at least in the beginning.

Certainly staples such as flour, sugar, grains, spices, canned goods, and frozen foods can be purchased in bulk and stocked on a long-term basis. But you won't be stocking food inventory the same way a restaurant does. Typically, you won't purchase foods until you have agreed on an exact menu with a client and determined the number of guests. Of course, as your business grows, you'll be able to stock more inventory and take advantage of the savings of volume purchasing.

The key to good shopping is organization. Sit down with your menu and make a list of everything you need to produce the party. If the preparation is going to require any new equipment you don't yet own, be sure to include that on your shopping list.

Once you've determined everything you need, organize your list by store and department; then figure out the most efficient order to visit each store. A single shopping excursion may take you to a farmers' market, a wholesale house, a general grocery store, a delicatessen, a bakery, and a gourmet shop. Most of your shopping should be done the day before the party, although some fresh items (lettuce, bread, etc.) should be purchased the day of the event.

Wholesale or Retail?

Depending on the size of your jobs, it may or may not be worth it to buy wholesale goods. There are dealers in every major city that can supply you with fresh produce, meat, poultry, etc., in large quantities at low prices. This can mean significant savings when you're buying for large jobs or several events at a time. Also, a big advantage of wholesalers is that most of them will deliver orders to your kitchen. But if you just need eight chicken breasts for a small dinner party, most wholesale dealers will not be enthused about the sale. It would probably be easier to visit your nearby supermarket.

Staffing

Most catering operations have a core permanent staff that is supplemented by part-timers on a per-project basis. To provide adequate service, you need to understand the basic structure and division of labor at a catered affair.

The three basic kinds of catered social affairs are the formal, sit-down dinner; the informal buffet dinner; and the cocktail party. Naturally, as individual events develop personalities of their own, these three definitions often vary or converge.

The majority of business affairs will require little or no service and mainly involve preparing platters of food for business luncheons that are either picked up at your facility or that you deliver to your clients. Some business events, however—such as office holiday parties or formal dinners for major clients—will be run the same way as social affairs.

> **Bright Idea**
>
> Allow for personnel shortages at every function by scheduling one or two extra people you may not need, on the assumption that at least one person won't show up due to illness, car trouble, or some other reason.

Typically, it takes two days to prepare food for any party. If all your ingredients are fresh and prepared from scratch at the last possible minute, those days will be full. An average party, serving 50 to 125 people, requires one chef plus one or two kitchen helpers, depending on the complexity of the setup.

Managers and Other Employees

The key employee at any catered affair (and this is going to be you in the beginning) is the project manager. This person organizes the food preparation and serving, hires the temporary help, and oversees the entire affair. The project manager must also be able to pitch in and prepare food in an emergency if the chef or one of the kitchen assistants fails to show.

If you supply bartenders for an event, a good ratio is one bartender for every 50 people. You will either employ these specialists yourself or subcontract their services, depending on your volume.

Waiters, buspersons, drivers, and warehouse personnel may be hired on either a temporary or permanent basis. Temporary means on a per-project basis; permanent means an employee who is paid regularly on a full- or part-time schedule. If you have ten waiters you can call to work as needed, they are typically paid as temporary workers.

Serving and food preparation personnel should be considered separate categories. A waiter might double as a driver and even as a busperson, but cooking and serving are two different areas of labor. Even with that in mind, you should look for employees who are flexible and who won't mind pitching in as needed in an emergency.

Clients who are trying to save money will frequently try to cut down on the number of service personnel for an event. Be firm and clear as you explain why this is not a good idea. Guests who can't get their dirty plates taken away, get another hors d'oeuvre, or get a fresh drink are unhappy guests. Nothing will ruin a party quicker than insufficient serving personnel.

Event Staffing Guidelines

There is no better teacher than experience when it comes to knowing how to staff various events. To help you get started, let's look at what experienced caterers would do when catering a party for about 100 people.

For a formal sit-down dinner with many courses, there will be eight or ten people per table and ten to 12 tables. You'll need two cooks or one cook plus one or two assistants. For most parties, one server per table will be sufficient, but this can also vary. Some caterers will have one server for every 15 people; others will put two at each table to keep everything running smoothly and quickly. Another option would be to have one server for each table, plus an extra server for every two tables to remove dirty dishes and glasses. The project manager will oversee the service of all tables.

An informal buffet dinner will require three or four serving people and one cook, plus the manager. All people on the job should be versatile enough to double on tasks after the job is completed—for example, clearing tables, storing food, and loading equipment. For both formal and informal dinners, if there is cocktail service, two bartenders would be required.

For a cocktail party for 100 people, have at least one bartender on hand, plus two service personnel. If both hot and cold hors d'oeuvres will be offered, upgrade to three or four servers. If serving a lot of blended drinks, your

Smart Tip

Tip...

Your employees should always be neat and presentable; after all, they are representing your company. They should dress unobtrusively, usually in dark pants or skirts with plain white shirts or blouses. You can add a discreet signature pin or apron to give personnel a distinctive look, but don't go overboard; you're there to serve, not to promote your company. If tuxedos are necessary for a formal affair, waiters are usually expected to provide their own.

best bet is to have two bartenders. For a party of this size, some caterers routinely have two bartenders, two servers, and a busperson, regardless of the type of drinks served. Still other operations have servers double as buspersons. Staffing requirements vary greatly depending on the type of cocktail party desired.

Some caterers don't provide the bartender or liquor for a cocktail party but will refer the client to available resources. Some provide ice, glasses, and bar setups, while others do not. Some provide beer and wine but no hard liquor or mixers.

These guidelines will help you plan your staffing until you are comfortable estimating your labor needs. No matter what kind of event you cater, having enough help on hand is crucial. Service can make or break a catered affair—and lack of it will surely kill your business.

Developing Menus and Setting Prices

Even though your clients will tell you what they want you to serve, you still need menus. Of course, none of those menus should be carved in stone; be flexible enough to accommodate your clients' preferences.

Sample menus will give you a solid base for meeting with clients, and they may give your clients some ideas about food combinations they would not have otherwise had. Also, you can cost out your sample menus beforehand, which will make figuring prices much easier, and you can provide your clients with more accurate estimates.

Nutritionally, you should strive to produce balanced meals with a good blend of the basic food groups. Each meal should contain about 1,000 calories.

You should also balance ingredients, textures, and tastes. If you serve leek and garlic soup as the opener, you should not serve garlic chicken as the main course. Similarly, if the main course is chicken mousse, chocolate mousse would be out of place as a dessert.

When creating sample menus, work with a variety of dishes and price ranges. If you specialize in something like Southern cooking or spectacular desserts, organize your menus to make this the focal point of your meals.

If you are planning on catering to the wedding market, you will need a wide range of menus for hot buffets, cold buffets, sit-down dinners, etc. A buffet table with a combination of hot and cold hors d'oeuvres, sliced meats, and bread, fruit, cheese and crackers is a very popular choice, and you should put together a

> **Smart Tip**
> *Tip...*
>
> Coordinate menus with the season. Serve lighter foods in summer (lobster and rice, Cobb salad) and heavier in winter (beef Wellington, cassoulet).

Now Presenting . . .

In addition to preparing delicious food, you must also be concerned with how it looks. Your clients hire you to create a special experience for them, to use your professional experience and abilities to design a meal they couldn't produce themselves.

This doesn't mean plopping a sprig of parsley or a tomato rosette on each plate before it goes out the kitchen door. It does mean planning your garnishes and arranging your plates so that your food looks as good as it tastes. You have only two rules when it comes to garnishing: Everything should be edible, and the garnish should taste good with the food. Beyond these rules, the only limit is your imagination.

list of hors d'oeuvres that your clients can choose from. You will also need a wide range of wedding cakes; you can contract out to a local baker if cake-decorating is not one of your talents. A photo album showing pictures of the kinds of cakes you can offer will help your clients select the cake they want. Punches, both champagne and nonalcoholic, are also a staple at weddings.

The corporate market leans more toward platters of food, suitable for business breakfasts and lunches. Middle management and below will tend to want deli plates with sandwiches, cookies, vegetables and dips, fresh fruit, and similar items. If you are working with the upper echelons, you may be called on to produce something more elaborate, perhaps even cooking part of the meal at their office and supplying a waiter to serve them. Develop several different menus based on these levels of formality.

Figuring out how much to charge is probably the most difficult thing you'll need to learn. When you're new, you may not have a solid feel for how much you can charge in your marketplace, how much ingredients for a particular dish will cost, or how much labor it will take to prepare a meal. You'll get better at this over time, but when you're starting out, it's important to carefully cost out your menus so you can make a respectable profit.

To cost a menu, sit down with the full menu. For each dish, break out the costs of the food by ingredients. Some of these will be easier than others. For example, if a recipe calls for a boneless breast of

Bright Idea

If you have a steady client who hires you for several events each year, change your menus monthly to offer variety and a new look.

chicken, a quick trip to the store can tell you exactly how much this will cost. It's much harder to figure out the cost of a teaspoon of salt or other seasoning. Estimate the cost of smaller quantities and staples (flour, sugar, etc.) as best you can.

Once you've determined the prices of all your ingredients, add them up. This is the total cost of the food you will need to prepare the full menu. Multiply this figure by three to get the price you will charge the client. Dividing this figure by the number of guests will give you the price per head for the meal.

This is the most basic method of figuring prices, and most of the time it should cover your food costs, labor, and overhead, and still leave you a net profit margin of between 10 and 20 percent.

Catering Price Worksheet

Food Costs

Item	Cost
_____	_____
_____	_____
_____	_____
_____	_____
_____	_____
_____	_____
_____	_____
Total food costs	_____
X 3	_____
Food price to client	_____
Liquor	_____
Rental equipment	_____
Serving staff	_____
Miscellaneous	_____
Total price	_____

You should check your prices to make sure they are acceptable in your market by calling other caterers to find out what they charge for a comparable menu. If your prices seem to be in line with your competition, you're probably figuring correctly.

There are, of course, instances where this method won't work entirely. For example, if you are preparing a menu that is very labor-intensive, even if the ingredients aren't particularly expensive, you won't be able to pull a profit simply by multiplying your food costs, because your time and employees' wages won't be adequately covered. In these cases, you should increase your prices so you are earning a decent hourly wage, based on the number of hours it's going to take to prepare the meal. Conversely, if you're making something like filet mignon, in which the ingredients are quite expensive but easy to prepare, you'll have difficulty justifying high prices. In this case, you might consider multiplying the cost of the steak by two, and the other ingredients by three, to arrive at a fair price.

Bright Idea

To check out the competition when you're doing your initial market research, give a few catered parties of your own. Hire the caterers you expect to be your strongest competitors so you can see exactly how they operate and what level of service they provide—it's a worthwhile investment in the future of your company.

The cost per person, arrived at by multiplying the cost of food and dividing by the number of guests, is the cost for the food and labor *only*. It does not include the cost of liquor, rental equipment, serving staff, or anything else. Be sure the final price you quote the client takes these expenses into consideration.

When the Customer Calls

When a client calls, you must be prepared to answer all their questions, make suggestions, and in general handle yourself in a pleasant and professional manner. The first phone call will rarely result in a sale for a number of reasons. First, the customer may be shopping several caterers. Second, you probably won't decide during that conversation exactly what is going to be served, so you won't be able to give a specific quote. Also, you'll want to inspect the site of the event before putting together your final proposal.

Many clients will pressure you for an exact price quote during the first phone call. Resist the temptation to do this. Even if the client knows exactly what they want served, you won't know how much the cost of food and labor is going to be until you've had a chance to do your own calculations. If you make up a quote on the spot, it may either be too high, in which case you'll lose the job, or too low, in which case you'll lose money—or you'll have to raise your quote later, which is not good for customer relations. Instead, try to satisfy the client with a general price range and promise a full written proposal later.

Use the checklist for initial client contact on page 135 as a guide for taking notes during your first conversation. Many clients will be reluctant to tell you their budget for an event, but try to get a fairly good idea of how much money they have to spend. You should be able to adjust your menus to suit their budget, but you'll have to know what that budget

Bright Idea

Offer to provide gifts for event attendees. You can help your clients choose a memento to be placed at each setting, perhaps something imprinted with a corporate logo, or help them choose special gifts for the guest of honor or committee members. You can purchase and wrap the gifts to provide a special service for your clients and increase your own revenue.

is first. There are many cost-cutting methods you can use if the client seems uncomfortable with your more expensive-sounding suggestions. For example, you can substitute lower-cost ingredients with a similar flavor or use dishes that are easy to prepare rather than more labor-intensive ones.

After the first telephone contact, your next meeting will likely be in person, preferably at the site where the event will be held. Bring your menus so the customer can review them and determine exactly what to serve. Get a firm number of guests and put it in writing; let the customer know that you will be planning your quote on that number and that any changes will affect the final price. Determine the style of the event (sit-down, buffet, cocktail) and any particular equipment or service needs the client will have.

Take a tour of the site to see what equipment is available for your use and what you'll need to bring. Decide where the buffet, if there is one, will be, and where the bar setup will go. Discuss staffing needs and be very specific about who is to provide

Timing Is Everything

You should have at least a week's notice for a catered event. A month's notice is quite common and not too much for an established caterer to ask. In fact, some catered affairs are booked as many as ten months in advance. Of course, if a client is in a bind—for example, a business needs a deli-style luncheon on trays for six people at the last minute—and you can handle the work, you'll build customer loyalty by doing so.

Checklist for Initial Client Contact

Name: _____

Address: _____

_____

Business phone: _____ Home phone: _____

Date of event: _____

Time of event: _____

Beginning: _____ Ending: _____

Location of event: _____

Type of occasion: _____

_____

Number of guests: _____

General age group of guests: _____

General mix of guests: _____

Type of service (cocktail, buffet, sit-down): _____

Foods client would like to have: _____

_____

_____

_____

Dishes to avoid: _____

_____

General budget of client: _____

Special services needed: _____

_____

_____

_____

_____

what to prevent any misunderstandings later. This information should also be included in your price proposal.

Take a day or two to calculate the final price, and be sure it includes everything. Call the customer with your quote; if it's acceptable, send out a detailed contract which itemizes the prices, outlines mutual responsibilities, and requires a deposit (typically 25 to 50 percent) on signing.

Once you've received the signed contract and deposit, you're ready to start arranging for staff and purchasing food. A few days before the event, call the customer to confirm the number of guests and other details. If the customer wants to make changes to the contract, be as accommodating as possible, but don't let it cause you to lose money.

Make a Packing List

Once the food for an event is prepared and ready to go, you'll need to pack it along with any serving dishes, utensils, linens, and other necessary equipment. To be sure you don't forget or lose anything, you'll need to prepare a packing list.

A day or so before the event, sit down with your menu. For each dish, list the equipment you'll need to finish preparing it on-site and serve it. When you're finished, double-check your figures, taking care to properly count multiple units of items, such as when different dishes require the same serving equipment. Don't forget miscellaneous supplies such as cocktail napkins, toothpicks, salt and pepper shakers. If you are taking care of rental furniture and/or flowers, make sure these are either going to be delivered to the event site or your kitchen, or will be available for you to pick up. Use the sample packing list on page 137 as a guide for organizing your events.

With your completed packing list, you can start assembling the food and supplies. Pack the items you'll need first on top so you don't have to dig through several boxes to find them. Pack items closely so nothing has room to shift and break. Use common sense: Don't put sacks of crushed ice on top of the bread. Make sure all containers of food are covered tightly so they won't spill if you have to turn or stop suddenly.

The packing list will also serve as a checklist to help you collect all of your items when the party is over. Leaving items behind can quickly eat up your profits. Maxine T. puts waterproof labels on trays and other items that identify each piece of equipment for inventory control purposes. "If something is missing, we go back through the inventory sheets to see what party it was used on last and contact the person who ordered the catering," she says. "It's amazing what we have found. One lady had coffee pots, trays, and serving pieces from a year before. It was a drop-off, and we forgot to go back and pick it up. She put it in a cupboard and forgot about it."

Sample Packing List

Client: _____

Date of event: _____

Address: _____

Item	Amount Needed	In	Out	Item	Amount Needed	In	Out
Glassware				*Accessories*			
Wine (10 oz.)				Blender			
Wine (6 oz.)				Stirrers			
Champagne				Corkscrew			
Martini				Strainers			
Old-fashioned				Toothpicks			
Highball				Paper umbrellas			
Brandy				Ice tongs			
Liqueur				Cork coasters			
Water goblets							
Water pitchers				*Dinnerware*			
				Cups			
Bar Mixes				Saucers			
Whiskey sour				Salad plates			
Bloody mary				Dinner plates			
Orange juice				Base plates			
Grapefruit juice				Dessert plates			
Piña colada							
Collins				*Flatware*			
Heavy cream				Teaspoons			
Bitter lemon				Salad forks			
Tonic				Dinner forks			
Thin tonic				Dinner knives			
Club soda				Soup spoons			
Perrier				Serving forks			
Coke				Serving spoons			
7 UP				Butter knives			
				Cheese knives			
Food Mixes							
Lemon twists				*Table Accessories*			
Olives				Creamer			
Onions				Sugar bowl			
Pineapple wedges				Salt shaker			
Red cherries				Pepper mill			
Green cherries				Bread basket			
Celery stalks				Cracker basket			

Sample Packing List, continued

Item	Amount Needed	In	Out	Item	Amount Needed	In	Out
Punch bowl set				Dinner napkins (paper)			
Candles				Toothpicks			
Candle holders				Garbage bags			
Ash trays				Paper doilies			
Toothpick holders				Dinner napkins (linen)			
Pots and Pans				Hand towels			
Omelette pans				Tin foil			
Small chafing dish				Matches			
Large chafing dish				Disinfectant			
Rectangular chafing dish				Dishwashing detergent			
Trays				Straight pins			
Pizza pans				Safety pins			
Cookie sheets				Masking tape			
Silver trays (round)				Scotch tape			
Silver trays (oblong)				Stapler			
Silver trays (square)				Ribbons			
Utility Equipment				*Staple Food Items*			
Coffee maker				Coffee (ground)			
Coffee mill				Coffee (beans)			
3-prong adaptors				Decaff coffee			
Sterno setup				Milk			
Heat lamp				Instant milk			
Coffee pitcher				Cream			
Serving tables				Artificial sweetener			
Ice buckets				Sugar			
Bus boxes				Tea bags			
Salad bowls				Saltines			
Coffee urn/burner				Sesame crackers			
Serving carts				Pretzels			
Cheese boards				Breadsticks			
Linens and Papers							
Cocktail napkins							

Beginning packer: _____   Double-checked by: _____

Time of delivery: _____

Ending packer: _____   Double-checked by: _____

At the Party

Once you've arrived at the event site, unpack everything and organize your service area. You'll want to arrive an average of 60 to 90 minutes in advance to make sure the food will be ready and available at precisely the right time.

If you are taking care of rental furniture, flowers, or the bar setup, make sure these are in place and arranged attractively. Start reheating or cooking anything that needs to be served hot. Make sure every tray that leaves the kitchen has been garnished and arranged to show to best advantage. Some caterers work with tweezers in the kitchen to arrange garnishes so that all platters look like pictures. It's an extra touch that will enhance your reputation.

As the party gets underway, keep an eye on what food is being consumed and have another tray ready to go out as the empty ones are returned. If you are serving from a buffet table, continually replenish the trays so they don't look picked over. Throughout the event, your serving staff should be picking up dirty dishes, cleaning used ashtrays, returning empty glasses to the bar, etc., so the party site does not look cluttered and untidy.

As your servers return the dirty dishes to you, rinse and pack them for later washing. After the event is over, clean up any of the client's dishes or utensils that have been used. Get out your packing list to make sure you retrieve all your own glassware, tableware, cookware, etc. Also, take care that you don't accidentally take any of the client's equipment. Check each item off on your packing list as you load it into your vehicle.

Leftover food should be wrapped and left with the client. Floors and counters should be clean if you have spilled anything, but you shouldn't be expected to function as a maid service. Just leave the facility as you found it; you are responsible only for your own messes.

Some caterers demand payment of the balance due immediately after the event; others will send the client a bill the day after the party. Whichever you choose, be sure the client knows in advance what to expect, and make it clear that the bill does not

> ## Smart Tip
> **Tip...**
>
> After you've billed each event, evaluate how things went. Collect all your receipts and figure out your total expenses. Were the costs close to the assumptions you made when you priced the event? If not, you may need to revise your menu prices or your method of estimating costs for a bid.
>
> How smoothly did the event itself go? Did you have adequate staffing? Were the guests satisfied? What comments did you get from the guests and your client? Make notes of things that went well, so you can be sure to repeat them, and of areas where you need improvement.

Catering to the Hungry

Unlike a retail food-service operation, the location of your catering business is not critical from a sales perspective. You'll be going to your clients' homes or offices to discuss the event and inspect their facilities; they will have little or no need to visit your kitchen. Even so, be sure your operation does not violate any zoning ordinances or rental agreements, or pose any threat to the community welfare.

Your location should be reasonably accessible by main thoroughfares, both for your employees to get to work and for you to get to various event sites. Be sure the parking lot is adequate and well-lighted; your employees may frequently be returning to their cars late at night.

The facility needs to be able to accommodate the regular food deliveries a successful caterer will get; standard loading docks make this significantly easier.

include gratuities for the serving staff. If the client decides to tip, this should be collected and divided among the staff after the party.

While you should always be on the alert for ways to promote your business, you should never do it at an event you're catering. "I never market myself at events," Maxine T. says. "We're there as a support to whatever event we're doing, and that is not the proper time for us to advertise." Her company name is on the aprons the staff wears but not on anything else. And while she'll provide a business card if asked, she does not put them on display. A truly professional caterer, she believes, is virtually invisible at the event, where the focus should be on the occasion itself. "We don't intrude. We are not guests; we are there to provide a service. I tell this to my service staff. Also, I don't allow them to talk to each other when they're in front of the client, other than to take care of business. Even if they have friends who are attending the event, I discourage them from stopping to talk. They are there for a purpose, and that purpose is to serve the client."

Inventory
Buying, Storing, and Tracking Supplies

Food and beverage inventory purchasing is one of the most mismanaged areas in the food-service industry, neglected by most because of lack of knowledge. Owners who never learned to implement proper inventory purchasing and control techniques can still enjoy success in the business, but they usually pay for it with reduced profits, constant frustration and years of repeated inventory ordering mistakes.

There are two key parts to inventory: acquisition and management. You must know how to find distributors you can count on to deliver quality products on time; you must be able to place accurate orders with them so you have enough of what you need when you need it; and you must be able to estimate how much inventory you will consume during any given period of time—daily, weekly, monthly, or yearly.

Poor inventory management is a primary reason for food-service business failure. Every shortfall or excess affects your bottom line. To succeed in the food-service business, you need good purchasing procedures and a system that will help you accurately control your inventory from acquisition through preparation.

Quality, prices, and availability often fluctuate in the seesaw food and beverage market. You need to study the market, pay attention to what's going on in the world, and track conditions so you can buy with confidence. With practice and diligent market research, you can identify your strongest menu items and order inventory accordingly.

You must also factor in lead time—the length of time between ordering and receiving a product—when you calculate basic stock. For instance, if your lead time is four weeks and a particular menu item requires ten units a week in inventory, then you must reorder before the basic inventory level falls below 40 units. If you do not reorder until you actually need the stock, the basic inventory will be depleted and you'll lose sales—and probably some customers, too.

One of the ways many small-business owners protect themselves from such shortfalls is by incorporating a safety margin into basic inventory figures. The right safety margin for your particular operation depends on the external factors that can contribute to delays. You must determine your safety margin based on past experience and anticipated delays.

> ### Smart Tip
> *Tip...*
>
> Pay attention to world events. Weather, natural disasters, and politics can all impact the price and availability of various food items, which affects what you can serve and how much you must charge for it to make a profit.

Caterer Ann C. says she works closely with her kitchen manager on inventory issues and discusses the challenge with other caterers. At one point, she discovered that another caterer stocked about a quarter of the amount of dry goods that she stocks. "She told me that most of her business had a week or two lead time, so she has plenty of time to order goods. I know another caterer who does small dinners for 10 or 20 people, and she just goes to the market that morning and picks up what she needs. But a lot of my business has just 24 to 48 hours' lead time, and we can't afford the time or money to go to the store and buy all that last-minute product. For our day-to-day breakfast and lunch business, we keep an enormous amount of goods on the shelf."

Beverage Systems

Soft drinks, milk, coffee, and iced tea are necessary beverages for most food-service operations. For soft drinks, you can either offer canned drinks or buy a dispensing system. Unless you expect an extremely low sales volume in this area, the dispensing system will be more profitable. You will typically pay 50 to 60 cents a can for soft drinks, which you can then sell for about 90 cents. While that's certainly an acceptable profit, a soft drink system will generate 10 to 15 cents more profit per drink. Syrups for colas, root beer, diet drinks, and other beverages can be obtained from a local beverage distributor.

Check with your local health department to see if you must serve milk in individual cartons or if it may be poured into glasses from a larger container. You'll make more money using the latter method.

Buy your coffee from a coffee wholesaler, who will also provide burners, coffee-brewing systems, coffee-bean grinders and all the other equipment you need to make fresh-brewed coffee. They're listed in the Yellow Pages under "Coffee Break Service and Supplies." Be sure to let them know you run a restaurant; you'll get a better price. Also, the coffee service can supply you with individual packets of sugar and artificial sweetener, nondairy creamer, stirrers, and other coffee-related items.

> ### Bright Idea
> If you have the demand, invest in an espresso/cappuccino machine. Even though these machines are fairly expensive and time-consuming to run, rich European coffees are extremely popular. Your coffee service supplier probably has both new and used machines available.

Avoid freeze-dried coffee dispensers. Although they reduce waste, they'll hurt sales. They do not offer the aroma and taste of freshly brewed coffees. Also, freeze-dried systems use much hotter water, which means customers can't drink the beverage right away. Finally, these systems often produce a bitter final product because operators put too much coffee in their machines. It's worth the money to go for fresh-brewed.

Iced tea should be made at the start of the day and placed in its own steel dispenser. Tea is remarkably cost-efficient; you can buy pre-measured bags to make any specified amount. Just as with coffee, remember individual packets of sugar, artificial sweetener, stirrers, and lemon slices.

Where to Buy

Purchase meats from a meat jobber who specializes in portion-controlled supplies for restaurants. A meat jobber will deliver five days a week, so, except for weekends and holidays, you won't need to stock a large quantity on-site. Though prices from this type of specialized distributor may be slightly higher than from wholesale distributors, the quality is usually excellent, and you can benefit from their expertise.

For dairy products, try to find a wholesale distributor that can handle many of your needs and negotiate a volume discount. If you purchase a great deal of cheese, milk, and eggs—as a pizzeria will—consider a daily trip to the local farmers' market to haggle with growers face-to-face. Often, this type of direct buying gives you the lowest price and the best quality available.

Canned foods can be purchased from a processed food distributor. These distributors function as wholesale grocers that specialize in packaged products. They can be found under "Grocers—Wholesale" in your local Yellow Pages.

Dealing with Suppliers

Regardless of what kinds of foods you offer, developing good relations with local food distributors is essential. They will be able to pass along vital information that will aid you in your purchasing activities. If you have a good rapport with your suppliers, they will also work harder on your behalf to provide you with quality products at competitive prices.

This doesn't mean wining and dining your suppliers' sales reps every day of the week. Actually, it doesn't mean wining and dining them at all. Good relations simply means paying your bills on time and being upfront with your suppliers about your needs and capabilities. You'll be pleasantly surprised at what adhering to the terms of your contracts will do for you, especially in an environment where so many businesses fail to live up to their part of the bargains.

Bright Idea

Always deal with the same person at each of your wholesalers. They will quickly learn what is acceptable to you and what is not, what you mean by "ripe," and how you like things handled. This will increase your chances of getting consistent quality and service.

Reliable suppliers are an asset to your operation. They can bail you out when your customers make difficult demands on you, but they will do so only as long as your business is profitable for them. Like you, suppliers are in business to make money. If you argue about every bill, ask them to shave prices on every item, if you fail to pay promptly after goods or services have been delivered, don't be surprised when they stop calling and leave you dangling.

Of course, the food-service business is competitive at all levels, and you must look for the best deal you can get on a consistent basis from your suppliers. No business arrangement can continue for long unless something of value is rendered and received by all involved. Don't be a doormat, but don't be excessively demanding. Tell your suppliers what you need and when you need it. Have specific understandings about costs, delivery schedules, and payment terms. Build a relationship based on fairness, integrity, and trust, and both you and your suppliers will profit.

Receiving Procedures

Only you or one of your most trusted employees should receive inventory. Compare all goods received with the purchase specifications and completed market quotation sheets. Weigh all products sold by weight and count all products sold by count. You should also break down all the cases to check for broken or deformed containers, full count, and spoilage. Containers of fresh produce and similar goods should be inspected thoroughly.

If you discover any shortages, spoilage, or damaged goods during the receiving process, make immediate adjustments to the invoice, which both you and the delivery person should initial. Check all mathematical calculations on the invoice, and when you're satisfied that everything is acceptable, stamp the invoice "received."

Goods should be placed immediately into their proper storage places. If you leave products strewn all over the floor, you'll find that they'll disappear. Effective storage will maintain adequate stocks of goods with minimum loss and pilferage. As stock is being put into storage, check it once again against your delivery report. As with receiving, this is a task only you or a trusted employee should do.

> **Tip...**
>
> **Smart Tip**
> Follow your receiving procedures consistently, without exception, no matter how well you get to know a vendor or delivery person, or how much you trust them. Finding damage or a shortage after the driver has left can create an awkward situation as you try to determine who is actually at fault. Avoid potential problems by inspecting, weighing, and counting all deliveries at the time they arrive.

Label all items and place them in the appropriately marked areas for easy retrieval. Make sure your inventory is constantly rotated; goods that come in first should be used first.

Hidden Inventory Costs

Excess inventory creates additional overhead, and that costs you money. In fact, it costs a restaurateur anywhere from 20 to 30 percent of the original investment in

▲

Enough Is Enough

The ideal in inventory control is to always have enough products on hand to meet customer demand while avoiding both shortage and excess. Unavoidably, in the course of operating a business, both will occur. Rather than viewing them as mistakes, the smart restaurateur will use a shortage or an excess as an indicator of sales trends and alter the inventory control system accordingly.

If a shortage occurs, you can:

○ review the preparation and cooking processes to locate any problems, if applicable

○ place a rush order

○ employ another supplier

○ use substitute ingredients, if necessary

○ remove an item from the menu if key ingredients are difficult or exceptionally expensive to acquire

You can address overstocking by returning excess stock to suppliers or creating a promotion to stimulate demand. But don't just deal with the fallout of excess stock; analyze your ordering system to understand why the overage occurred. If you conduct purchasing and reordering correctly, you should be able to keep both excesses and shortages to a minimum.

---

inventory just to maintain it. Inventory that sits in your storeroom does not generate sales or profits; it generates losses in the form of:

- food spoilage from excess shelf life
- debt service on loans used to purchase the excess inventory
- increased insurance costs on the greater value of the inventory in stock

The natural reaction of many restaurateurs to excess inventory is to move it out. While that solves your overstocking problem, it reduces your return on investment. In all your financial projections, you based your figures on using specific ingredients in dishes that would be sold at full retail price. If you opt to clear out excess inventory by reducing menu item prices and offering specials and one-time-only meal discounts, you're ultimately taking money out of your own pocket.

Responding to spoilage and inventory excesses with overly cautious reordering is understandable. The problem there is that, when you reduce your reordering, you run the significant risk of creating a stock shortage. Remember, we didn't promise this would be easy.

You need to plan carefully, establish a realistic safety margin, and do your best to order only what you're sure you'll use to prepare your foods.

Tracking Inventory

A critical part of managing inventory is tracking it—that means knowing what you have on hand, what's on order and when it will arrive, and what you have sold. This information allows you to plan your purchases intelligently, quickly recognize fast-moving items that need to be reordered, and identify slow-moving merchandise that should be marked down and moved out.

There are a variety of inventory tracking methods you can use, from basic hand-written records to computerized bar code systems. The food-service business owners we talked to use simple systems, most on basic computer databases. Your accountant can help you develop a system that will work for your particular situation.

Controlling Bar Losses

Managing liquor inventory is one of the most challenging aspects of having a bar in your food-service business. Losses from spillage, theft, and honest mistakes can cost a single outlet thousands of dollars per week—dollars that fall straight to the bottom line in the form of lost profits.

One popular solution is a computerized inventory auditing system. Bevinco, a Canadian-based company with franchises in the United States and 11 other countries, provides such a service using portable electronic scales and a notebook computer. "When I started the business, we conducted a study, and I was amazed to learn that the accepted loss level in alcoholic beverages in the restaurant and bar business is 20 percent," says Barry Driedger, Bevinco's founder and president. "When you look at the volume most places do—even the smaller bars and restaurants—that's a lot of money."

Driedger is quick to point out that bar losses are not exclusively related to deliberate and calculated theft by employees. A significant amount of shrinkage can be traced to spills and carelessness in preparation, misplaced "good intentions" of bartenders who over-pour drinks for regular customers, and external fraud or theft. He also notes that although the primary reason for liquor-loss control is profitability, staff morale is likely to rise when control methods are implemented. "Most bars and restaurants have fairly large staffs, and it's usually only a small number of people who are causing the problem," he says. "The honest, hard-working people on the staff will appreciate having the dishonest people weeded out."

Bevinco's service starts with a baseline audit; then audits are conducted regularly—usually weekly or biweekly. All open liquor bottles, wine bottles, and beer kegs are weighed; other inventory is counted; sales and purchase figures are factored in; and the auditor is then able to generate a report identifying the source and volume of losses. With that information, a plan can be developed and implemented to correct the problem. Bevinco audits typically range from $150 to $250, depending on the size of the inventory and frequency of the audit. Although the Bevinco system is proprietary, if you want to audit yourself, you can purchase the necessary equipment through other companies. One is Digital Weighing Instruments Inc. in Dayton, Ohio. The company offers a system that uses a PC, portable scale, and bar code scanner. You can opt for a self-contained scale and a software package that does not require a PC, but that only tracks inventory and does not include the full range of reports a PC can generate. Cost for the full system is $3,900 for the scale, $2,995 for the software, and $500 for installation, which, concedes Sean C. Hathaway, Digital Weighing's president, is expensive for small restaurants. However, he says larger operations have reported recovering the initial cost of the system in six to nine months.

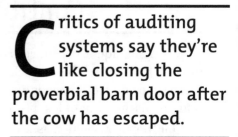

Critics of auditing systems say they're like closing the proverbial barn door after the cow has escaped. An alternative is liquor control systems, which are designed to prevent rather than simply identify losses, and use a variety of techniques to measure and track product use. One of the most recent entries in the liquor control market is Barmate Corp., based in San Francisco. The Barmate system consists of wireless spouts that dispense a pre-measured amount of liquor and immediately transmit the information to a computer. At a cost of $125 per spout, the total price of a Barmate system depends on the number of bottles in the bar.

If you're shopping for a liquor control system, consider these points:

- *Flexibility*. The bartenders should be able to move around comfortably while they're working and be able to pour more than one drink at a time.
- *Compatibility with other systems*. Be sure the liquor control system can communicate data to your cash register and inventory system.
- *Reliability*. Check the vendor's references carefully to evaluate the performance record of the system.
- *Training*. Be sure the vendor will provide thorough training on the system.

• *Warranty and ongoing support.* Find out the details of the warranty, and make sure the company will answer questions and respond to problems after the sale.

Of course, technology can go a long way toward reducing bar area losses, but it can't replace common sense. Here are some simple, easy-to-implement suggestions that can improve profits and customer service:

• Restrict access to the bar: allow only bartenders behind the bar, and be sure that bartenders are the only personnel making drinks.

• Require drink purchases to be entered into the register before they are made.

• Watch back-door security: Check in and put away deliveries promptly; never allow inventory to sit unsupervised in loading areas. Install an alarm on the back door that will alert you if an unauthorized person attempts to leave the facility.

• Provide lockers for employees to store their personal belongings, and do not allow them to bring bags or containers into the bar or serving area.

• Make people accountable for mistakes: Require mistakes, such as mixing the wrong drink, spills, etc., to be logged in and signed off by the manager on duty. Such accountability increases awareness and leads to a reduction in these types of losses.

• Cushion surfaces to reduce breakage: quality floor mats not only prevent slipping and ease the back and leg stress on bartenders, but they can also provide a cushion that reduces breakage if bottles or glasses are dropped.

• Be sure spouts fit securely: sometimes they can loosen and leak, especially when used on odd-shaped bottles.

• Check the ice: be sure the ice is free from trash and debris that would cause the drink to be refused.

• Provide incentives for loss reduction: come up with ways to reward employees for positive performance in this area.

• Encourage employees to report theft: consider setting up a system where such reports can be made either anonymously or, at the very least, in strict confidence.

• Hire carefully: screen prospective employees thoroughly, conduct complete background checks, and contact references.

Structuring
Your Business

No doubt you're attracted to the food-service business because you enjoy food preparation and service. And while that is a big part of the business, there are plenty of other mundane issues you'll have to address both in the start-up phase and in the long run.

Legal Structure

One of the first decisions you'll need to make about your new food-service business is the legal structure of your company. This is an important decision, and it can affect your financial liability, the amount of taxes you pay, the degree of ultimate control you have over the company, as well as your ability to raise money, attract investors, and ultimately sell the business. However, legal structure shouldn't be confused with operating structure. Attorney Robert S. Bernstein, managing partner with Bernstein Bernstein Krawec & Wymard P.C. explains the difference: "The legal structure is the ownership structure—who actually owns the company. The operating structure defines who makes management decisions and runs the company."

A sole proprietorship is owned by the proprietor; a partnership is owned by the partners; and a corporation is owned by the shareholders. Sole proprietorships and partnerships can be operated however the owners choose. In a corporation, the shareholders typically elect directors, who in turn elect officers, who then employ other people to run and work in the company. But it's entirely possible for a corporation to have only one shareholder and to essentially function as a sole proprietorship. In any case, how you plan to operate the company should not be a major factor in your choice of legal structures.

So what goes into choosing a legal structure? The first point, says Bernstein, is who is actually making the decision on the legal structure. If you're starting the company by yourself, you don't need to take anyone else's preferences into consideration. "But if there are multiple people involved, you need to consider how you're going to relate to each other in the business," he says. "You also need to consider the issue of asset protection and limiting your liability in the event things don't go well."

Something else to think about is your target customer and what their perception will be of your structure. While it's not necessarily true, Bernstein says, "There is a tendency to believe that the legal form of a business has some relationship to the sophistication of the owners, with the sole proprietor as the least and the corporation as the most sophisticated." If your target market is going to be other businesses, it might enhance your image if you incorporate.

Stat Fact

More than four out of ten food-and-drink establishments are sole proprietorships or partnerships.

Your image notwithstanding, the biggest advantage of forming a corporation is asset protection, which, says Bernstein, is ensuring that the assets you don't want to put into the business aren't liable for business debt. However, to take advantage of the protection a corporation offers, you must respect the corporation's identity. That means maintaining the corporation as a separate entity; keeping your corporate and personal funds separate, even if you are the sole shareholder; and following your state's rules regarding holding annual meetings and other record-keeping requirements.

Is any one structure better than another? No. We found food-service businesses operating as sole proprietors, partners, and corporations, and they made their choices based on what was best for their particular situation. Choose the form that is most appropriate for your particular needs.

Do you need an attorney to set up your business's legal structure? Again, no. Bernstein says there are plenty of good do-it-yourself books and kits on the market, and most of the state agencies that oversee corporations have guidelines you can use. Even so, it's always a good idea to have a lawyer at least look over your documents before you file them, just to make sure they are complete and will allow you to truly function as you want.

Finally, remember that your choice of legal structure is not an irrevocable decision, although if you're going to make a switch, it's easier to go from the simpler forms to the more sophisticated ones than the other way around. Bernstein says the typical pattern is to start as a sole proprietor, then switch to a corporation as the business grows. But if you need the asset protection of a corporation from the beginning, start out that way. Says Bernstein, "If you're going to the trouble to start a business, decide on a structure, and put it all together, it's worth the extra effort to make sure it's really going to work."

Naming Your Company

One of the most important marketing tools you will ever have is your company's name. A well-chosen name can work very hard for you; an ineffective name means you have to work much harder at marketing your company.

There is no sure-fire formula for naming a food-service business. Names range from the name of the owner to the name of a place to the wildest name the owner could think of. You should pick a name in keeping with the theme of your restaurant, so that it is compatible with the food and atmosphere. A dramatic example of this is the Rainforest Café at Walt Disney World in Florida; the entire restaurant is designed to create the atmosphere of a jungle, complete with lush vegetation, animals, volcanoes, and sound effects. You probably won't go to such an extreme, but if your goal is a fine-dining restaurant, you won't want to name it something like Road Kill Café.

Your company name should also very clearly identify what you do in a way that will appeal to your target market. If you're going to use your own name, add a

Bright Idea

Once you've narrowed down your name search to three or four choices, test-market your ideas by asking a small group of people who fit the profile of your potential customer what they think of the names you're considering. Find out what kind of company the name makes them think of and if they'd feel comfortable patronizing a food-service business with that name. Finally, get them to explain the reasoning behind their answers.

description. For example, instead of just Angelo's, call your pizzeria Angelo's Pizza and Pasta. As you become known in the community, people will likely drop the description when they refer to you, but until that time, it will pay to avoid confusing the public.

The name should be short, catchy, and memorable—and it doesn't hurt to make it fun. It should also be easy to pronounce and spell—people who can't say your restaurant's name may patronize you, but they probably won't tell anyone else about you.

Though naming your food-service company is without a doubt a creative process, it helps to take a systematic approach. Once you've decided on two or three possibilities, take the following steps:

- *Check the name for effectiveness and functionality.* Does it quickly and easily convey what you do? Is it easy to say and spell? Is it memorable in a positive way? Ask several of your friends and associates to serve as a focus group to help you evaluate the name's impact.

- *Search for potential conflicts in your local market.* Find out if any other local or regional food-service business serving your market area has a name so similar that yours might confuse the public.

- *Check for legal availability.* Exactly how you do this depends on the legal structure you choose. Typically, sole proprietorships and partnerships operating under a name other than that of the owner(s) are required by the county, city, or state to register their fictitious name. Even if it's not required, it's a good idea, because that means no one else can use that name. Corporations usually operate under their corporate name. In either case, you need to check with the appropriate regulatory agency to be sure the name you choose is available. Bakery owner Jim A. says one of his biggest mistakes was in not checking the availability of the first name he chose for his company; he used that name for two years and then had to change it when he was challenged by the trademark owner.

- *Check for use on the World Wide Web.* If someone else is already using your name as a domain site on the World Wide Web, consider coming up with something else. Even if you have no intention of developing a Web site of your own, the use could be confusing to your customers.

- *Check to see if the name conflicts with any name listed on your state's trademark register.* Your state department of commerce can either help you or direct you to the correct agency. You should also check with the trademark register maintained by the U.S. Patent and Trademark Office (PTO).

Once the name you've chosen passes these tests, you need to protect it by registering it with the appropriate state agency; again, your state department of commerce can help you. If you expect to be doing business on a national level—for example, if you'll be handling mail orders or operating on the World Wide Web—you should also register the name with the PTO.

> **Tip...**
>
> **Smart Tip**
>
> When you purchase insurance on your equipment and inventory, ask what documentation the insurance company requires for filing a claim. That way, you'll be sure to maintain appropriate records, and the claims process will be easier if it is ever necessary.

Business Insurance

It takes a lot to start a business, even a small one, so protect your investment with adequate insurance. If you maintain your office at home—as many food-service business operators do—don't assume your homeowner's or renter's policy covers your business equipment; chances are it doesn't. If you're located in a commercial facility, be prepared for your landlord to require proof of certain levels of liability insurance when you sign the lease. And in either case, you need coverage for your inventory, equipment, fixtures, and other valuables.

A smart approach to insurance is to find an agent who works with businesses similar to yours. The agent should be willing to help you analyze your needs, evaluate what risks you're willing to accept and what risks you need to insure against, and work with you to keep your insurance costs down.

> **Tip...**
>
> **Smart Tip**
>
> Sit down with your insurance agent every year and review your insurance needs. As your company grows, your needs are sure to change. Also, insurance companies are always developing new products for the growing small-business market, and it's possible one of these new policies will be appropriate for you.

Once your business is up and running, consider business interruption insurance to replace lost revenue and cover related costs if you are ever unable to operate due to covered circumstances.

If the Unthinkable Happens

Ypu buy insurance hoping you'll never need it, but if you do, be sure to take the appropriate steps to make sure you get the full benefit from your coverage. Notify your agent or carrier immediately if you suffer a property loss or if something happens that could turn into a liability claim. In the case of a property claim, be prepared to provide the appropriate documentation and proof of loss.

In the case of potential liability, there doesn't have to be an actual loss before you get your insurance company involved. For example, if a customer slips and falls on your premises, even if he or she says there is no injury, get their name, address, and telephone number, as well as contact information on any witnesses, and pass this information on to your insurance company. Don't wait until you are served with legal papers.

Professional Services

As a business owner, you may be the boss, but you can't be expected to know everything. You'll occasionally need to turn to professionals for information and assistance. It's a good idea to establish a relationship with these professionals *before* you get into a crisis situation.

Anthony A. says his first experience in the food-service business, which was his pizzeria, proved the value of quality professional advice. He was inadequately protected by his first lease, and when the lease expired, the landlord refused to renew the lease and opened his own successful pizzeria in that location. "I simply wasn't protected," he says. "When you're setting up, it pays to spend the money on an attorney. And make sure you use one who has experience in the type of thing you are doing."

To shop for a professional service provider, ask friends and associates for recommendations. You might also check with your local chamber of commerce or trade association for referrals. Find someone who understands your industry and specific business, and appears eager to work with you. Check them out with the Better Business Bureau and the appropriate state licensing agency before committing yourself.

As a food-service business owner, the professional service providers you're likely to need include:

- *Attorney.* You need a lawyer who understands and practices in the area of business law, who is honest, and who appreciates your patronage. In most parts of the United States, there is an abundance of lawyers willing to compete fiercely for the privilege of serving you. Interview several and choose one you feel comfortable with. Be sure to clarify the fee schedule ahead of time, and get your agreement in writing. Keep in mind that good commercial lawyers don't come cheap; if you want good advice, you must be willing to pay for it. Your attorney should review all contracts, leases, letters of intent, and other legal documents before you sign them. They can also help you with collecting bad debts and establishing personnel policies and procedures. Of course, if you are unsure of the legal ramifications of any situation, call your attorney immediately.

- *Accountant.* Among your outside advisors, your accountant is likely to have the greatest impact on the success or failure of your business. If you are forming a corporation, your accountant should counsel you on tax issues during start-up. On an ongoing basis, your accountant can help your organize the statistical data concerning your business, assist in charting future actions based on past performance, and advise you on your overall financial strategy regarding purchasing, capital investment, and other matters related to your business goals. A good accountant will also serve as a tax advisor, making sure you are in compliance with all applicable regulations, but also that you don't overpay any taxes.

> **A**mong your outside advisors, your accountant is likely to have the greatest impact on the success or failure of your business.

- *Insurance agent.* A good independent insurance agent can assist you with all aspects of your business insurance, from general liability to employee benefits, and probably even handle your personal policies, as well. Look for an agent who works with a wide range of insurers and understands your particular business. This agent should be willing to explain the details of various types of coverage, consult with you to determine the most appropriate coverage, help you understand the degree of risk you are taking, work with you in developing risk-reduction programs, and assist in expediting any claims.

- *Banker.* You need a business bank account and a relationship with a banker. Don't just choose the bank you've always done your personal banking with; it may not be the best bank for your business. Interview several bankers before making a decision on where to place your business. Once your account is opened, maintain a relationship with the banker. Periodically sit down and review your accounts and the services you use to make sure you are getting the package most appropriate for your situation. Ask for advice if you have financial questions or problems. When you need a loan, or you need a bank reference to provide to creditors, the relationship you've established will work in your favor.

- *Consultants.* The consulting industry is booming—and for good reason. Consultants can provide valuable, objective input on all aspects of your business. Consider hiring a business consultant to evaluate your business plan, a marketing consultant to assist you in that area, and a restaurant consultant to help you design your facility. When you are ready to hire employees, a human resources consultant may help you avoid some costly mistakes. Consulting fees vary widely, depending on the individual's experience, location, and field of expertise. If you can't afford to hire a consultant, consider contacting the business school at the nearest college or university and hiring an MBA student to help you.

- *Computer expert.* If you don't know much about computers, find someone to help you select a system and the appropriate software, and who will be available to help you maintain, trouble-shoot, and expand your system as you need it. If you're going to pursue Internet sales, use a professional Web page designer to set up and maintain your site. Just as you wouldn't serve sloppily prepared food, you shouldn't put up an unprofessional Web page.

Create Your Own Advisory Board

Not even the president of the United States is expected to know everything. That's why he surrounds himself with advisors—experts in particular areas who provide knowledge and information to help him make decisions. Savvy small-business owners use a similar strategy.

When Maxine T. decided to expand her catering company to include a delicatessen, she made some serious mistakes and nearly bankrupted her company. In the middle of her crisis, she realized that the way to get a handle on her own company was to get help from other business owners. She formed an advisory board of successful small-business owners, offering them nothing but good food at their meetings and her personal commitment to return the kindness by helping others in the future. "We met once a month, and the first meeting was about the biggest jolt I had ever had in my life," she recalls. At her request, her advisors were completely candid. She realized how much she was doing wrong that she thought she had been doing right and came up with a strategy to correct her problems. Today, she believes that if she had started her company with an advisory board in place, she would never have had the problems she did. "I think it's a great idea to have an advisory board before you open your doors, while you're still putting together your business plan," she says. And if you're seeking financing, having such a support network will likely weigh heavily in your favor with potential lenders.

You can assemble a team of volunteer advisors to meet with you periodically to offer advice and direction. Because this isn't an official or legal entity, you have a great deal of latitude in how you set it up. Advisory boards can be structured to help with the operation of your company as well as keep you informed on various business, legal, and financial trends that may affect you. Use these tips to set up your board:

- *Structure a board that meets your needs.* Generally, you'll want a legal advisor, an accountant, a marketing expert, a human resources person, and perhaps a financial advisor. You may also want successful entrepreneurs from other industries who understand the basics of business and will view your operation with a fresh eye.

- *Ask the most successful people you can find, even if you don't know them well.* You'll be surprised how willing people are to help other businesses succeed.

- *Be clear about what you are trying to do.* Let your prospective advisors know what your goals are and that you don't expect them to take on an active management role or to assume any liability for your company or for the advice they offer.

- *Don't worry about compensation.* Advisory board members are rarely compensated with more than lunch or dinner—something you can easily provide. Of course, if a member of your board provides a direct service—for example, if an attorney reviews a contract or an accountant prepares a financial statement—then they should be paid at their normal rate. But that's not part of their job as an advisory board member. Keep in mind that, even though you don't write them a check, your advisory board members will likely benefit in a variety of tangible and intangible ways. Being on your board will expose them to ideas and perspectives they may not otherwise see and will also expand their own network.

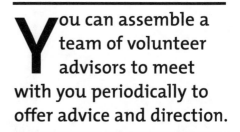

You can assemble a team of volunteer advisors to meet with you periodically to offer advice and direction.

- *Consider the group dynamics when holding meetings.* You may want to meet with all the members together or in small groups of one or two. It all depends on how they relate to each other and what you need to accomplish.

- *Ask for honesty and don't be offended when you get it.* Your pride might be hurt when someone points out something you're doing wrong, but the awareness will be beneficial in the long run.

- *Learn from failure as well as success.* Encourage board members to tell you about their mistakes so you can avoid making them yourself.

- *Respect the contribution your board members are making.* Let them know you appreciate how busy they are, and don't abuse or waste their time.

- *Make it fun.* You are, after all, asking these people to donate their time, so create a pleasant atmosphere.

- *Listen to every piece of advice.* Stop talking and listen. You don't have to follow every piece of advice, but you need to hear it.
- *Provide feedback to the board.* Good or bad, let the board know what you did and what the results were.

13

Locating and Setting Up Your Business

Successful food-service businesses can occupy a wide array of facilities, from free-standing buildings constructed especially to house a specific operation to existing buildings converted to suit the particular operation. Train stations, retail stores, and even banks are among the numerous structures that have been successfully converted to food-service businesses.

With most restaurants, the owner begins by coming up with the concept, then determines the market for that concept, and finally finds a location for the restaurant. After determining the general location, the next step is to find a specific facility in the area. This is when you must decide whether you will convert an existing structure or build an entirely new facility. Typically, converting will cost less than building. Even if you gut an entire building and install completely new fixtures, it will be cheaper than buying the vacant land, building the structure, and adding the fixtures you need.

Of course, a little bit of creativity can go a long way toward saving start-up capital. When Maxine T. started her Salt Lake City catering operation, she was working out of a school cafeteria. She leased the space, provided lunches for the school, and used the kitchen to prepare foods for her corporate clients. That setup worked successfully for ten years, until she decided to open a retail deli and moved her commercial kitchen to the same location.

Depending on how much money you have to invest in a food-service business and the particular type of business you choose, you can spend anywhere between $30,000 and $1.5 million on a facility.

Retail Locations

Not every food-service operation needs to be in a retail location, but for those that depend on retail traffic, here are some factors to consider when deciding on a location:

- *Anticipated sales volume.* How will the location contribute to your sales volume? Consider the presence or potential presence of other food-service businesses that will compete with you, and be sure the market is strong enough to support both of you.

- *Accessibility to potential customers.* Consider how easy it will be for customers to get into your business. If vehicle traffic is often heavy, or if the speed limit nearby is more than 35 mph, drivers may have difficulty entering or leaving your site. Narrow entrances and exits, turns that are hard to negotiate, and parking lots that are always full can prevent would-be customers from patronizing your business.

If you are relying on strong pedestrian traffic, consider whether or not nearby businesses will generate foot traffic for you. Large department stores will

> **Dollar Stretcher**
>
> To help keep your overhead as low as possible, don't spend a lot of money on fancy fixtures and décor in your work, storage, and administration areas—places your customers never see.

draw shoppers who may then stop in your restaurant for a meal or snack, and shopping centers in busy office districts might attract pedestrian customers, particularly during weekday lunch hours. By contrast, a strip center anchored by a supermarket may not be the best location; grocery shoppers typically go directly to the grocery store and back to their cars.

> ## Smart Tip *Tip...*
> In addition to finding the right location, it's important to negotiate the right deal on the real estate. You may find the best spot on a main street, but if you're paying too much rent, you won't be profitable.

Consider the entrance to the site. Is it on the street level or an upper floor? Can it be reached from a main street, or is it difficult to find?

Analyze the site. Monitor foot and auto traffic patterns at different times of the day. See if those patterns fit the hours when you want to do business. Visit the prospective site on several different days to assess any changes in the pattern.

- *The rent-paying capacity of your business.* The best locations will usually command the highest rents. If you have done a sales-and-profit projection for your first year of operation, you will know approximately how much revenue you can expect to generate, and you can use that information to decide how much rent you can afford to pay.

- *Restrictive ordinances.* You may encounter unusually restrictive ordinances that make an otherwise strong site less than ideal, such as limitations on the hours of the day when trucks can legally load or unload. Cities and towns are composed of areas—from a few blocks to many acres in size—zoned only for commercial, industrial, or residential development. Each zone may have further restrictions. A commercial zone may permit one type of business but not another, so check the zoning codes of any potential location before pursuing a specific site or spending a lot of time and money on a market survey.

- *Traffic density.* Modern site analysis distinguishes between automobile and pedestrian traffic. If only auto traffic were important, most businesses would be located near highways or main roads. With careful examination of foot traffic, you can determine the approximate sales potential of each pedestrian passing a given location. Two factors are especially important in this analysis: total pedestrian traffic during business hours and the percentage of it that is likely to patronize your food-service business.

To make pedestrian traffic counts, select a few half-hour periods during busy hours of the day. You should only count potential customers for your business; total numbers of passersby are not the most significant factor. You need to know if these are the types of people who are either dining out or picking up prepared food to take home. Why are they at the location at this time? To find

▲

And the Answer Is . . .

As you analyze the pedestrian traffic at a retail location you're considering, use this as a model for your interviews:

Begin by dressing professionally and carry a clipboard on which you can make notes. Approach people very courteously and say, "Excuse me, I'm considering opening a restaurant in this shopping center, and I'm trying to decide if this is a good location for my type of operation. May I have two minutes of your time to ask a few questions?"

If they refuse, thank them anyway, and move on to the next person. However, most people will agree. When they do, quickly ask your questions and let them get on with their business. Make your survey very simple; the following questions should tell you what you need to know:

○ What is your primary purpose for being at this shopping center today?

○ Which store or stores have you visited or will you visit?

○ Do you think this shopping center needs a [name the specific type of food-service business you intend to open]?

○ If a [name the specific type of food-service business you intend to open] opened in this location, would you patronize it?

out, ask them. Conduct a brief interview. Ask them if they feel there is a need for a food-service business of the type you want to start at that location, and would they patronize such a business if it existed.

Take your sample periods and multiply the results out over a week, month, and quarter, and use those figures in your financial forecasts. Certainly this process involves some guessing in your calculations, but if you are careful with your questions and honest in your analysis, you should get a reasonably accurate picture of what to expect.

- *Customer parking facilities.* The site should provide convenient, adequate parking as well as easy access for customers. Storefront parking is always better than a rear lot; people like to be able to see the parking lot before they turn off the main thoroughfare. The lot should be well-lighted and secure, with adequate spaces for patrons with disabilities. Consider whether the parking area will need expansion, resurfacing, or striping—possibly at an additional cost. If you are looking at a free-standing location, think big and envision how you will accommodate the hordes of customers your restaurant will eventually attract. Generally speaking, you should have one parking spot for every three seats in your restaurant. If you do a substantial amount of take-out business, you may want to reserve two or three places near the entrance for take-out customers to park briefly when they pick up their orders.

If construction costs and acquiring land for parking are a problem, consider offering valet parking. Once reserved for elegant, fine-dining establishments, this service is becoming more common at casual-dining and even family-oriented operations. Check out nearby parking facilities and research the costs involved; then compare that to the cost of constructing and maintaining your own lot, and make a decision on what is most efficient and effective for your particular circumstances.

> ## Bright Idea
> Let your location complement your concept. Robert O.'s casual seafood restaurant is located on the water—literally, on 10-foot pilings. "I've got great sunsets, crab pots in the water, all kinds of wildlife—herrings, turtles, muskrats, you name it," he says. "I've got a great location."

- *Proximity to other businesses.* Neighboring businesses may influence your store's volume, and their presence can work for you or against you. Studies of the natural clustering of businesses show that certain types of companies do well when located close to one another. For example, men's and women's apparel and variety stores are commonly located near department stores. Florists are often grouped with shoe stores and women's clothing stores. Restaurants, barber shops, candy, tobacco, and jewelry stores are often found near theaters.

- *History of the site.* Find out the recent history of each site under consideration before you make a final selection. Who were the previous tenants, and why are they no longer there? There are sites—in malls and shopping centers as well as free-standing locations—that have been occupied by numerous business failures. The reasons for the failures may be completely unrelated to the success potential of your food-service operation, or they could mean your business will meet the same fate. You need to understand why previous tenants failed so you can avoid making the same mistakes.

- *Terms of the lease.* Be sure you understand all the details of the lease because it's possible an excellent site may have unacceptable leasing terms. The time to negotiate terms is before you sign the lease; don't wait until you've moved in to try to change the terms.

- *The rent-advertising relationship.* You may need to account for up to six months of advertising and promotion expenditures in your working capital. Few businesses can succeed without any sales promotion, and the larger the sum you

Streetwise

The sunny side of the street is generally less desirable for retail operations than the shady side, especially in warm climates. Research shows rents to be higher on the shady side in high-priced shopping areas. Merchants acknowledge the sunny-side-of-the-street principle by installing expensive awnings to combat the sun and make customers more comfortable.

Marketing research has also demonstrated that the going-home side of the street is usually preferable to the going-to-work side. People have more time to stop at your food-service business on the way home than when they are rushing to work—unless, of course, you offer coffee and breakfast foods, in which case even the busiest person will take time to stop.

can afford for well-placed, well-targeted advertising and promotions, the greater your chances of success.

The amount you plan to spend on advertising may be closely related to your choice of site and the proposed rent. If you locate in a shopping center or mall supported by huge ad budgets and the presence of large, popular chain and department stores, you will most likely generate revenue from the first day you open your doors—with no individual advertising at all. Of course, your rental expenses will be proportionately higher than those for an independent location.

If you do not locate in an area that attracts high foot traffic, you will experience a slower growth rate, even if your business fronts a high-traffic street. Your real profits will come as you develop a clientele—and this will require advertising and promotion.

Bright Idea

If you're opening an independent operation in a food-service business with a lot of national competition, take a look at where the national chains are locating. They invest in a tremendous amount of market research. Study the characteristics of their sites, and then look for a site for your own business that is similar, perhaps even nearby, and offer a better product or service.

Additional Retail Options

An alternative to a traditional retail store is a cart or kiosk. Carts and kiosks are a great way to test your business before moving into a regular store, and in some cases, they could be a permanent part of your operating strategy. One of the hottest trends in mall retailing is the temporary tenant—a retailer that comes into a mall, sometimes in a store but often with a cart or kiosk, for a specified period, usually to capture holiday or seasonal sales.

If you have a retail store, such as a bakery or coffeehouse, a temporary cart at another location can generate immediate sales and serve as a marketing tool for your year-round location.

Renting cart or kiosk space usually costs significantly less than the rent for an in-line store, but rates vary dramatically depending on the location and season. Mall space in particular can be pricey. For example, a class-C mall off-peak season may cost

Holding (Food) Court

A food court is a congregation of six to 20 restaurants, usually quick-service establishments, in one location. The primary attraction of the concept is the wide assortment of menus from which to choose. In addition, food courts are appealing due to their diversity, convenience, atmosphere, quality, and value.

Food courts are often located in large shopping malls, but they are also found in office buildings, sports arenas, and universities, where large numbers of people congregate. Food courts can also serve as anchors for strip malls. Some food courts insist that all restaurant tenants operate from in-line stores; others allow some to operate from kiosks or carts. Popular food court restaurants include those specializing in pizza and Italian food, Chinese food, ice cream, Mexican food, soups and salads, baked potatoes, and hamburgers and hot dogs.

Food court rents tend to be on the high end of retail locations. Even though most food courts are in heavy-traffic areas, that's no guarantee that you'll get enough business to justify the cost of the location. Do careful market research before signing a lease.

as little as $400 a month for cart space, but a class-A mall in December might charge $4,000 to $5,000 per month for the same amount of space.

Carts can be leased or purchased. New carts can be purchased for $3,000 to $5,000 and up, depending on how they are equipped; monthly lease fees will typically run 8 to 12 percent of the new price. You can probably get a good deal on a used cart; just be sure it will suit your needs. If a used cart needs significant modifications to work for you, it may be better to buy new and get exactly what you need.

Though kiosks are often occupied by temporary tenants, they have a greater sense of permanency than carts. They typically offer more space and more design flexibility. They're also more expensive—expect to pay $9,000 to $10,000 or more to purchase a new kiosk. As with carts, you may be able to lease a kiosk, or find a used one to purchase for less money.

Carts and kiosks are available from a variety of sources. Check out manufacturers' and brokers' ads in a variety of retail trade publications; you can also contact the manufacturers listed in this book's appendix.

> **Though kiosks are often occupied by temporary tenants, they have a greater sense of permanency than carts.**

Signage

When you're ready to order signs for your food-service business, keep this in mind: A one-inch letter is easily seen ten feet away, two-inch letters can be seen at 20 feet, and so on. A common mistake is creating a sign with letters so small that your customers can't easily read them.

It's also important to have a professional proofreader check your sign for errors. Don't spend a lot of money just to make a poor impression.

If you're going to put up banner-type signs outside, don't hang them with rope, nails, and hooks. Rope doesn't hold on a windy day, which means your sign will double as a sail and quickly become battered and tattered. Instead, use Bungee cords; they'll allow your sign to flex in the wind and retain its original shape.

Mail Order

Setting up a mail order operation makes the entire world your market. If you have food products that are appropriate for shipping, you can take orders over the phone, by mail, by fax, or on the Internet, and send items virtually anywhere.

The All-Important Mailing List

You'll develop your customer base by mailing your catalog or brochure to people who fit your target market profile. How do you find these folks? The easiest way is to buy mailing lists. As you probably know from the amount of marketing mail you receive yourself, developing, maintaining, and selling mailing lists is big business. And the list companies can provide you with names and addresses of potential customers who meet your desired demographics.

Buying a list can be expensive, so take the time to do it right. Contact several list brokers before making a decision. Find out what guarantees they offer. Ask how they acquire data and what techniques are in place to assure accuracy and currency of the information. In today's mobile society, a list that is even one year old will likely contain a sizable percentage of names of people who have moved. Ask for the list broker's references and check them before making a final selection.

Once you've found a good list broker, stick with him or her. A good broker is a valuable partner in growing a mail order business, because you'll always be trying new lists, even after you're established and profitable.

Your most valuable list will be your in-house list—the people who have become your customers. You need to mail frequently to this list, and be creative in developing ideas for ways they can purchase your products. As this list grows, you'll find maintaining it a complex, time-consuming, and critical task. Consider hiring an outside company to take over your database management. After all, you're starting a food-service business because you love the business; if you're an expert at database management, perhaps you should consider starting a company offering that service.

> **Tip...**
>
> ## Smart Tip
>
> Whenever you try a new list, test the potential response by mailing to a small segment before you spend the money on mailing to the entire list.

Selling on the Internet

As e-commerce grows in popularity and acceptance, you may want to set up a Web site to market your food-service business and even sell specific products. For example, a bakery in Louisiana offers Creole fruitcake on its Web site and ships the famous holiday treat and other baked goods—formerly available only through select retail outlets—worldwide.

Packing and Shipping Tips

Get your orders out the door and on their way as quickly as possible; people want immediate gratification, and the faster you deliver, the more orders you'll get.

Package your products with extreme care, and be sure the exterior of the box can take a serious beating without damaging the contents. No matter how many "fragile" and "handle with care" stamps you put on the outside, you can be assured that while it's in transit, the box will be shaken, turned upside down, tossed, and have things stacked on top of it—that's simply the nature of the shipping business.

Be Creative

Look for ways to add revenue without substantially increasing your overhead. If you make a unique sauce, for example, have it bottled and available for sale in your restaurant.

Bright Idea

Want to offer delivery without having to buy or lease a vehicle and hire a driver? Set up an arrangement with an independent delivery service. In many communities, delivery services that focus on restaurant food are springing up. These services distribute menus from a variety of quick-service and midrange restaurants; the consumer places an order with the service, which sends a driver to the restaurant to pick up the food and deliver it to the customer for the menu price of the food plus a small service charge.

Caterer Ann C. only has to stock a few extra items to offer a gift basket service. She already has the food contents—fresh bakery items, fruit, cheeses, and crackers—and just keeps baskets and brightly colored seasonal ribbons on hand.

When Rebecca S. and her mother started their retail gourmet pasta shop, they listened to customer requests and began to add services. Over the years, their operation has grown to include a restaurant, a cooking school, a catering business, private labeling of food, special product development, and wholesale distribution, along with their retail store. Their primary criterion is that any new business idea be linked to pasta.

Should You Buy an Existing Operation?

If you find the start-up process a bit overwhelming, you may think taking over an existing food-service operation seems like a simple shortcut to getting your own business up and running. It can be, but you must proceed with extreme caution.

You can find various types of food-service businesses for sale advertised in trade publications, shopping center publications, and your local newspaper. You might also want to check with a business broker—they're listed in the Yellow Pages—to see what they have available.

Buyers frequently purchase food-service businesses "lock, stock, and barrel," including store fixtures, equipment, inventory, and supplies. Others negotiate for portions of theses items, preferring to remain free to create their own inventory and image.

Be careful not to select a business that is already doomed, perhaps by a poor location or the unfavorable reputation of the former owner. Especially in the case of the latter, it's much easier to start with a clean slate than to try to clean up after someone else. Before buying an existing business, take the following steps:

- *Find out why the business is for sale.* Many entrepreneurs sell thriving businesses because they're ready to do something else or they want to retire. Others will try to sell a declining business in the hopes of cutting their losses.

- *Do a thorough site analysis to determine if the location is suitable for your type of food-service business.* Has damaging competition moved in since the business originally opened?

- *Examine the store's financial records for the last three years and for the current year to date.* Compare sales tax records with the owner's claims.

- *Sit in on the store's operation for a few days, observing daily business volume and clientele.*

- *Evaluate the worth of existing store fixtures.* They must be in good condition and consistent with your plans for image and food products.

- *Determine the costs of remodeling and redecorating if the store's décor is to be changed.* Will these costs negate the advantage of buying?

Be sure any business you're considering buying is worth the price. If you're going to make substantial changes, it may make more sense to start from scratch. But if you do decide to buy, include a noncompete clause in your contract so the seller can't go out and start a competing operation in your service area. And remember that no seller can guarantee that the customers they have when they sell you the business will stick around.

Franchise

Another alternative to starting from scratch is to purchase a franchise. Many people do very well with this option, but there are significant risks involved.

Franchising is a method of marketing a product or service within a structure dictated by the franchisor. When you buy a franchise, you are entering into an agreement either to distribute products or to operate under a format identified with and structured by the parent company. One major advantage of franchising is that you have the opportunity to buy into a product or system that is established, rather than having to create everything yourself. There is, of course, a price for this—in addition to your start-up equipment and inventory, you'll have to pay a franchise fee. Also, most franchise companies collect ongoing royalties, usually a percentage of your gross sales. They also, however, provide you with ongoing support.

Franchises are regulated by the Federal Trade Commission (FTC) and also by a number of states. There are many food-service franchises available, and it's likely that you'll be able to find one that meets your vision of the type of operation you want to open. Thoroughly research any franchise you are considering, and expect the franchisor to want to know a lot about you, too. After all, if you're going to be responsible for operating under their name, they'll want to be sure you'll do it right.

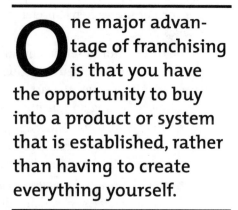

One major advantage of franchising is that you have the opportunity to buy into a product or system that is established, rather than having to create everything yourself.

Is Two Better Than One?

One of the hottest trends in the food-service industry is *dual-branding* or dual-concepting. The basic idea is to pair two restaurants that offer complementary menu items, which maximizes the use of your facility and increases customer satisfaction. For example, frozen-treat companies and quick-service chains have benefited from this trend. Florida-based Miami Subs Corp. was one of the first restaurant chains to experiment with dual-branding. In the late 1980s, the company was searching for a new strategy to boost sales and to strengthen some of the weaker *dayparts*, a restaurant industry term that refers to various meal cycles that occur throughout the day. Rather than investing time and capital into menu research and development, the chain decided to add a familiar product customers enjoyed but could not previously purchase at Miami Subs: Baskin-Robbins ice cream and frozen yogurt. Baskin-Robbins filled the afternoon and early-evening dayparts that account for Miami Subs' downtime, and the dual-brand arrangement dovetailed with the frozen-treat chain's expansion plans.

Such pairings also make sense to help companies deal with seasonal fluctuations and provide a vehicle for menu expansion. And if dual-branding is good, does that mean multibranding is better? The popularity of food courts would indicate that consumers will not only accept but enthusiastically embrace the idea.

While its benefits are numerous, dual-branding does have its risks. Here are some guidelines to keep in mind before you join forces with another company:

The Bump-Out Option

More and more convenience stores and gas stations are incorporating various food-service businesses in their operations, often by partnering with a franchise or leasing space to an independent restaurateur. A relatively new configuration worth considering for a pizzeria, deli/sandwich shop, or limited-menu restaurant is known as a bump-out. Similar to a porch or sunroom on a house, a bump-out is an extension of the existing floor space so the restaurant is adjacent to, rather than housed within, the convenience store or gas station.

Such partnering creates a win-win situation, because the restaurant and the store can benefit from each other's traffic and combine marketing efforts. The bump-out configuration gives the restaurant greater visibility and more of its own identity, even though it's under the same roof as the convenience store or gas station.

- *Make sure you're ready for the expansion.* Be sure the base operation is solid enough to function on its own before taking on a partner. Adding another concept to an already-floundering operation can cause both to fail.
- *Complement, don't compete.* Look for a partner that won't undercut your existing sales. You want to dual-brand with a product line that won't force customers to choose. If you're selling burgers, you can dual-brand with a line of vegetarian items or desserts. But if you're selling ice cream, don't dual-brand with a frozen yogurt company.
- *Seek comparable quality.* Any dual-branding partner should offer the same quality that you do.
- *Consider company culture.* The corporate culture of any dual-branding partner must be compatible with your own for the relationship to work.

Human
Resources

One of the biggest challenges businesses in all industries face is a lack of qualified labor. As the food-service industry in general continues to grow and thrive, the demand for workers in an already-diminished labor pool is also increasing. Finding qualified workers and rising labor costs are two key concerns for food-service business owners.

The first step in a comprehensive human resources program is to decide exactly what you want someone to do. The job description doesn't have to be as formal as one you might expect from a large corporation, but it needs to clearly outline the person's duties and responsibilities. It should also list any special skills or other required credentials, such as a valid driver's license and clean driving record for someone who is going to make deliveries for you.

Next, you need to establish a pay scale. We've indicated the pay ranges for many of the positions you're going to need to fill. You should also do some research on your own to find out what the pay rates are in your area. You'll want to establish a minimum and maximum rate for each position; you'll pay more even at the start for better qualified and more experienced workers. Of course, the pay scale will be affected by whether or not the position is one that is regularly tipped.

You'll also need a job application form. You can get a basic form at most office supply stores or create your own. In any case, have your attorney review the form you'll be using for compliance with the most current employment laws.

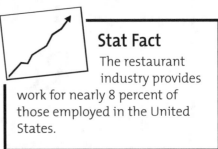

Stat Fact
The restaurant industry provides work for nearly 8 percent of those employed in the United States.

Every prospective employee should fill out an application—even if it's someone you already know, and even if they have submitted a detailed resume. A resume is not a signed, sworn statement acknowledging that you can fire them if they lie; the application is. The application will also help you verify their resumes; compare the two and make sure the information is consistent.

Now you're ready to start looking for candidates.

Look in the Right Places

Picture the ideal candidate in your mind. Is this person likely to be unemployed and reading the classified ads? It's possible, but you'll probably improve your chances for a successful hire if you are more creative in your searching techniques than simply writing a "help wanted" ad.

Sources for prospective employees include vendors, customers, and professional associations. Check with nearby colleges and perhaps even high schools for part-time help. Put the word out among your social contacts as well—you never know who might know the perfect person for your food-service business.

Roughly 80 percent of food-service business operators say that the most common resources for hourly employees are walk-in inquiries, word-of-mouth, and newspaper ads, according to a National Restaurant Association survey. Restaurants with average check amounts of $25 or higher are more likely to recruit hourly employees from vocational schools, while operators of establishments with average check amounts of $8 or less are more likely than others to use signage in their businesses to attract employees.

Consider using a temporary help or employment agency. Many small businesses shy away from agencies because they think they can't afford the fee—but if the agency handles the advertising, initial screening, and background checks, their fee may be well worth paying.

Use caution if you decide to hire friends and relatives—many personal relationships are not strong enough to survive an employee-employer relationship. Small-business owners in all industries tell of nightmarish experiences when a friend or relative refused to accept direction or otherwise abused a personal relationship in the course of business.

The key to success as an employer is making it clear from the start that you are the one in charge. You don't need to act like a dictator, of course. Be diplomatic, but set the ground rules in advance, and stick to them.

Recruiting Young People

If current recruiting initiatives and educational programs continue to expand and pay off as expected, the food-service industry should see a sizable influx of young people. And the timing couldn't be better. Though the population of 16- to 24-year-olds declined 3 percent during the first half of the 1990s, that group is expected to grow 18 percent between 1996 and 2010. But just because this anticipated demographic shift will increase the size of a targeted labor group, restaurateurs can't afford to relax their recruitment efforts.

Too often, young people see food-service jobs as a way to work toward their "real" career without realizing the tremendous potential and varied opportunities the industry offers. The solution is a combination of awareness and educational programs that will introduce high school and middle school students to hospitality careers and provide them with training that will allow them to move smoothly from school to the workplace.

Across the country, restaurateurs and educators are joining forces to attract and train young people for food-service careers. At the national level, there are two key players in developing such programs: the Hospitality Business Alliance (HBA) and the National Academy Foundation (NAF). (See this book's appendix for contact information.)

In addition to developing school-based curricula, the HBA is aggressively working to introduce young people to the opportunities in food service. The organization is a key participant in Groundhog Job Shadow Day, which was started by General Colin Powell's volunteer organization, America's Promise, the National School-to-Work Opportunities Office, the American Society of Association Executives, Junior Achievement, and the National Employer Leadership Council. The HBA and participating organizations use Groundhog Day to focus on providing young people with job-shadowing experience in restaurants and other hospitality venues.

The HBA has also developed a tool kit to help restaurateurs be more effective in marketing careers in the industry. The kit includes a booklet with suggestions for ways restaurateurs can get involved with young people, a brochure outlining available opportunities, and posters and/or videos for operators and teachers to use when communicating with students.

Evaluating Applicants

What kinds of people make good employees for food-service businesses? It depends on what you want them to do. If you're hiring a delivery person, you need someone with a good driving record who knows the city. If you're hiring someone to help with administrative tasks, they need to be computer-literate and be able to learn your operating system. If you're hiring someone to wait tables, they need to be friendly, people-oriented, and able to handle the physical demands of the job. Bartenders need to know how to make drinks, cooks need to know how to cook, and managers need to know how to manage. What is really important is that the people you hire are committed to giving you their best effort while they're working so that your customers receive the best service.

When you actually begin the hiring process, don't be surprised if you're as nervous at the prospect of interviewing potential employees as they are about being

Hire Education

Under the Immigration Reform and Control Act of 1986, you may only hire people who may legally work in the United States, which means citizens and nationals of the United States, and aliens authorized to work in the United States. As an employer, you must verify the identity and employment eligibility of everyone you hire. You must complete and retain the Employment Eligibility Verification Form (I-9) on file for at least three years, or one year after employment ends, whichever period of time is longer.

The Immigration and Nationality Act protects U.S. citizens and aliens authorized to accept employment in the United States from discrimination in hiring or discharge on the basis of national origin and citizenship status.

interviewed. After all, they may need a job—but the future of your company is at stake.

It's a good idea to prepare your interview questions in advance. Develop open-ended questions that encourage the candidate to talk. In addition to knowing *what* they've done, you want to find out *how* they did it. Ask each candidate for a particular position the same set of questions, and make notes as they respond so you can make an accurate assessment and comparison later.

When the interview is over, let the candidate know what to expect. Is it going to take you several weeks to interview other candidates, check references, and make a decision? Will you want the top candidates to return for a second interview? Will you call the candidate, or should they call you? This is not only a good business practice; it's also common courtesy.

Always check former employers and personal references. Though for legal reasons many companies restrict the information they'll verify, you may be surprised at what you can find out. You should at least confirm that the applicant told the truth about dates and positions held. Personal references are likely to give you some additional insight into the general character and personality of the candidate; this will help you decide if they'll fit into your operation.

Be sure to document every step of the interview and reference-checking process. Even very

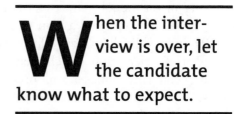

When the interview is over, let the candidate know what to expect.

small companies are finding themselves targets of employment discrimination suits; good records are your best defense if it happens to you.

Once They're on Board

The hiring process is only the beginning of the challenge of having employees. The next thing you need to do is train them.

Many small businesses conduct their "training" just by throwing someone into the job, but that's not fair to the employee, and it's certainly not good for your business. And if you think you can't afford to spend time on training, think again—can you afford *not* to adequately train your employees? Do you really want them preparing food or interacting with your customers when you haven't told them how you want things done?

In an ideal world, employees could be hired already knowing everything they need to know. But this isn't an ideal world, and if you want the job done right, you have to teach your people how to do it. Bakery owner Jim A. says he looks for people with food-service experience because they're used to being on their feet in a fast-paced environment, but he expects to have to train people in the art of sourdough bread-making. "Because we do so much training, we really look for people who we think are going to be around for a couple of years or more," he says.

Virtually all table-service restaurant operators provide employees with some sort of on-the-job training, with about 90 percent providing ongoing training and 80 percent offering formal job training.

Whether done in a formal classroom setting or on the job, effective training begins with a clear goal and a plan for reaching it. Training will fall into one of three major categories: orientation, which includes explaining company policies and procedures; job skills, which focuses on how to do specific tasks; and ongoing development, which enhances the basic job skills and grooms

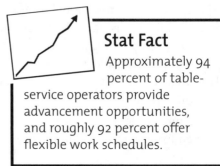

employees for future challenges and opportunities. These tips will help you maximize your training efforts:

Bright Idea

Post the duties of all positions clearly so new people can quickly see what they are supposed to do each day and also have a clear picture as to how their positions interact with others.

- *Find out how people learn best.* Delivering training is not a one-size-fits-all proposition. People absorb and process information differently, and your training method needs to be compatible with their individual preferences. Some people can read a manual, others prefer a verbal explanation, and still others need to see a demonstration. In a group training situation, your best strategy is to use a combination of methods; when you're working one-on-one, tailor your delivery to fit the needs of the person you're training.

  With some employees, figuring out how they learn best can be a simple matter of asking them. Others may not be able to tell you because they don't understand it themselves; in those cases, experiment with various training styles and see what works best for the specific employee.

- *Use simulation and role-playing to train, practice, and reinforce.* One of the most effective training techniques is simulation, which involves showing an employee how to do something, then allowing them to practice it in a safe, controlled environment. If the task includes interpersonal skills, let the employee role-play with a co-worker to practice what they should say and do in various situations.

- *Be a strong role model.* Don't expect more from your employees than you are willing to do. You're a good role model when you do things the way they should be done, all the time. Don't take shortcuts you don't want your employees to take or behave in any way that you don't want them to behave. On the other hand, don't assume that simply doing things the right way is enough to teach others how to do things. Role-modeling is not a substitute for training; it reinforces training. If you only role-model but never train, employees aren't likely to get the message.

- *Look for training opportunities.* Once you get beyond basic orientation and job skills training, you need to constantly be on the lookout for opportunities to enhance the skills and performance levels of your people.

- *Make it real.* Whenever possible, use real-life situations to train—but avoid letting customers know they've become a training experience for employees.

- *Anticipate questions.* Don't assume that employees know what to ask. In a new situation, people often don't understand enough to formulate questions. Anticipate their questions and answer them in advance.

- *Ask for feedback.* Finally, encourage employees to let you know how you're doing as a trainer. Just as you evaluate their performance, convince them that it's OK to tell you the truth, ask them what they thought of the training and your techniques, and use that information to improve your own skills.

Employee Benefits

The actual wages you pay may be only part of your employees' total compensation. While many very small companies do not offer a formal benefits program, more and more business owners have recognized that benefits—particularly in the area of insurance—are extremely important when it comes to attracting and retaining quality employees. In most parts of the country, the employment rate is higher than it's been in decades, which means competition for good people is stiff.

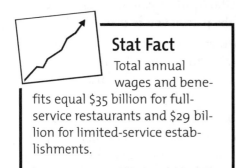

Stat Fact
Total annual wages and benefits equal $35 billion for full-service restaurants and $29 billion for limited-service establishments.

Typical benefit packages include group insurance (your employees may pay all or a portion of their premiums), paid holidays, and vacations. You can build employee loyalty by seeking additional benefits that may be somewhat unusual—and they don't have to cost much. For example, if you're in a retail location, talk to other store owners in your shopping center to see if they're interested in providing reciprocal employee discounts. You'll not only provide your own employees with a benefit, but you may get some new customers out of the arrangement.

If the Unthinkable Happens . . .

In most states, if you have three or more employees, you are required by law to carry workers' compensation insurance. This coverage pays medical expenses and replaces a portion of the employee's wages if he or she is injured on the job. Even if you have only one or two employees, you may want to consider this coverage to protect both them and you in the event of an accident.

Details and requirements vary by state; contact your state's insurance office or your own insurance agent for information so you can be sure to be in compliance.

Beyond tangible benefits, look for ways to provide positive working conditions. "We're not just about making bread; we're about creating a good work environment where people feel like they are making some progress in their own lives in terms of developing skills and becoming better people," says Jim A., whose three wholesale and retail bakeries in Portland, Maine, employ 50 people. "We don't just look at the financial bottom line, we look at what the employees are doing and what is the value being added for the employees and the customers." His bakery not only provides a strong benefits package that includes health insurance, paid vacations, and holidays, but he also pays employees for doing volunteer work at their regular hourly rate for up to three hours a month.

Caterer Ann C. sends her full-time staffers to seminars to help sharpen their skills. She also provides extras, such as the time she bought tickets to Disneyland for the staff and their families. And periodically, she brings lunch in from another restaurant; since staff members cook their own lunches every day, "ordering out" is a treat.

Child Labor Issues

Teenagers make up a significant portion of the food-service industry's labor force, and it's important that you understand the child labor laws that apply to your operation. The Fair Labor Standards Act has set four provisions designed to protect the educational opportunities of youths and prohibit their employment in jobs and under conditions that are detrimental to their health and well-being.

The minimum age for most nonfarm work is 16; however, 14- and 15-year-olds may be employed outside of school hours in certain occupations under certain conditions. At any age, youths may work for their parents in their solely owned nonfarm business (except in mining, manufacturing, or in any other occupation declared hazardous by the Secretary of Labor); this means your minor children can work in your food-service business if you are the sole owner, and as long as they are not violating other age-related laws, such as serving alcohol.

The basic age-related guidelines of the Fair Labor Standards Act are:

- Youths 18 years or older may perform any job for unlimited hours.
- Youths age 16 and 17 may perform any job not declared hazardous by the Secretary of Labor for unlimited hours.
- Youths age 14 and 15 may work outside school hours in various nonmanufacturing, nonmining, nonhazardous jobs under the following conditions: no more than 3 hours on a school day, 18 hours in a school week, 8 hours on a nonschool day, or 40 hours in a nonschool week. In addition, they may not

begin work before 7 A.M. or work after 7 P.M., except from June 1 through Labor Day, when evening work hours are extended until 9 P.M.

- Youths age 14 and 15 who are enrolled in an approved Work Experience and Career Exploration Program (WECEP) may be employed for up to 23 hours in school weeks and three hours on school days, including during school hours.

Department of Labor regulations require employers to keep records of the date of birth of employees under age 19, their daily starting and quitting times, daily and weekly hours of work, and their occupation. Protect yourself from unintentional violation of the child labor provisions by keeping on file an employment or age certificate for each youth employed to show that they are the minimum age for the job.

> **Keep in mind that, in addition to the federal statutes, most states also have child labor laws.**

Keep in mind that, in addition to the federal statutes, most states also have child labor laws. Check with your own state labor department to see what state regulations apply to your business. When both federal and state laws apply, the law setting the higher standards must be observed.

Stat Fact

Average earnings for employees in the restaurant industry are similar to the U.S. average for all household incomes. Of those employed in food preparation and service occupations, 31 percent have household incomes of $50,000 or more; 32 percent have household incomes between $25,000 and $49,999; 19 percent have incomes between $15,000 and $24,999; and 18 percent have incomes of $15,000 or less.

Minimum Wage

The Fair Labor Standards Act also establishes minimum wage, overtime pay, and record-keeping standards. The act requires employers of covered employees who are not otherwise exempt to pay these employees a minimum wage. Youths under 20 years of age may be paid a youth minimum wage that is lower than the standard minimum wage during the first 90 consecutive calendar days of employment. Employers may not displace any employee to hire someone else at the youth minimum wage. Because minimum wage laws change, be sure to check with your state labor board and/or the U.S. Department of Labor Wage and Hour Division for the current minimum wage amounts.

Employers of tipped employees, which are defined as employees who customarily and regularly receive more than $30 a month in tips, may consider the tips of these employees part of their wages, but must pay a direct wage of at least $2.13 per hour if they claim a tip credit. Certain other conditions also must be met; check with your accountant or the appropriate agency to be sure you're in compliance.

The act also permits the employment of certain individuals at wage rates below the statutory minimum wage, but they must be working under certificates issued by the Department of Labor. Those individuals include student learners (vocational education students); full-time students in retail or service establishments; and individuals whose earning or productive capacity is impaired by a physical or mental disability, including those related to age or injury.

Tips and Taxes

Tips received by your employees are generally subject to withholding. Your employees must report all cash tips they've received to you by the tenth of the month after the month the tips are received. This report should include tips employees receive directly in cash as well as tips you paid from charge receipts. Also include the tips employees receive from other employees and through tip-splitting.

Employees should report their tips on IRS Form 4070, Employee's Report of Tips to Employer, or on form 4070-A, Employee's Daily Record of Tips, or on a similar statement. The statement must be signed by the employee and include the employee's name, address, and social security number; your name and address; the month or period the report covers; and the total tips received. No report is required when tips are less than $20.

As an employer, you must collect income tax, employee social security tax, and employee Medicare tax on employees' tips. You can collect these taxes from wages or from other funds the employee makes available. You are also responsible for paying the employer social security tax on wages and tips.

You must file Form 941 to report withholding on tips. Your accountant can help you set up a system to be sure you are in compliance with IRS reporting and payment requirements.

Certain establishments are required to report allocated tips under certain circumstances. The IRS requires that large food and beverage establishments, which are defined as providing "food or beverages for consumption on the premises, where tipping is customary, and where there are normally more than ten employees on a typical business day during the preceding year," report allocated tips (which can be calculated by hours worked, gross receipts, or good-faith agreement) but do not withhold income, social security, or Medicare taxes on allocated tips. Check with your accountant or the IRS for more information.

When You Suspect an Employee of Stealing

Employee theft can have a serious impact on your bottom line as well as on the morale of other employees who may be aware of what's going on. When you become aware of actual or suspected employee theft, you need to act quickly—but carefully—to resolve the situation.

"Treat the complaint as valid until it is established otherwise, and treat the accused as innocent until proven guilty," says Michael P. O'Brien, a labor and employment attorney with Jones, Waldo, Holbrook, & McDonough in Salt Lake City. "Also, treat the matter confidentially to the greatest extent possible." In today's litigious world, protecting the privacy of a suspect is essential; failing to do so can leave you vulnerable if that individual decides to sue later—regardless of whether or not the person was actually guilty.

The first step is to conduct a thorough investigation, including a review of all relevant documents, such as personnel files, time sheets, performance evaluations of involved persons, inventory and delivery records, and any applicable financial records. If your security system includes video surveillance, you'll want to review the tapes. You may also want to interview witnesses and others who may have knowledge of the situation. Of course, you should also interview the accused—without making an

You Deserve a Break

No matter how much you enjoy your work, you need an occasional break from it. This is a challenge for small-business owners, but it's critical. You need to be able to be away from your operation occasionally, not only for vacations, but for business reasons, such as attending conferences and trade shows. Also, you need a plan in place in case of illness, accidents, or other emergencies. Be sure your people are well-trained and committed to maintaining your service levels when you aren't there.

accusation. When conducting interviews, be very clear that the issue under investigation is not to be discussed with unconcerned parties. "If a witness can't be trusted, think carefully about involving that person [in the investigation] in order to avoid possible defamation problems," says O'Brien.

Regardless of how much you trust a particular witness, avoid disclosing information unnecessarily, and don't ask questions that indicate the direction of your inquiry. Document every step of the investigation, and maintain those records in a secure place separate from your personnel records. Do not make details of an investigation part of an employee's personnel file unless and until the results are in and misconduct has been proven.

If your investigation confirms misconduct of any sort, take immediate and appropriate disciplinary action that is consistent with your general policies. "The worst thing you can do is nothing," O'Brien says. "You need to take some sort of disciplinary action against the individual you've concluded has done an inappropriate act." Certainly you'll want to consider the severity, frequency, and pervasiveness of the conduct—for example, occasionally over-pouring drinks for regular customers is certainly less severe than skimming cash out of the register—but whatever remedy you apply must end the offensive behavior. Keep in mind that whatever

> **If your investigation confirms misconduct of any sort, take immediate and appropriate disciplinary action that is consistent with your general policies.**

you do may eventually wind up in court, so maintain good records and be sure you can always justify your actions.

You must also decide whether or not to involve law enforcement. Weigh the potential for negative publicity against the potential good, which could include restitution and the fact that the perpetrator may receive some much-needed rehabilitation.

Regulatory
Issues

Because of the significant impact food-service businesses can have on the health and safety of their patrons, they are subject to a wide range of regulatory requirements, which often vary by city and state. You are responsible for knowing what specific regulations apply to your particular operation and complying with them. Don't try to bend or break the regulations; if you get caught, you'll be subject to civil and perhaps even criminal liability, along with the potential of negative publicity that could put you out of business.

Licenses and Permits

Most cities and counties require food-service business operators to obtain various licenses and permits to comply with local regulations. Requirements vary by municipality; use this information as a guide, but do your own research to make sure your business is in full compliance.

Business License

City business license departments operate as tax-collecting bureaus and do not perform any public service. You simply pay a fee to operate your business in that city. Some cities also claim a percentage of your gross sales.

The planning or zoning department will process your license application and check to make sure applicable zoning laws allow the proposed use and that there are enough parking spaces to meet the code.

Health Department Permit

To purvey and distribute food, you will need a food establishment permit from your state or county health department. All food-service operations, including temporary food-service establishments and mobile units such as carts, must obtain this permit before beginning operation. The health department will inspect your facilities before issuing your initial permit, and on an ongoing basis as long as you are in business.

Health inspectors will want to make sure all areas of your operation meet legal standards. They will be concerned with food storage, food preparation, food display, employee health and cleanliness, the design and installation of equipment, the cleaning and storage of equipment and utensils, sanitary facilities, and the construction and maintenance of the facility. The type of food your restaurant specializes in is not an issue; what is important is how you store and prepare that food. Your local or state health department can provide you with guidelines.

> **Tip...**
>
> ### Smart Tip
> While you're still in the planning stages, contact your local health department for information on their requirements. They'll be happy to give you the information you need to set up so you'll qualify for all the necessary permits.

Liquor, Wine, and Beer Licenses

Most states require you to obtain one type of license to serve wine and beer, and another to serve hard liquor. A liquor license is more difficult to obtain than a beer-and-wine license. In some areas, no new liquor licenses are being issued at all, which means you can only obtain one by buying it from an existing license holder.

One advantage of buying an existing restaurant is that if it served liquor, you may be able to acquire the license as part of the deal. Typically, you will have to file an application with the state beverage control board, then post notice on the premises of your intent to serve liquor.

In some states, the beverage control board requires holders of liquor licenses to keep all purchase records for a specific number of years, during which time they are subject to inspection by the control board and/or the Internal Revenue Service.

Under most circumstances, it's much easier to obtain a license to serve wine and beer than a hard-liquor license. Beer-and-wine licenses are usually issued for an annual period and are easy to renew if you haven't committed any offenses, such as selling alcoholic drinks to minors. The government section of your telephone directory will have the number for the nearest beverage control agency, which can provide you with the information you need.

Fire Department Permit

Your fire department may require you to obtain a permit if your business uses any flammable materials or if your premises will be open to the public. In some cities, you must secure a permit before you open for business. Other jurisdictions don't require permits; instead, they schedule periodic inspections of the premises to see if you meet regulations. Restaurants, theaters, clubs, bars, retirement homes, day-care centers, and schools are subject to especially close and frequent scrutiny by the fire department.

Sign Permit

Many municipalities have sign ordinances that restrict the size, location, and sometimes the lighting and type of sign you can use in front of your business. Landlords may also impose their own restrictions. You'll likely find sign restrictions most stringent in malls and upscale shopping areas. Avoid costly mistakes by checking regulations and securing the written approval of your landlord *before* you invest in a sign.

County Permit

County governments often require the same types of permits and licenses as cities. These permits apply to commercial enterprises located outside city limits.

▲

State Licenses

Many states require persons engaged in certain occupations to hold licenses or occupational permits. Food-service employees generally are not required to hold licenses, but you should check with your state government for a complete list of occupations that require licensing to make sure you are in compliance.

Zoning Laws

In most cases, if you locate your food-service business in a structure previously used for commercial purposes, zoning regulations will not be a problem. However, if you intend to construct a new facility, use an existing building for a different purpose, or perform extensive remodeling, you should carefully check local building and zoning codes. If zoning regulations do not allow operation of the type of food-service business you wish to open, you may file for a zoning variance, a conditional-use permit, or a zone change.

Music Licenses

If you plan to play music in your restaurant—whether you hire a live performer or just play on-hold music on your telephone—you will need to obtain the appropriate licenses. Federal copyright laws require that any business that plays copyrighted music pay a fee. Fees are collected by the American Society of Composers, Authors, and Publishers, Broadcast Music Inc., and SESAC Inc. (formerly the Society of European Stage Authors and Composers). (See this book's appendix for contact information.)

United States copyright law requires you to obtain permission from, and negotiate a fee with, the composer and publisher of a musical piece before you can reproduce or perform the material. Since contacting each composer and publisher is impossible, especially if the composer is deceased, the previously listed organizations work on behalf of their members. They require business owners who play music in their establishments to obtain licenses through them instead of directly from the composers and publishers. The fees for these licenses are used to pay composers and publishers royalties for the performance of their material. By going through these performance rights organizations, you will pay a general fee which will cover the performance of all their members' songs. You must obtain a license from each of these organizations because they represent different artists. If you play copyrighted music without having a license to do so, the appropriate agency could levy a $5,000 to $20,000 fine.

The organizations base their fees on a number of factors, including the seating capacity in your establishment, the number of days or evenings each week you play music, whether you charge patrons for admission, and whether the music is performed live or by mechanical means.

The Legalities of Liquor Vending

Most food-service businesses find that serving alcoholic beverages can help improve their profit margins and offset the costs associated with some of the less profitable aspects of the business. Over the last decade or so, however, there has been a marked increase in the sociopolitical pressure and legal trouble facing businesses that sell alcoholic beverages. Some are calling this the "new temperance era" and "a time of neoprohibitionism." On both state and federal levels, legislators, public health officials, and special-interest groups are warring against alcohol abuse and bringing to light the fatalities and injuries caused by drunk driving. The effect on those who serve liquor, regardless of their personal beliefs, has been profound.

As a part of this movement, old statutes are being dusted off and new laws promulgated to place pressure on not just the alcohol abuser but on the supplier, too. It has always been incumbent upon the owners of liquor-vending establishments to observe state liquor laws or face criminal penalties. However, businesses selling liquor also face the threat of increased popular and legal support for those filing civil suits against liquor vendors.

It used to be that the average bartender or liquor-store owner just had to worry about getting caught serving minors or someone obviously intoxicated, and bought special liquor-liability insurance for coverage in the event of a lawsuit from a drunken patron. Lately, the liquor vendor has become potentially financially liable when a third party is injured.

Beware!
Regardless of what the laws say in terms of liability, just about anyone can sue anyone else in civil court for just about any reason. And although you may win the verdict in a lawsuit where the plaintiff had insufficient grounds, fighting a lawsuit is still expensive and time-consuming. Your best strategy is to avoid situations that could result in potential liability of any kind.

Simply stated, *dramshop laws* and other types of third-party liability work this way: if you, the server of alcoholic beverages, act irresponsibly and overserve a patron, and that patron is later involved in an automobile crash, then the individual server, as well as the establishment, can be held financially liable for the death or injury of not only an innocent third party but of the intoxicated patron as well.

Laws regarding liquor liability vary by state and can change quickly. Your state's liquor board or alcoholic beverage commission should be able to tell you what the current laws in your particular state are.

Whether your state exposes you to high or low risks of liability, or whether your type of establishment puts you in jeopardy of civil suits, you must be cognizant of, and take precautions against, legal action. Progressive owners and management take steps to minimize the risk of criminal charges and civil litigation.

One step is learning to perceive intoxication and cutting off customers as soon as it becomes necessary. Most liquor vendors (and drinkers) are familiar with the signs, but all sellers/servers should be acquainted with them. Among the more common are staggering, slurred speech, impaired thinking, heavy eyelids, silence, talking too much or too loudly, tearfulness, hostility, acting out, nausea, sudden mood changes, physical imbalance, and verbal or physical confrontations.

Steps You Can Take

Most liquor vendors can stand some reform to protect customers and themselves from accidents that can turn into lawsuits. The general idea is to control the quantity of alcohol consumed by individual patrons and the ways in which drinking is encouraged. Though it may appear counterproductive for a liquor vendor to restrict the sale of alcoholic beverages, the trouble caused by not doing so costs more, in the long run, than any negligible decrease in liquor sales.

Here's one way to think of the situation: for every drunk you throw out of your place, think of how many customers are made more relaxed by his or her absence and are likely to return.

Preventive measures employed by many liquor vendors include:

> **Bright Idea**
>
> Consider a program that offers free nonalcoholic beverages to the designated driver in groups of patrons. Your investment will be minimal, but the impact on your potential liability, as well as the marketing benefit, will be significant.

- *Don't serve minors.* Drunk driving is a primary killer of teenagers in this country. Observe the legal drinking age, and check ID on any patron who appears to be under 30.

- *Dealing with intoxicated patrons.* You should develop and implement consistent, diplomatic procedures for denying alcohol to customers who arrive drunk or who are becoming so, and for making last calls. Each employee, from the bus-person to the manager, should be familiar with these procedures and the philosophy behind them.

- *Bar layout.* Your bar cannot become so crowded that bartenders can't keep track of who and how much they have served. You cannot allow customers in inconspicuous areas of your establishment to drink all night without being monitored at least casually. Adding bartenders and servers or changing the layout of your bar can help you avoid this situation.

- *Controlling the flow.* Free-pouring (as opposed to measuring) drinks is not economical, makes it difficult to control inventory, and hampers your servers' abilities to monitor alcohol consumption. Also, a free-pour bar may be in a difficult spot if you must legally account for the quantity of alcohol consumed by a particular customer. Consider cutting back on the happy-hour and closing-time two-for-one or all-you-can-drink specials, while promoting your nonalcoholic drinks. You can make them inexpensively, with an even greater profit margin than alcoholic beverages. Try putting more emphasis on food items and encourage the safe consumption of alcohol by selling snacks or providing complimentary hors d'oeuvres.

- *Alternative transportation.* Serving liquor responsibly may include ensuring that inebriated customers get home safely. Some establishments provide complimentary taxi service or will assist in calling a cab for a customer. Some taverns and restaurants band together to provide carpool service. Cab companies and community organizations may be willing to help provide transportation for free or at a nominal cost.

Despite your best precautions, any time alcohol and people mix in your establishment, you have the potential for danger to the public and liability to you. An important step in self-protection is becoming familiar with the liquor-liability laws in your state and purchasing adequate insurance. Your lawyer or insurer should be able to inform you of the relevant state laws and evaluate your risk.

> **S**erving liquor responsibly may include ensuring that inebriated customers get home safely.

Sanitation

Sanitation is extremely important to a successful food-service operation, not only for health and safety reasons, but for image reasons as well. Your storage area, kitchen preparation area, serving areas, waiting area, lounge, restrooms, and dining area should be clean and in good repair from floor to ceiling.

Set standards for all employees and reinforce them with charts, labels, and placards placed in areas where the staff will be reminded of sanitation issues. (Certain sanitation-related signs are required by law; your health department can give you the necessary information on that.) The National Restaurant Association produces a wide range of training materials dealing with various aspects of sanitation; contact the association for more information.

You or your manager should also perform thorough sanitation inspections at least once every six months. This inspection should focus on the storage of food; employees' personal hygiene; the cleanliness of all equipment and utensils; all floors, walls, and ceilings; lighting; ventilation; the dishwashing facility; water, sewage, and plumbing; restrooms; garbage and refuse disposal; insect and animal control; and linens.

Proper food storage is vitally important. A single case of food poisoning can put a restaurant out of business. Nothing should be placed directly on the floor, whether it's food in dry storage, frozen, or refrigerated. Use pallets, racks or anything else that

---

Preventive Medicine

The possibility that someone could get sick from eating food you served is a food-service business owner's worst nightmare. First, there's the fact that you—however unintentionally—caused someone to suffer. Then there's the potential liability, in terms of both paying direct medical costs and additional punitive damages. Finally, there's the bottom-line damage, because when word gets out—and it will—your business will suffer; sales can plummet.

Preventing food-borne illnesses begins with awareness. Everyone in your operation needs to understand how to prevent problems and the consequences of failing to do so. It's not enough just to tell workers that salads need to be kept at a certain temperature and that they need to wash their hands thoroughly after using the restroom; they need to know what can happen if they fail to follow these health and safety regulations.

The National Restaurant Association offers a number of training programs and other educational materials, such as signs and posters, that can help you maintain an operation that is safe for both your employees and your customers.

You might also consider providing inoculations for employees. For example, many restaurants in high-risk areas require employees to be vaccinated against hepatitis A. While seldom fatal, the virus can cause diarrhea, nausea, cramping, fatigue, and jaundice. The cost of the vaccine is about $80 per person but may be available for less through the National Restaurant Association or some local public health programs.

will raise your inventory off the floor. This makes it easier to clean the floors and protects the food from vermin and from being splashed by chemicals or dirty water.

To keep food free from contamination, place it in an area where you can maintain the proper temperature—keep hot food hot and cold food cold. Cover all refrigerated food. Don't leave anything out longer than necessary during the preparation period.

Whether you serve them raw or cooked, wash all fruits and vegetables thoroughly. Use proper utensils during preparation so human contact with food is kept to a minimum.

Your employees' personal hygiene is also important. Employees with cuts, abrasions, dirty fingernails, any type of skin disease, or a communicable disease should certainly not be involved in preparing or serving food. Employees involved in food preparation or serving should have clean uniforms, clean hair, and clean hands and fingernails. Employees with long hair should either wear a hairnet or at least pull their hair back away from their faces to prevent hairs from falling into the food.

Smart Tip

Tip...

Too many incidences of food contamination that leads to illness can be traced to workers failing to wash their hands after using the restroom. Stress to all employees who handle or serve food the importance of thorough hand-washing.

Emphasize to the dishwasher and all your servers that all pots, pans, preparation utensils, plates, silverware, glassware, and serving utensils should be spotless before they are used. All production equipment should be checked and cleaned regularly by your cooks. Maintain proper hot water temperatures, and make sure your water source is safe.

All your floors, walls, and ceilings should be cleaned regularly. Check them to make sure that all surfaces are smooth and free of dust, grease and cobwebs. Set up a service contract with a local exterminator to ensure that your facility is free of insects and rodents. Clean drains regularly. Rubber mats should be easy to move for cleaning.

Don't neglect your garbage area. All trash containers should be leak-proof and nonabsorbent, and have tight-fitting covers. Wash your containers thoroughly inside and out when you empty them.

16

Equipment

For most food-service businesses, the focus is on the food preparation and service equipment. For your office, as we've said in previous chapters, chances are a small desk, a chair, a couple of locking filing cabinets, and a few bookshelves for catalogs and pricing guides will be sufficient in the beginning. Your office furnishings should be comfortable and efficient, but don't worry about how they look—your customers aren't going to see your office, so don't waste money in this area that could be more effectively spent in the front of the house. Speaking of the front of the house, keep the following in mind when purchasing major equipment for your food-service business.

Major Equipment

While each of the food-service operations discussed in this guide has specific equipment requirements, there are many items that are basic to just about any type of food-service business. Food-service equipment dealers are often good sources for finding out what you need and what particular piece of equipment will do it best. A good salesperson will also function as a consultant, helping you make a wise decision; after all, if you're satisfied, you're likely to come back when you need more equipment—and you'll refer others. However, you still need to be somewhat cautious when accepting advice and guidance from a salesperson. Get several opinions and price quotes before making a final decision.

Careful and thoughtful equipment selection will mean a cost-effective and productive operation over the long run. Don't buy based on price alone. You can cut down on labor costs by purchasing equipment that is fully automatic and self-cleaning, even though it may cost more upfront. Install as much modern, energy-efficient equipment as possible; as gas and electricity costs rise, your energy-saving equipment will help keep your utility bills reasonable.

Buy from a well-known manufacturer that has reliable equipment and a network of repair facilities. Look for standard lines of equipment that are both versatile and mobile. Avoid custom-designed lines whenever possible. Standard equipment is generally lower-priced and less expensive to install. It's also easier and less expensive to replace at the end of its service life.

Most food-service operations will need a walk-in refrigerator/freezer at the rear of the facility near the receiving door for primary food storage. You'll also need a smaller reach-in refrigerator/freezer in your production area to keep the food supplies you need that day or for that meal period fresh and easily accessible.

Your receiving area should also include a scale to verify weights of deliveries; a breakdown

> ## Smart Tip
> **Tip...**
>
> Resist the temptation to fritter away time on your computer. The abundance of easy-to-use software on the market today gives us fun ways to turn out impressive documents, tempting you and your employees to add artwork, color, and even motion to your materials. While a certain amount of creativity helps your competitive position, take care that it doesn't get out of control and become a serious time-waster.

Meals on Wheels

If you plan to offer delivery, you'll need a company vehicle. The type and style will vary depending on the specific food-service business you have and exactly what you're delivering. A pizzeria, for example, can have employees use their own personal cars to make deliveries. But a wholesale bakery or a catering service will likely need commercial vehicles with greater capacity than the typical passenger car.

Whether you lease or buy depends on exactly what you need, your cash flow, and your tax situation. Do a needs analysis, research the costs of buying both new and used vehicles, check out lease deals, and consult with your tax advisor before making a final decision. For example, caterer Ann C. owns six vehicles, including a refrigerated lift-gate truck, and does not feel she's overloaded with equipment.

table; at least one dolly or hand truck; dry shelving; and shelving for the walk-in refrigerator/freezer. You may find wheeled carts a convenient tool for managing your inventory.

Buying Used Equipment

Heavy-duty restaurant hardware does not wear out quickly, so why buy brand-new when "seasoned" used merchandise can be as good or even better? You can buy secondhand equipment for a fraction of what it would cost new. And there's plenty available from other food-service businesses that have failed, merged, or grown to the point where they require larger or more modern equipment.

Since Ann C. bought her catering company, she's been expanding at a healthy pace. When she needed additional equipment to support her growing business, she says, "I couldn't afford to go out and buy all new equipment. The only thing I bought new was my walk-in refrigerator and the overhead hood for the cooking line. Everything else is used."

Caterer Maxine T. also buys used equipment. She used to go to auctions but got burned a few times when she bought

Dollar Stretcher

Shopping for used equipment? Don't overlook new-equipment suppliers. They frequently have trade-ins or repossessions that they're willing to sell at discounts of 75 percent or more.

equipment that wasn't as good as she thought. Now she only buys at auction if she knows who she's working with and is extremely familiar with the equipment being sold. She also learned how to work with equipment dealers, particularly new-equipment dealers that have departments that sell the used items they accept as trade-ins.

Buying used equipment is normally a good cost-cutting measure, but there are some pitfalls. Consider that some major equipment has a useful lifetime of only ten years. If you buy a used walk-in refrigerator/freezer that is near the end of its useful life, you run the risk of repeated breakdowns, resulting in costly maintenance and food spoilage. Also, newer equipment is generally going to be more cost-efficient to operate.

Before buying a piece of used equipment, perform a cost analysis of the item you're considering over its expected lifetime versus that of a comparable new item. When you factor in maintenance and operating costs, it's possible new equipment may actually be less expensive in the long run.

Look for standard lines of equipment that are both versatile and mobile so you won't have to duplicate hardware. Try to avoid custom-designed lines. Standard equipment is generally less expensive to buy, install, and replace. Also, try to install as much energy-efficient equipment as possible, so long as it's affordable.

When shopping for used equipment, carefully check it for wear, and buy only from reputable dealers. Judicious shopping may turn up some excellent bargains. Check the classified section of your local newspaper for a wide range of used furniture and equipment for sale. Also look under the "Business Opportunities" classification, because businesses that are being liquidated or sold may have fixtures or equipment for sale at substantial savings.

Basic Office Equipment

Many entrepreneurs find a trip to the local office supply store more exciting than any mall. It's easy to get carried away when you're surrounded with an abundance of clever gadgets, all designed to make your working life easier and more fun. But if, like most new business owners, you're starting on a budget, discipline yourself and buy only what you need. Consider these primary basic items:

- *Typewriter.* You may think most typewriters are in museums these days, but they actually remain quite useful to businesses that deal frequently with preprinted and multipart forms, such as order forms and shipping documents.

Tip...

Smart Tip

If you're going to accept orders via fax, be sure the fax machine is visible and checked at least every five minutes. You don't want someone arriving to pick up a faxed order that you haven't even started to prepare.

The determination of whether or not you need a typewriter is one only you can make based on your specific operation. A good electric typewriter can be purchased for $100 to $220.

- *Computer and printer.* A computer can help you manage complex bookkeeping and inventory control tasks, maintain customer records, and produce marketing materials. A computer is an extremely valuable management and marketing tool and an essential element for growing a strong and profitable business.

- *Software.* Think of software as your computer's "brains," the instructions that tell your computer how to accomplish the functions you need. There are a myriad of programs on the market that will handle your accounting, inventory, customer information management, and other administrative requirements. Software can be a significant investment, so do a careful analysis of your own needs then study the market and examine a variety of products before making a final decision.

- *Modem.* Modems are necessary to access online services and the Internet and have become a standard component of most computers. If you are going to conduct any business on-line, whether it's creating your own Web site to attract customers, doing research or visiting your suppliers' Web sites, or simply communicating via e-mail, you must have a modem.

- *Photocopier.* The photocopier is a fixture of the modern office; whether or not you need one depends on the specific type of food-service operation you're starting. Chances are a deli or pizzeria can do without a copier, but a wholesale bakery or catering service will likely find one useful. You can get a basic, no-frills personal copier for less than $500 in just about any office supply store. More elaborate models increase proportionally in price. If you anticipate a heavy volume, consider leasing.

> **Beware!**
> Although multi-function devices—such as a copier/printer/fax machine or a fax/telephone/answering machine—may be cost- and space-efficient, you risk losing all of these functions simultaneously if the equipment fails. Also, consider your anticipated volume with the machine's efficiency rating and cost to operate, and compare that with stand-alone items before making a decision.

> **Dollar Stretcher**
> Just about any type of secondhand business equipment can be purchased for a fraction of its original retail cost. Check the classified section of your local newspaper, and ask new equipment dealers if they have trade-ins or repossessions for sale. Careful shopping for used items can save hundreds of dollars.

- *Fax machine.* For most food-service businesses, fax capability is essential. You'll want to be able to fax orders to your suppliers, and you may want to be able to receive faxed orders from your customers. You can either add a fax card to your computer or buy a stand-alone machine. If you use your computer, it must be on to send or receive faxes, and the transmission may interrupt other work. For most businesses, a stand-alone machine on a dedicated telephone line is a wise investment. Expect to pay around $250 for a high-quality fax machine, $700 for a multi-functional device.

Stat Fact

Food-service business owners use computers for a range of operational needs, including accounting, payroll records, sales analysis, inventory control, menu planning, employee scheduling, and online services. More than 80 percent of table-service operators use a computer in some fashion, and 98 percent of operators with five or more establishments use computers.

- *Postage scale.* Unless all of your mail is identical, a postage scale is a valuable investment. An accurate scale takes the guesswork out of postage and will quickly pay for itself. It's a good idea to weigh every piece of mail to eliminate the risk of items being returned for insufficient postage or overpaying when you're unsure of the weight. If you're averaging 12 to 24 items per day, consider a digital scale, which generally costs $50 to $200. If you send more than 24 items per day or use priority or expedited services frequently, invest in an electronic computing scale, which weighs the item and then calculates the rate via the carrier of your choice,

To Lease or Not to Lease?

If your initial equipment investment will be large, you may want to consider leasing rather than purchasing. Leasing is an excellent alternative when start-up capital is limited. You should also check with your tax advisor to determine what type of tax advantages leasing offers.

The disadvantage to leasing is that if you have a tax-deductible lease, you do not build equity in your equipment and therefore do not build up your balance sheet. A financial statement showing a strong net worth is important to any business. In addition, the total cost of leasing over a period of years is going to be higher than if the same items were purchased. Consult with your accountant to make the best choice based on your tax status and cash situation.

making it easy for you to make comparisons. Programmable electronic scales cost $80 to $250.

- *Postage meter.* Postage meters allow you to pay for postage in advance and print the exact amount on the mailing piece when it is used. Many postage meters can print in increments of one-tenth of a cent, which can add up to big savings for bulk-mail users. Meters also provide a "big company" professional image, are more convenient than stamps and can save you money in a number of ways. Postage meters are leased, not sold, with rates starting at about $30 per month. They require a license, which is available from your local post office. Only four manufacturers are licensed by the USPS to manufacture and lease postage meters; your local post office can provide you with contact information.

- *Paper shredder.* A response to both a growing concern for privacy and the need to recycle and conserve space in landfills, shredders are becoming increasingly common in both homes and offices. They allow you to efficiently destroy incoming unsolicited direct mail, as well as sensitive internal documents. Shredded paper can be compacted much tighter than paper tossed in a wastebasket, and it can also be used as packing material. Light-duty shredders start at about $25, and heavier-capacity shredders run $150 to $500.

> **Bright Idea**
>
> Postage stamps come in a variety of sizes, designs, and themes and can add an element of color, whimsy, and thoughtfulness to your mail. Some mailers prefer stamps because they look personal; others prefer metered mail because it looks "corporate." Suggestion: use metered mail for invoices, statements, and other "official" business, and stamps for thank-you notes and marketing correspondence that could use a personal touch.

Telecommunications

The ability to communicate quickly with your customers and suppliers is essential to any business, but especially for a food-service business where customers often have last-minute needs and questions. Advancing technology gives you a wide range of telecommunications options. Most telephone companies have created departments dedicated to small and homebased businesses; contact your local service provider and ask to speak with someone who can review your needs and help you put together a service and equipment package that will work for you. Specific elements to keep in mind include:

- *Telephone.* A single voice telephone line should be adequate during the start-up period for a smaller operation. As you grow and your call volume increases, you'll add more lines.

  The telephone itself can be a tremendous productivity tool, and most of the models on the market today are rich in features you will find useful. Such features include automatic redial, which redials the last number called at regular intervals until the call is completed; programmable memory for storing frequently called numbers; and a speakerphone for hands-free use. You may also want call forwarding, which allows you to forward calls to another number when you're not at your desk, and call waiting, which signals you that another call is coming in while you are on the phone. These services are typically available through your telephone company for a monthly fee.

> ### Bright Idea
> Be sure the announcement on your answering machine or voice mail includes your business name, location, hours of operation, and fax number. If a caller just wants that basic information, they won't have to call back when you're open to get it.

  If you're going to be spending a great deal of time on the phone, perhaps doing marketing or handling customer service, consider purchasing a headset for comfort and efficiency. A cordless phone lets you move around freely while talking, but these units vary widely in price and quality, so research them thoroughly before making a purchase.

- *Answering machine/voice mail.* Because your business phone should never go unanswered, you need some sort of reliable answering device to take calls when you can't do it yourself. Whether you buy an answering machine (expect to pay $40 to $150 for one that is suitable for a business) or use a voice-mail service provided by your telephone company is a choice you must make depending on your personal preferences, work style, and needs.

- *Cellular phone.* Once considered a luxury, cellular phones have become standard equipment for most business owners. Most have features similar to your office phone—such as caller ID, call waiting, and voice mail—and equipment and services packages are very reasonably priced. You may want delivery personnel or catering crews to have cellular phones. You may also feel more comfortable if you know your staff can reach you at any time. On the other hand, if you have a small family-style restaurant and are not out of the store often, a cellular phone may not be necessary.

- *Pager.* A pager lets you know that someone is trying to reach you and gives you the option of when to return the call. Many people use pagers in conjunction

Get with the Program

The birth of online communications has been one of the most significant technological breakthroughs in personal computing. The ability to link millions (and potentially billions) of computers allows individuals and businesses to communicate in ways never before possible and gain access to unlimited information.

You can use online services for research about your specific type of food-service business, or about small business and entrepreneurship in general. Most professional associations, equipment manufacturers, and other industry suppliers have Web sites that provide a wealth of information about how they can help you. Take the time to visit these sites and study the information they contain. You can also network online with food-service business owners across the country and around the world through electronic mailing lists, bulletin board services, message boards, and chat rooms.

It's well worth your while to get comfortable with the electronic world; it will give you a distinct advantage over those who are not.

---

with cellular phones to conserve the cost of air time. As with cellular phones, the pager industry is very competitive, so shop around for the best deal.

- *Toll-free number.* If you are targeting a customer base outside your local calling area, you'll want to provide them with a toll-free number so they can reach you without having to make a long-distance call. Most long-distance service providers offer toll-free numbers, and they have a wide range of service and price packages. Shop around to find the best deal for you.

- *E-mail.* E-mail is rapidly becoming a standard element in a company's communication package. It allows for fast, efficient, 24-hour communication. If you have e-mail, check your messages regularly and reply to them promptly.

Other Equipment

In addition to these basics, there are other items you may need, depending on your particular operation. They include:

- *Cash register.* For a retail operation, you need a way to track sales, collect money, and make change. You can do this with something as simple as a divided cash drawer and a printing calculator, or you can purchase a sophisticated, state-of-the-art point-of-sale system that is networked with your computer; this type of register is ideally suited for a multiregister operation, with a bar and main dining area, or a multiunit chain. Of course, the latter will cost somewhere between $1,200 and $5,000 per terminal and may not be a practical investment for a start-up operation. A preferable option is an electronic cash register (ECR), which ranges in price from $600 to $3,000, and can be purchased outright, leased, or acquired under a lease-purchase agreement. Many ECRs offer such options as payment records to designate whether a customer paid by cash, check, or credit card; department price groupings; sign-in keys to help managers monitor cashiers; and product price groupings for tracking inventory more effectively. To free capital in the early stages of your business, check on a lease-purchase arrangement, which will run about $100 to $150 per month, or consider leasing a mechanical cash register in the early stages and make your purchasing decision later. You may be able to justify the investment in an ECR because it can perform several bookkeeping functions and track inventory and customer preferences. A word of caution: many business owners believe any cash register is a highly visible invitation to thieves, so you should consider security options not only for your cash receipts, but also for the safety of your employees and customers.

* *Credit and debit card processing equipment.* This could range from a simple imprint machine to an online terminal. Consult with several merchant status providers to determine the most appropriate and cost-effective equipment for your business.

Security

Small merchandise, office equipment, and cash attract burglars, robbers, and shoplifters. Not only do you need to protect your inventory and equipment with alarms and lighting and through the careful selection of employees, but you also need to ensure your personal safety as well as that of your employees.

Begin by investigating your area's crime history to determine what kind of measures you need to take. To learn whether your proposed or existing location has a high crime rate, check with the local police department's community relations department or crime prevention officer. Most will gladly provide free information on safeguarding your business and may even visit your site to discuss specific crime prevention strategies. Many also offer training seminars for small retailers and their employees on workplace safety and crime prevention.

Common techniques merchants use to enhance security and reduce shoplifting include mirrors, alarms, and video cameras. Technology is bringing the cost of these items down rapidly, and installing them may earn you the fringe benefit of discounts on your insurance. You can also increase the effectiveness of your security system by posting signs in your store window and discreetly around the store announcing the presence of the equipment.

17

Marketing

Every business needs a marketing plan, and your food-service business is no exception. But even as you consider various marketing vehicles, keep this in mind: Research conducted by the National Restaurant Association reveals that word-of-mouth is still the best method of advertising. More than four out of five consumers are likely to choose a table-service restaurant they haven't patronized before on the basis of a recommendation from a family member or friend. So make the foundation of your marketing program an absolutely dazzling dining experience that customers will want to talk about and repeat.

Ask every new customer how they found out about you, and make a note of this information so you know how well your various marketing efforts are working. You can then decide to increase certain programs and eliminate those that aren't working.

There are issues and ideas specific to various types of food-service businesses that you need to know as you develop your plan.

A key question for restaurant owners is this: Do your marketing materials—menus, signs, table tents, ads, etc.—send an accurate message about who you are and what you do? Or are they confusing and misleading?

Marketing is the process of communicating with your existing and prospective customers. A key component of successful restaurant marketing is being sure your message is consistent with what you really are. Certainly a fine-dining establishment isn't going to put its menus in clear vinyl sleeves and illustrate them with photographs of children enjoying burgers and fries. But the same restaurateur who chuckles at the absurdity of that image may well be guilty of a variety of other far more subtle marketing sins.

Beware!

If someone says they can design a menu or an ad or some other marketing piece without visiting your restaurant, don't hire them. Anyone you hire to assist with your marketing materials should spend time in your restaurant so they know what you're trying to do.

For example, if senior citizens are a key segment of your market, do your menus and signs consider the physical changes, such as declining vision, that come with age? If you are trying to attract families, are your photographs and illustrations contemporary and relative to your market? Does each element of your marketing package—from décor to menu selections to printed materials—reflect a consistent marketing message? Have you taken societal changes into account when designing your marketing materials? It's possible that what worked well for you a few years ago may be having a negative impact on your business today.

The first step in creating a complete marketing package is to know your market, and it's not enough to gather demographics once. Markets change, and food-service businesses that don't change their marketing strategies with population shifts are missing out on a lot of opportunities.

Next, step back and take a look at each element in your facility. Everything from the parking lot to the interior décor to the printed items contributes to your marketing message—and each should be an accurate reflection of what your message is.

Samples Sell

Provide diners with samples of menu items to encourage them to order those items. One restaurant sends servers into the bar area with platters of bite-sized bits of main dishes; people in the bar waiting for tables have a chance to sample several different entrees while waiting for their tables. Another restaurant owner places small portions of desserts on the table when patrons are seated; they get to eat dessert first—and last! Tasting a bit of a delicious dessert at the beginning of the meal seems to whet customers' appetites for a full-size portion afterward.

If you wholesale your food products, help your customers promote your items with a sampling program. Baker Jim A. sends his own employees into new wholesale accounts to conduct a sampling promotion. Generally, two or three times during the first month a new retailer is carrying his bread, Jim sends his own people into the store to pass out samples. "We know we've got a good product," he says. "If we get it into people's hands and mouths in a no-risk situation, we'll see a return in sales."

It's not enough for each marketing component to be relevant to the audience; the elements must create a sense of continuity. Colors and textures should blend comfortably. Your printed materials should have enough common elements so there is no question that they represent the same restaurant.

Keep Up with the Trends

Staying in step with market trends is standard business advice; restaurants can accomplish this in a variety of subtle ways. Certainly an increasing number of diners are looking for healthy, low-fat fare, but you can take advantage of trends that go beyond food selection.

People are concerned about the environment; you can let them know you share their feelings by using recycled stock for all your printed items. Include a small line that says, "Because we care about the future, this menu [or whatever] has been printed on recycled paper." Expressing support for a particular chari-

Bright Idea
Entertainment enhances the dining experience, which increases customer loyalty and repeat business. Popular forms of entertainment in restaurants include live music, display kitchens, video or board games, cooking classes, and cigar rooms.

ty is a popular business trend; choose one that is consistent with your image and not controversial.

To appeal to parents, a family restaurant may provide crayons, coloring books, balloons, or toys for children; be sure each carries your logo and basic marketing message, and has been chosen with safety in mind.

Make Your Grand Opening Grand

You should actually open for business a few weeks *before* your grand opening. This "soft opening" gives you a chance to get things arranged properly in your facility and train your employees. At the time of your soft opening, you should have your business sign(s) up and most or all of your inventory in stock. Customers will wander in, and if they are pleased with your business, they will start spreading the word. As both a soft opening exercise and marketing technique, one pizzeria distributed coupons for free pizzas in its target delivery area, explaining on the coupon that the restaurant was in the soft opening phase and that the coupons were good for a specific day and time only.

Use every possible means to attract customers during your grand opening. Have daily drawings for door prizes such as free meals or a free dessert with a meal purchase. Keep liberal supplies of promotional flyers (perhaps with first-purchase discount coupons), business cards, gift certificates, and specialty advertising items in the restaurant. Complimentary coffee, refreshments, and food samples will add to the excitement. You might even consider throwing a party and inviting local dignitaries and celebrities. Whatever you do, open your food-service business with a huge splash.

Look for Marketing Opportunities

Marketing opportunities are often where you least expect them, and it pays to pay attention. Maxine T. saw her deli business decrease sharply when the road in front of her building was under construction one summer. "It was very hot, so we put out a flier to all of the businesses here in our own complex and all around us, targeting all the people who come into our deli but who were frustrated because the construction made it difficult for them to get here," she recalls. "We did a 'beat the heat, beat the construction, bring a friend,

Bright Idea

Promote holidays that are not necessarily recognized as popular restaurant holidays. For example, Maxine T. promotes a Halloween menu in her deli and catering operation and is seeing a significant increase in the number of clients using her for that holiday.

Smart Tip

Coupons are among the most popular marketing tools food-service businesses use. You can include coupons with any print media or direct-mail advertisements you produce. Direct-mail advertising uses computer-selected mailing lists and blanket mailings to entire ZIP codes to distribute fliers, coupon mailers, and other advertisements. Special mailing rates make this a highly effective, low-cost medium.

and have lunch on us' campaign. It was a two-for-one promotion—just a reminder that we are here and serving the community. Our business increased by 30 percent immediately, and it was amazing to see how many people came in without the two-for-one card."

Maxine also pays close attention to what's going on in the offices around her store. "If someone is moving in, we send them a little complimentary lunch to introduce ourselves and to welcome them to our business community," she says. "We try to do anything we can to put our name in front of people."

Rebecca S. looks for ways to tie other events into dinner at her restaurant. For example, she offers a Theater Plus Dinner package that includes a multicourse gourmet dinner, tickets to a show, and transportation—typically in a small bus or van—from her restaurant to the civic center or downtown

Today's Specials

Let your customers gamble for a free meal. Keep a set of dice by the cash register, and put up a few signs that read:

Win a FREE meal today!
Roll the dice and win!
Two sixes—your meal is free!
Two fives—take 55% off
Two fours—take 44% off
Two threes—take 33% off
Two twos—take 22% off
Two ones—11% off

If you calculate the odds, the total discounts work out to an average of 1.2 percent on each order. But the contest produces excitement, and when someone wins a free meal, your cost is minimal, but the word-of-mouth advertising is priceless. Besides, the winner is likely to come in with at least one friend to claim his or her prize.

theater and back. "Parking is always a problem downtown, and dining there is also a problem," she says. "We always get great seats for the show, they have a wonderful meal with us, and they meet other people and make new friends. It's a fabulous package."

Public Relations and Promotions

An easy way to promote your food-service business is by giving away gift certificates—such as dinner for two, coffee, and bagels for ten or a free pizza. Call local radio stations that reach the demographics of your target market and ask to speak to their promotions manager. Offer to provide gift certificates or coupons to use as prizes for on-air contests and promotions. Your company name and location will be announced several times on the air during the contest, providing you with valuable, free exposure, and it's always possible that the winner will become a paying customer.

You can also donate coupons and gift certificates to be used as door prizes at professional meetings or for nonprofit organizations to use as raffle prizes. Just be sure every coupon or gift certificate clearly identifies your business name, location, hours of operation, and any restrictions on the prize.

Make being active in the community part of your overall marketing strategy. "You have to leave your store to bring people in," says Rebecca S. Get out and be visible, and people will follow you back to your business.

Some other promotional methods you can try include:

- *Gift certificates.* Gift certificates are convenient for gift-giving, especially around holidays. Current customers may give gift certificates to friends or relatives who have never tried your restaurant. Employers may give gift certificates as employee incentives. Many people will gladly try a new eating establishment for a free meal. If you give them good food and service, they'll happily return as paying customers.

- *Sponsorships.* By sponsoring a local event or sports team, you can put your restaurant's name in front of a whole new group of customers. Your name will appear on advertisements promoting the event or on team members' uniforms. This constant exposure will keep your name in customers' minds. Because people are typically drawn to establishments they are familiar with, you may attract customers who have never visited your restaurant but feel familiar with it due to the exposure from your sponsorship.

- *Discount coupon books.* Many communities have companies that produce books of coupons for participating businesses that schools and nonprofit organizations sell as fund-raisers. As with gift certificates, many people will try a new

Time for a Makeover

Maintaining a consistent marketing message is an ongoing effort. In the craziness of dealing with deliveries that don't arrive on time, cooks who don't show up, and servers who drop trays of food on their way out of the kitchen, it's easy to overlook a messy parking lot or a faded poster—so schedule a regular checkup of your facility. At least once a year, step back and look at your restaurant through the eyes of someone who has never eaten there.

Answer these questions during your annual image overhaul:

○ What are the most recent demographics of your trading area?

○ What is the profile of your target market?

○ Is your parking lot clean, easily accessible, well-marked, and well-lighted for safety and comfort?

○ Are your exterior signs in good condition and easy to read?

○ Is your waste disposal equipment visible and, if so, how does the area look and smell?

○ Is your flooring clean and in good condition?

○ Are your restrooms clean and functioning properly?

○ Do your restrooms provide adequate accommodations for your target market—such as diaper-changing stations, lighted vanities, telephones, vending machines with personal products, etc.?

○ Are your menus clean, attractive, readable, and designed for your target market?

○ Do all of your promotional materials—including banners, in-house signs, table tents, menu inserts, etc.—clearly identify your restaurant and share a common theme?

○ Do the photographs on your walls, menu boards, and pass-out menus reflect what you are offering?

○ Do your posters and signs look fresh, new, and appetizing?

○ Are your ads easily recognizable with art and copy that appeal to your target market?

establishment if they know they're getting a significant discount, and they'll return as full-paying customers if you give them good food and service.

- *Frequent-dining clubs.* Reward your regular customers with free food. For example, you can issue a card with 12 spaces so you can mark off each visit; when the customer has purchased 12 entrees, give him or her a free entree.

- *Menu promotions.* By offering regular lunch or dinner specials, you can appeal to those who are on a limited budget or who just like saving money. You can also offer early-bird specials (typically dinner at a discounted price, usually from 4 to 6 P.M.), or two-for-one specials during certain periods. These specials not only attract customers but can also help you reduce your inventory of over-stocked items.

- *Contests.* The most common restaurant contest involves placing a fish bowl (or other glass container) near the cash register where patrons can drop their business card for a drawing for a free lunch or dinner. The winners may bring along friends when they come in for their free meal. Also, the cards give you a list of customers to use for direct mail campaigns.

Be Media Savvy

When your name is mentioned in the newspaper and on local radio and television broadcasts, it means one of two things: Either you've done something wrong and gotten caught, or you have a strong, positive relationship with the local media. Assuming that you're going to work hard to avoid the former, here are some tips for achieving the latter:

- *Build a media list.* Find out the names of local journalists who might include you in a story; this would include the food and business editors and reporters at your local newspaper, and the feature editors and reporters at television stations. Make a list of these people, and then call them and find out how they would like to receive information from you. Be brief and professional; simply say, "I have a [description] business, and I'd like to send you periodic news releases. How do you prefer to receive that information?" Typically, they'll want it by regular mail, e-mail, or fax.

> **Bright Idea**
> Take professional photos of yourself and your operation so you have them available to provide to publications that may write articles about your establishment. That way you can control the quality and image that goes into print. Also, many local publications are on limited budgets and cannot afford to send a photographer out but will use photos you provide.

- *Make your news releases newsworthy.* Avoid news releases that are obvious bids for self-promotion. Your releases should have a news "hook"; the person reading the release should have a clear answer to the question, "So what?" You can tie your releases into a national event or a holiday to provide a local connection.

- *Be available as a local expert.* Let your media contacts know you can be counted on as a local expert. For example, if a national wholesale food supplier has a problem with contaminated products, offer to be a resource for a feature on what local food-service operations can do to protect the health and safety of their customers.

- *Take media calls immediately and return them promptly.* Reporters are usually on tight deadlines; when they call, they need to talk to you right away. If you're not available, they'll find someone who is—and that's who they'll call next time.

- *Only give away compliments.* If a reporter does a particularly good story, either about your operation or the industry in general, write them a brief note letting them know you appreciate their work. But never send gifts or food; most reporters are not allowed to accept them, and you'll only create an awkward situation.

Trade Shows

In addition to attending trade shows to find merchandise and learn more about running your business, consider exhibiting in trade shows to market your business. Local trade shows can provide a tremendous amount of exposure at a very affordable cost.

There are two types of shows—consumer (which focus on home, garden, and other consumer themes) and business-to-business (where exhibitors market their products and services to other companies). Both can work for a food-service business.

"When you go to a show, you're tapping into an audience that is typically outside your network," says trade show consultant Allen Konopacki. "The other important thing is that the individuals who are going to shows are usually driven by a need. In fact, 76 percent of the people who go to a show are looking to make some kind of a decision on a purchase in the near future."

To find out about local shows in your area, call your local chamber of commerce or convention center and ask for a calendar. You can also check out *Trade Show Week Show Directory*, which should be available in your public library, or do an Internet search.

When you've identified potential shows, contact the sponsors for details. Find out who will attend—show sponsors should be able to estimate the total number and give you demographics so you can tell if the attendees fit your target market profile.

Give as much thought to the setup of your booth as you did to the design of your facility. Your exhibit does not need to be elaborate or expensive, but it does need to be professional and inviting. Avoid trying to cram so much into your booth that it

Trade Secrets

Trade shows and conventions are valuable business tools, whether you're attending to shop and learn or exhibiting to get more business. For more information on how to get more out of trade shows, and to find show schedules, visit these trade show Web sites: Incomm Research Center, www.tradeshowresearch.com; Trade Show Central, www.tscentral.com; Trade Show News Network, www.tsnn.com; and Tradeshow Week On-Line, www.tradeshowweek.com.

looks cluttered. If possible and appropriate, bring food samples, but be sure they can be properly stored at correct temperatures to avoid the risk of contamination.

Your signage should focus first on the problems you solve for clients, then list your company name. For example, if you operate a coffeehouse, the prominent words on your booth signage might be "Great Coffee and Entertainment," and then your establishment's name.

Even though the show sponsors may provide one, do not put a table across the front of your exhibit space; that creates a visual and psychological barrier and will discourage visitors from coming in.

Don't leave your booth unattended during exhibit hours. First, it's a security risk—during a busy show, it would be easy for someone to walk off with valuable merchandise. More important, you could miss a tremendous sales opportunity.

Consider some sort of giveaway item such as pens, mugs, or notepads imprinted with your company name. But, says Konopacki, do not display these items openly; that will only crowd your booth with "trade show tourists" who are not really prospective customers. Instead, store them discreetly out of sight, and present them individually as appropriate. You should also have a stock of brochures, business cards, and perhaps discount coupons.

Financial
Management

There are two key sides to the issue of money: How much do you need to start and operate, and how much can you expect to take in. Doing this analysis is often extremely difficult for small-business owners who would rather be in the trenches getting the work done than bound to a desk dealing with tiresome numbers. But force yourself to do it anyway.

One of the primary indicators of the overall health of your business is its financial status, and it's important that you monitor your financial progress closely. The only way you can do that is to keep good records. There are a number of excellent computer accounting programs on the market; another option is to handle the process manually. You might want to ask your accountant for assistance getting your system set up. The key is to do that from the very beginning and keep your records current and accurate throughout the life of your company.

Keeping good records helps generate the financial statements that tell you exactly where you stand and what you need to do next. The key financial statements you need to understand and use regularly are:

- *Profit and loss statement* (also called the P&L or the income statement), which illustrates how much your company is making or losing over a designated period—monthly, quarterly, or annually—by subtracting expenses from revenue to arrive at a net result, which is either a profit or a loss.

Beware!
Don't even think about inflating your financial statements to cover a lack of references. This is a felony, and it's easily detected by most credit managers.

- *Balance sheet*, which is a table showing your assets, liabilities, and capital at a specific point. A balance sheet is typically generated monthly, quarterly, or annually when the books are closed.

The Tax Man Cometh

Businesses are required to pay a wide range of taxes, and there are no exceptions for food-service business owners. Keep good records so you can offset your local, state, and federal income taxes with the expenses of operating your company. If you sell retail, you'll probably be required by your state to charge and collect sales tax. If you have employees, you'll be responsible for payroll taxes. If you operate as a corporation, you'll have to pay payroll taxes for yourself; as a sole proprietor, you'll pay self-employment tax. Then there are property taxes, taxes on your equipment and inventory, fees and taxes to maintain your corporate status, your business license fee (which is really a tax), and other lesser-known taxes. Take the time to review all of your tax liabilities with your accountant.

- *Cash flow statement*, which summarizes the operating, investing, and financing activities of your business as they relate to the inflow and outflow of cash. As with the profit and loss statement, a cash flow statement is prepared to reflect a specific accounting period, such as monthly, quarterly, or annually.

Successful food-service business owners review these reports regularly, at least monthly, so they always know where they stand and can quickly correct minor difficulties before they become major financial problems. If you wait until November to figure out whether or not you made a profit last February, you won't be in business long.

Sources of Start-Up Funds

How much money you need to start depends on the type of business, the facility, how much equipment you need, whether you buy new or used, your inventory, marketing, and necessary operating capital (the amount of cash you need on hand to carry you until your business starts generating cash). It's easy to spend hundreds of thousands of dollars starting a restaurant. By contrast, when Jim A. started his first bakery in Maine, he rented a space that had been a commercial bakery and was complete with mixers, benches, ovens, and other equipment. He was able to start with just $10,000 he borrowed from family and friends and used that primarily on inventory. Or you can probably start a coffee cart for $15,000 to $20,000.

Regardless of how much, you *will* need cash to start your food-service business. Here are some suggestions of where to go to raise your start-up funds:

- *Your own resources.* Do a thorough inventory of your assets. People generally have more assets than they realize. This could include savings accounts, equity in real estate, retirement accounts, vehicles, recreation equipment, collections, and other investments. You may opt to sell assets for cash, or use them as collateral for a loan. Take a look, too, at your personal line of credit. Many a successful business has been started with credit cards.

- *Family and friends.* The logical next step after gathering your own resources is to approach friends and relatives who believe in you and want to help you succeed. Be cautious with these arrangements; no matter how close you are, present yourself professionally, put everything in writing, and be sure the individuals you approach can afford to take the risk of investing in your business.

- *Partners.* Using the "strength in numbers" principle, look around for someone who may want to team up with you in your venture. You may choose someone who has financial resources and wants to work side-by-side with you in the business. Or you may find someone who has money to invest but no interest in doing the actual work. Be sure to create a written partnership agreement that clearly defines your respective responsibilities and obligations.

Cold, Hard Cash

If you think finding start-up funds is difficult, be prepared: Finding money to fund expansion after you're up and running can be even more challenging. "As hard as it is to open, it's almost harder to get second-tier financing," says West Des Moines, Iowa, restaurateur/caterer/retailer/wholesaler Rebecca S.

The real difficulty will come when you're trying to make the first expansion. That's a time when your personal resources are most likely stretched to the limit, and most of your assets are already pledged as collateral. But, says Rebecca, if you can hang in there and continue building a profitable operation, "You'll reach a point where people are throwing money at you."

But just because lenders want you to borrow from them doesn't mean you should. "There's always a price to money," Rebecca points out. Sometimes it's simply the interest you'll have to pay; sometimes it's something else. For example, you may find someone who wants to invest in your business, but the money will come with strings—such as this person wanting to take an active role in managing the operation, and you don't agree on strategies and methods. His daughter may have just graduated from culinary school or his wife has always wanted to run a bakery, and you end up with employees you didn't bargain for and are having trouble working with.

If someone expresses an interest in investing in your business, find out what their motives are. Are they looking for a job for their spouse or kids? Are they looking for a place they can bring their friends to eat for free and show off? Or do they simply see a good investment opportunity? Says Rebecca, "Make sure you understand what you're getting into."

- *Government programs.* Take advantage of the abundance of local, state, and federal programs designed to support small businesses. Make your first stop the U.S. Small Business Administration; then investigate various other programs. Women, minorities, and veterans should check out niche financing possibilities designed to help them get into business. The business section of your local library is a good place to begin your research.

Billing

If you're extending credit to your customers—and it's likely you will if you have corporate accounts, especially if you're a bakery or in the catering business—you need to establish and follow sound billing procedures.

Coordinate your billing system with your customers' payable procedures. Candidly ask what you can do to ensure prompt payment; that may include confirming the correct billing address and finding out what documentation may be required to help the customer determine the validity of the invoice. Keep in mind that many large companies pay certain types of invoices on certain days of the month; find out if your customers do that, and schedule your invoices to arrive in time for the next payment cycle.

Smart Tip

Tip...

If possible, bill on delivery. That's when the appreciation of your work is highest; when customers are thinking about you in a positive way, they're more likely to process your invoice faster.

Most computer bookkeeping software programs include basic invoices. If you design your own invoices and statements, be sure they're clear and easy to understand. Detail each item and indicate the amount due in bold with the words "Please pay" in front of the total. A confusing invoice may be set aside for clarification, and your payment will be delayed.

Beware!

Including fliers or brochures with your invoices is a great marketing tool, but remember that adding an insert may cause the envelope to require extra postage. Certainly getting out the marketing message is probably well worth the extra few cents in mailing costs; just be sure you check the total weight before you mail so your invoices aren't returned to you for insufficient postage—or worse, delivered "postage due."

Finally, use your invoices as marketing tools. Print reminders of upcoming specials or new products on them. Add a flier or brochure to the envelope—even though the invoice is going to an existing customer, you never know where your brochures will end up.

Setting Credit Policies

When you extend credit to someone, you are essentially providing them with an interest-free loan. You wouldn't expect someone to lend you money without getting information from you about where you live and work and your potential ability to repay. It just makes sense to get this information from someone you are lending money to.

Reputable companies will not object to providing you with credit information or even paying a deposit on large orders. If you don't feel comfortable asking for at least part of the money upfront, just think how uncomfortable you'll feel if you deliver an expensive order and don't get paid at all. The business owners we talked to all agreed they felt awkward asking for deposits—until they got burned the first time.

Certainly extending credit involves some risk, but the advantages of judiciously granted credit far outweigh the potential losses. Extending credit promotes customer loyalty. People will call you over a competitor because they already have an account set up and it's easy for them. Customers also often spend money more easily when they don't have to pay cash. Finally, if you ever decide to sell your business, it will have a greater value because you can show steady accounts.

Typically, you will only extend credit to commercial accounts. Individuals will likely pay cash (or by check) at the time of purchase, or use a credit card. You need to decide how much risk you are willing to take by setting limits on how much credit you will allow each account.

Your credit policy should include a clear collection strategy. Do not ignore overdue bills; the older a bill gets, the less likely it will ever be paid. Be prepared to take action on past-due accounts as soon as they become past-due.

> **Tip...**
>
> **Smart Tip**
> Check the account status when taking an order from a customer on open credit. If the account is past-due or the balance is unusually high, you may want to negotiate different terms before increasing the amount owed.

Red Flags

Even though a customer passed your first credit check with flying colors, that doesn't mean you should never re-evaluate his or her credit status—in fact, you should do it on a regular basis.

Tell customers when you initially grant their credit applications that you have a policy of periodically reviewing accounts so when you do it, it's not a surprise. Remember, things can change very quickly in the business world, and a company that is on sound financial footing this year may be quite wobbly next year.

An annual re-evaluation of all customers on open account is a good idea—but if you start to see trouble in the interim, don't wait to take action. Another time to re-evaluate a customer's credit is when they request an increase in their credit line.

Some key trouble signs are a slow-down in payments, increased returns, and difficulty getting answers to your payment inquiries. Even a sharp increase in ordering could signal trouble; companies concerned that they may lose their credit privileges may try to stock up while they can. Pay attention to what your customers are doing; a major change in their customer base or product line is something you may want to monitor.

Take the same approach to a credit review that you do to a new credit application. Most of the time, you can use what you have on file to conduct the check, but if you're concerned for any reason, you may want to ask the customer for updated information.

Most customers will understand routine credit reviews and accept them as a sound business practice. A customer who objects may well have something to hide—and that's something you need to know.

Accepting Credit and Debit Cards

Unless you are exclusively wholesale, most food-service businesses need to be able to accept credit and debit cards. It's much easier now to get merchant status than it has been in the past; in fact, these days merchant status providers are competing aggressively for your business.

To get a credit card merchant account, start with your own bank. Also check with various professional associations that offer merchant status as a member benefit. Shop around; this is a competitive industry, and it's worth taking the time to get the best deal.

Accepting Checks

Because losses for retailers from bad checks amount to more than $1 billion annually, many restaurants do not accept checks.

If you choose to accept checks, look for several key items. Make sure the check is drawn on a local bank. Check the date for accuracy. Do not accept a check that is undated, postdated, or more than 30 days old. Be sure the written amount and numerical amount agree.

Post your check-cashing procedures in a highly visible place. Most customers are aware of the bad-check problem and are willing to follow your rules. If your customers don't know what your rules are until they reach the cash register, however, you may annoy them when, for example, you ask for two forms of identification before accepting a check.

Bright Idea

Consider putting an ATM in your facility. Your customers will appreciate the convenience of a safe place to get cash, and the machine can also generate income for you in the form of transaction surcharges.

Your main reason for asking for identification is so you can locate the customer in case you have a problem with the check. The most valid and valuable piece of identification is a driver's license. In most states, this will include the driver's picture, signature, and address. If the signature, address, and name agree with what is printed on the check, you are probably safe. If the information does not agree, ask which is accurate and record that information on the check.

You can get insurance against bad checks. Typically, a check-reporting service charges a fee for check verification, usually 4 to 6 percent of the face value of the check, depending on the volume of checks you send through the system. If you called in a $60 check, for example, the service would cost you $2.40. If you weigh that charge against the possibility of losing the entire $60, the service has merit.

If you do not use a check-verification system, you should ask for a second piece of identification, such as a check-guarantee card, a bank card, or other identification. Retail merchants' associations often provide lists of stolen driver's licenses and credit cards, so if you are dealing with a customer you don't know, you should check the list.

You might want to check out the latest in point-of-sale check readers; they will significantly speed up the amount of time it takes to accept a check from a customer.

Dealing with Your Own Creditors

Most business start-up advice focuses on dealing with your customers, but you're also going to become a customer for your suppliers. That means you'll have to pay for what you buy. Find out in advance what your suppliers' credit policies are. Most will accept credit cards but will not put you on an open account until they've had a chance to run a check on you. If you open an account with a supplier, be sure you understand their terms and preserve your credit standing by paying on time. Typically, you'll have 30 days to pay, but many companies offer a discount if you pay early.

Hold the Line on Costs

When you think about how to improve your bottom-line profit, your first thought is probably to increase sales. An equally important and often easier route to greater

Dollar Stretcher

Ask suppliers if payment terms can be part of your price negotiation. For example, can you get a discount for paying cash in advance?

profitability comes from reducing costs. David Cohen, president of Expense Reduction Group Inc. in Boca Raton, Florida, offers this illustration: Your restaurant generates $1 million a year in sales at a net profit margin of 10 percent. Reduce expenses by $5,000, and you have accomplished the same bottom-line result as you would had you increased sales by $50,000. Cohen asks, "What's easier—finding $50,000 worth of new business or trimming costs by $5,000?"

The first step in a cost reduction program is to identify the purchases that represent the greatest opportunity for savings. Typically, Cohen says, these are the items that are purchased repetitively in sizable quantities.

"Run a vendor report to identify the larger suppliers and to see whether there is any correlation in product purchases from one supplier to another," Cohen advises. Though many business owners believe using multiple sources for the same item keeps vendors honest, he disagrees. "If you're buying the same product from more than one supplier, consolidating those purchases with a single source will give you the opportunity to take advantage of quantity discounts and also earn you more negotiating strength with the vendor you choose."

Keep seasonal price fluctuations and availability in mind. A restaurant owner in North Carolina buys seafood in bulk when prices are down and freezes it for later use. She also buys dry goods in bulk and stores them.

If you are buying multiple products from a single source, consider whether or not you would be better off taking some of those purchases to a specialty vendor, which may offer better pricing. Cohen says segregating specific paper products and purchasing them at lower prices from specialty paper companies is a good example of how this can work.

Be sure the products you buy are the most appropriate and cost-effective for your needs. It's often worthwhile to spend more money for a higher-quality cleaning or paper product because it does a better job or lasts longer. You may spend more per unit, but less overall.

Regardless of how good your vendor relationships are, Cohen recommends an annual review of your overall purchasing process. "Put your major product purchases out for bid every year," he says. "Let two or three companies, plus your current vendor, bid on your business. If your current vendor is giving you good service and pricing, they should have nothing to fear. If they're treating you fairly, stay with them—don't change for the sake of change. But if they've gotten greedy or careless, they're going to get caught." The idea is to build loyalty but keep vendors on their toes. The way to keep vendors from becoming complacent about your business is to not be complacent yourself.

Set up an internal system to stay on top of rebates and manufacturer promotions. A lot of items have rebates with deadlines that are easy to overlook. Also, manufacturers might have end-of-year surpluses that will let you pick up a little extra quantity at a substantial savings.

Throughout the year, look to your vendors for co-op promotional support. If you're going to run a special of some sort, you can generally get co-op funds in the way of either a price reduction on the product, rebates, or even free products.

Once you reach an agreement on a purchase, follow up to make sure your invoices actually reflect the stipulated terms and that the arithmetic is accurate. Beyond the actual dollars involved, check the product itself. Weigh what is sold by weight; count what is sold by unit.

Be aware of the details of your contracts. Some business owners automatically renew; be smart and review the terms and consider renegotiating before that happens. Many have escalator clauses that increase prices; again, this is a point for serious negotiation.

> Set up an internal system to stay on top of rebates and manufacturer promotions.

Shopping for Vendors

The process of putting purchases out for bid is not complicated, but it does take some thought. Use a written request for proposal (RFP) that clearly defines your parameters. The RFP (or request for quote, RFQ) forces you to document your criteria and address all your needs, while also allowing you to make a more accurate comparison of vendors because everyone is responding to the same information. Formalizing your purchasing process in this manner also strengthens your own negotiating position because it lets vendors know you understand and are committed to using professional procurement procedures.

Evaluate each vendor on quality, service, and price. Look at the product itself, as well as the supplementary services and support the company provides. Confirm that the vendor has the resources to meet your needs from both a production and delivery perspective. Remember, a great product at a good price doesn't mean anything if the vendor can't produce enough or is unable to get it to you on time.

Verify the company's claims before making a purchase commitment. Ask for references and do a credit check on the vendor—just as the vendor will probably do on you. Product and service claims can be verified through references. You can confirm the company's general reputation and financial stability by calling the Better Business Bureau, any appropriate licensing agencies, trade associations, and Dun & Bradstreet.

A credit check will tell you how well the supplier you're going to be using pays their suppliers. This is important because it could ultimately affect you. If your vendor is not paying his own vendors, he may have trouble getting raw materials, and that may delay delivery on your order. Or he may simply go out of business without any advance notice, leaving you in a lurch.

Know Your Negotiating Points

As you negotiate your vendor agreements, consider the cost of the item itself; the quantity discounts; add-ons such as freight and insurance; and the payment terms. To determine the true value of a quantity discount, calculate how long you can expect to have the material on hand and what your cost of carrying that inventory is. Quantity discounts are often available if you make a long-term purchase commitment, which may also allow you to lock in prices on volatile commodities.

In many cases, payment terms are an important consideration. Some vendors offer substantial discounts for early payment; others will extend amounts to an interest-free, short-term loan by offering lengthier terms.

Freight is an excellent and often overlooked negotiating point. If you're paying the freight, you should be selecting the carrier and negotiating the rates. If the vendor is delivering on their own trucks, you can negotiate the delivery fee as part of your overall price.

Every element of the sale is open for negotiation. At all stages of the process, leave room for some give and take. For example, if you are asking for a lower price or more liberal payment terms, can you agree to a more relaxed delivery schedule?

Finalize the Deal in Writing

Contracts are an excellent way to make sure both you and the vendor are clear on the details of the sale. This is not "just a formality" that can be brushed aside. Read all agreements and support documents carefully, and consider having them reviewed by an attorney. Make sure everything that's important to you is in writing. Remember, if it's not part of the contract, it's not part of the deal—no matter what the salesperson says. And if it's in the contract, it's probably enforceable.

Any contract the vendor writes is naturally going to favor the vendor, but you don't have to agree to all the standard "boilerplate" terms. In addition, you can demand the inclusion of details that are appropriate to your specific situation. Here's some advice on contracts:

- *Make standard provisions apply to both parties.* If, for example, the contract exempts the supplier from specific liabilities, request that the language be revised to exempt you, too.
- *Use precise language.* It's difficult to enforce vague language, so be specific. A clause that states the vendor is not responsible for failures due to causes "beyond the vendor's control" leaves a lot of room for interpretation; more precise language forces a greater level of accountability.
- *Include a "vendor default" provision.* The vendor's contract probably describes the circumstances under which you would be considered to be in default; include the same protection for yourself.
- *Be wary of supplier representatives who have to get any contract changes approved by "corporate" or some other higher authority.* This is a negotiating technique that generally works against the customer. Insist that the vendor make personnel with the authority to negotiate available.

Finally, Cohen advises including an escape clause. "If you are not pleased with the quality and service levels, you want a way to get out of the contract. You also need to know if there are any other circumstances that could release either party from the agreement, and what the liability is." In any case, don't substitute an escape clause for thorough and careful vendor selection.

Tales from the Trenches

By now, you should know how to get started and have a good idea of what to do—and not to do—in your own food-service business. But nothing teaches as well as the voice of experience. So we asked established food-service business operators to tell us what has contributed to their success and what they think causes some companies to fail. Here are their stories:

▲

Do Basic Market Research

When Jim A. decided to start a wholesale bakery specializing in sourdough bread, no one else was doing anything similar in Maine. To find out if there was a market for the breads he wanted to bake, he called restaurants and retailers, explained his idea, and asked if they'd be interested in buying his breads. "I came up with about 15 accounts that said they would be interested," he says. And that was enough to get him started.

Provide Employees with Feedback and Recognition

Employees need to know how they're doing—both good and bad—and that their contributions are appreciated. "Our employees know they are coming to a job where a certain level of professionalism is expected, and in return, they are treated as professionals," says Jim A. Managers provide regular verbal feedback, both for jobs well done and when improvement is necessary. "We also do a lot of off-the-cuff stuff," Jim says. "If somebody has done a really good job at something, we might give them a gift certificate to go out to dinner or something like that. We also have company events where we all go bowling or sailing."

Caterer Ann C. says she makes it a point to pass along customer compliments immediately. When a customer calls to praise a staff member, she immediately contacts that staff person and relays the comments. When customers write positive letters, they are also shared with staffers.

It's often just a matter of treating your employees the way you'd like to be treated, says Robert O. "Most people don't even say 'thank you' in today's world. They take the simplest things for granted. You've got to pay people competitively, but you also have to tell them you appreciate them and don't belittle them," he says. "If you treat people how you want to be treated, most of them will treat you the same way."

Rebecca S. sees employees as another market you have to please. "In a way, employees are like customers," she says. "There has to be mutual respect."

Michael G. says that in addition to individual feedback, it helps to give your staff the opportunity to discuss problems and possible solutions as a group. Even after a situation has been resolved, you can use those circumstances as a training tool, letting employees talk about how a better resolution could have been achieved and what can be done to prevent a reoccurrence of a problem.

Find Your Market Niche and Stay Focused

Jim A. says one of the key things he's done that has contributed to his success is finding a market niche that no other baker occupies. "We've positioned ourselves as having a unique product. We don't have a lot of competitors, and that has allowed us to maintain fairly high wholesale prices."

Though Rebecca S.'s company provides a wide range of food service-related products and services, they are all focused on pasta. "We have been asked to do a lot of things that are very far off of our path," Rebecca says. "We think the way to survive is to become an expert in something. We've seen places that go too far out on a limb from their core business and get lost, and then they can't be distinguished from others in the marketplace."

Get It in Writing

If you're in the catering or wholesale food business, never assume you have an order until you have a signed contract or purchase order. Caterer Ann C. recalls making a bid on a very upscale party. It was a new client, and she had taken her art director and florist with her to meet with the client—and they all left with the impression that they had the job. But the client was accepting bids from three other caterers. Don't take anything for granted; find out who you're competing against and when you can expect a final decision. And don't buy any supplies or materials until you have a signed contract and a deposit.

Give Back to the Community

Baker Jim A. encourages his employees to do volunteer work in the community by paying them for up to three hours of volunteer work (at their regular pay rate) each month. Caterer Ann C. is a strong believer in giving back to the community and serves on a variety of nonprofit boards. She says it opens her up to being asked to provide food at a discount, but it also exposes her to potential customers. "One of the more positive things that has come from volunteering is when I have underwritten a party for a nonprofit organization, the people who attend are the same people I want to taste my food, and the word-of-mouth benefit from that has been substantial."

At Rebecca S.'s gourmet pasta shop and restaurant, all tips are donated to charity. The business does not provide table service, and employees are not dependent on tips for income, but customers frequently leave gratuities behind. The tips are collected, and at the end of each month the employees choose what organization gets the money.

Don't Take Your Eyes off the Business

Marie H., owner of a chain of barbecue restaurants in California, says you can never stop running your restaurants, no matter how big you get. As your company grows, and especially if you eventually want to go public, it's easy to get distracted by financial issues and stock prices. But if you lose sight of your primary purpose, which is running your food-service business and satisfying your customers, you'll end up in trouble.

Don't Go It Alone

Take advantage of all the experience and information that is available to you. "The biggest mistake I made was thinking I could invent this business from the ground up by myself," says coffeehouse founder Phyllis J. "There is a wealth of information out there on how to run a restaurant, no matter which part of the business you're in. A lot of what is true in one food-service business applies to another. I would have been much better off if I had brought people into my organization early who had previous restaurant experience."

Keep Customer Requests in Perspective

Certainly providing outstanding customer service is a worthwhile goal, but you won't be able to meet every single customer request. Trying to do so will stretch your resources to an unmanageable point. As an example, Phyllis J. says, if a few people want you to extend your hours, you have to be able to generate enough business to cover the additional overhead and make a profit, or it's not worth doing. Or if a few customers ask for certain products, be sure the overall demand is strong enough to make purchasing those items worthwhile. Phyllis says a few people have asked her to carry goat's milk and soy milk, but in her market, stocking those milks would not be profitable. But years ago, when customers began asking for skim milk, she realized that the market was strong enough to justify adjusting her inventory.

Test Your Real Market

When Anthony A. opened his first pizzeria, he did some market testing of various dough recipes. "One of my test batches was a Portuguese sweetbread dough recipe, and I happened to do my test-marketing on a night that all of the high school kids were coming out of a basketball game," he recalls. "They all loved the sweet dough, so I made that my dough." But high school kids were not his primary market, and his older patrons didn't care for the sweet dough at all.

Be sure when you are test-marketing that you conduct your tests on sample groups that truly represent the market you plan to target. And remember that many people will compliment free food because they think it's the polite thing to do. So ask questions that will get you information that you can work with. It's not enough for people to say they like something; find out why they like it, if there's anything they don't like, if there's anything they would change, and if they'd be willing to buy it.

Choose Your Partners Carefully

Because of the financial investment most food-service businesses require, many people opt to form partnerships to raise the capital. Be very cautious if these partners are friends or family members. "When you go into business with a friend or family member, it really changes the relationship," says Michael G. "Sometimes you find out that you can't stay friends." Don't assume that just because you like someone that you can run a business together. Draw up a detailed partnership agreement, and be sure you're clear on your mutual goals and working styles.

Similarly, be careful when you hire friends and family to work for you. Draw a clear line between your professional and personal relationships, and understand that you may be risking the relationship if the job doesn't work out.

Watch What You Say—and Who You Say It To

Food service is a stressful business, and it's easy to get frustrated with customers who are overly demanding or who want you to do things their way when yours is better. But no matter how you feel, be careful what you say and who can hear it.

Michael G. tells this story on himself: Years ago, he was running a private club and dealing with a particularly difficult client who was planning a private party. The client represented a significant amount of business, but the contact person was asking for a physical layout that was not efficient or effective, refusing to listen to advice, making extensive menu revisions, and in general being extraordinarily irritating.

One day, a messenger arrived with an envelope from the client. Thinking that the delivery person was with an independent service, when Michael accepted the envelope, he muttered, "What is she bothering me with now?" It turned out the messenger was an employee of the client, and Michael's remarks and attitude were promptly conveyed back to the decision maker. And to make matters worse, the envelope contained a check. He apologized, the account was saved, and a valuable lesson was learned.

No Negatives

Michael G. points out that a basic rule of salesmanship is to never ask a question the prospect can answer with "No." He likes to take the technique a step further. "We don't want a customer to ask a question we have to say 'no' to. Even if they are asking for something they cannot get, don't tell them 'I can't do that.' Instead, tell them what you can do," he says.

Appendix
Restaurant Resources

They say you can never be too rich or too young. While these could be argued, we believe "You can never have too many resources." Therefore, we present for your consideration a wealth of sources for you to check into, check out, and harness for your own personal information blitz.

These sources are tidbits, ideas to get you started on your research. They are by no means the only sources out there, and they should not be taken as the Ultimate Answer. We have done our research, but businesses—like patients—do tend to move, change, fold, and expand. As we have repeatedly stressed, do your homework. Get out and start investigating.

As an additional tidbit to get you going, we strongly suggest the following: If you haven't yet joined the Internet Age, do it! Surfing the Net is like waltzing through a library, with a breathtaking array of resources literally at your fingertips.

Associations

Bakery-Net, the professional baker's online magazine: www. bakery-net.com

Coffee Science Source, Web site created by the National Coffee Association: 110 Wall St., New York, NY 10005, info@coffeescience.org, www.coffeescience.org

Coffee Universe, (800) 655-3955, www.coffeeuniverse.com

Hospitality Business Alliance, 250 S. Wacker Dr., #1400, Chicago, IL 60606, (800) 765-2122, ext. 340.

International Dairy-Deli-Bakery Association, 313 Price Pl., #202, Madison, WI 53705-0528, (608) 238-7908, fax: (608) 238-6330.

National Academy Foundation, 235 Park Ave. South, 7th Floor, New York, NY 10003, (212) 420-8400, fax: (212) 475-7375, www.naf-education.org

National Association of Pizza Operators, 137 E. Market St., New Albany, IN 47150, (812) 949-0909, fax: (812) 941-9711, www.napo.com

National Barbecue Association, P.O. Box 9685, Kansas City, MO 64134-9865, (816) 767-8311, fax: (816) 765-5860, www.ribman.com/nbbqa

National Caterers Association, 860 Bay St., Staten Island, NY 10304, (800) 622-0029

National Pasta Association, 2101 Wilson Blvd., #920, Arlington, VA 22201, (703) 841-0818

National Restaurant Association, 1200 17th St., NW, Washington, DC 20036-3097, (800) 424-5156, (202) 331-5900, fax: (202) 331-5950, www.restaurant.org

Specialty Coffee Association of America, 1 World Trade Center, #1200, Long Beach, CA 90831-1200, (562) 624-4100, fax: (562) 624-4101, coffee@scaa.org, www.scaa.org

Consultants and Other Experts

Robert S. Bernstein, Esq., Bernstein Bernstein Krawec & Wymard P.C., 1133 Penn Ave., Pittsburgh, PA 15222, (412) 456-8100, fax: (412) 456-8135, bob@bernstein law.com

David Cohen, President, Expense Reduction Group Inc., 7777 Glades Rd., #317, Boca Raton, FL 33434, (561) 852-1099, ext. 20, erg5@aol.com

Allen Konopacki, Ph.D., trade show consultant, Incomm Research Center, 1005 N. LaSalle Dr., #100, Chicago, IL 60610, (312) 642-9377, www.tradeshowresearch.com

Credit Card Services

American Express Merchant Services, (888) 829-7302, www.americanexpress.com

Discover Card Merchant Services, (800) 347-6673

MasterCard, (914) 249-4843, www.mastercard.com

Visa, (800) VISA-311, ext. 96, www.visa.com

World Cash Providers LLC, electronic transaction products: 3649 W. Beechwood Ave.,Fresno, CA 93711, (800) 257-CASH, fax: (559) 261-2012, www.worldcash providers.com

XtraCash ATM, National Bankcard Association, 8787 Complex Dr., #400; San Diego, CA 92123, (800) 217-8110, (619) 712-1649, fax: (619) 712-1617, www.xtracash.com

Equipment Suppliers

AEI Music Network Inc., music services, sound, and video systems: 900 E. Pine St., Seattle, WA 98122, (800) 234-6874, (206) 329-1400, fax: (206) 329-9952, www.aeimusic.com

All A Cart Manufacturing Inc., custom-designed and manufactured carts, kiosks, and other custom vending vehicles: 700 N. James Rd., Columbus, OH 43219, (614) 237-3767, fax: (614) 237-7779, jjmorris@allacart.com, www.allacart.com

Barmate Corp., liquor control systems: 33 New Montgomery St., #210, San Francisco, CA 94105, (415) 543-7747, fax: (415) 543-7585, www.barmate.com

Bevinco, liquor inventory systems: 250 Consumers Rd., #1103, Toronto, ON, CAN M2J 4V6, (888) 238-4626, (416) 490-6266, fax: (416) 490-6899, barry@bevinco.com, www.bevinco.com

Bunn Commercial Products, coffee-making equipment: P.O. Box 3227, Springfield, IL 62708, (800) 637-8606, www.bunnomatic.com

Consolidated Plastics Co., Inc., commercial matting: 881 Darrow Rd., Twinsburg, OH 44087, (800) 362-1000

EquipCo, used food-service equipment sales and installation: P.O. Box 543, Cederhurst, NY 11516, (888) 571-7100, www.equipco-corp.com

Fetco Corp., beverage service equipment: 640 Heathrow Dr., Lincolnshire, IL 60069-0199, (847) 821-1177, fax: (847) 821-1178

Globe Food Equipment Co., food slicers: P.O. Box 3209, Dayton, OH, 45401-3209, (800) 347-5423, (937) 299-5493, fax: (937) 299-4147, www.globe-food.com

Grindmaster Corp., beverage systems, coffee makers, espresso machines, tea equipment, grinders: 4003 Collins Ln., Louisville, KY 40245, (800) 695-4500, (502) 425-4776, fax: (502) 425-4664, (502) 425-4776

Hollowick Inc., liquid candle lamps and lamp fuel: 316 Fayette St., Manlius, NY 13104, (800) 367-3015, (315) 682-2163, fax: (315) 682-6948, www.hollowick.com

Howard Co., menu systems, point-of-purchase displays, visual merchandising systems: 1375 N. Barker Rd., Brookfield, WI 53045, (800) 782-6222, (414) 782-6000, fax: (414) 782-6515, www.mainstreetmenus.com

Rapids Wholesale Co., restaurant and bar equipment, commercial food-service supplies: 1011 Second Ave. SW, Cedar Rapids, IA 52404, (800) 472-7431, www.4rapid1.com

Renato Specialty Products Inc., display cooking equipment including brick ovens and rotisseries: 2775 W. Kingsley Rd., Garland, TX 75040, (800) 876-9731, (972) 864-8800, fax: (972) 864-8900, www.renatos.com

Plymold Seating, food-service furniture: 615 Centennial Dr., Kenyon, MN 55946, (800) 789-5111, fax: (507) 789-8315, www.plymold.com

SerVend International, ice and beverage systems: 2100 Future Dr., Sellersburg, IN 47172, (812) 246-7000, fax: (812) 246-9922, www.servend.com

Sicom Systems Inc., PC point-of-sale equipment: 4140 Skyron Dr., Doylestown, PA 18901, (800) 547-4266, fax: (215) 489-2769, www.sicom-systems.com

Skorr Products Inc., catering equipment: 90 George St., Paterson, NJ 07503, (973) 523-2606, fax: (973) 523-3009, www.skorrproducts.com

The Trane Company, heating, ventilation, air conditioning equipment: 2550 Corporate Exchange Dr., #200, Columbus, OH 43231, (614) 899-5100, fax: (614) 882-5456, www.trane.com

21st Century Carts and Kiosks Inc., cart and kiosk supplier, coffee cart consultants: 9930-21 Sailview Ct., Fort Myers, FL 33905, (941) 694-7574, fax: (941) 693-7670, 21stcentury@chesulwind.com, www.yhp.com/21stcentury/index.htm

Franchise and Business Opportunities

Atlanta Bread Co. (upscale bakery and cafe), 1200 A Wilson Wy., #100, Smyrna, GA 30082, (800) 398-3728, (770) 432-0933, fax: (770) 444-1991, www.atlanta bread.com

Cinnamon Street Bakery & Coffee Co. (bakery and coffeehouse), Orion Food Systems, 2930 W. Maple Ave., Sioux Falls, SD 57107, (800) 336-1320, (605) 336-6961, fax: (605) 336-0141, www.orionfoodsys.com

Cousins Subs, N83 W13400 Leon Rd., Menomonee Falls, WI 53051, (800) 238-9736, (414) 253-7700, fax: (414) 253-7705, www.cousinssubs.com

Donatos Pizza, 935 Taylor Station Rd., Columbus, OH 43230, (800) 366-2867, (614) 864-2444, fax: (614) 575-4480

Love's Barbeque Restaurants, Custom Food Franchise Group Inc., 270 N. Canon Dr., 3rd Floor, Beverly Hills, CA 90210, (888) 79-LOVES, (310) 247-1588, www.lovesb bq.com

Manchu Wok (quick-service Chinese restaurant), 816 S. Military Trail, Bldg. 6, Deerfield Beach, FL 33442, (800) 423-4009, (954) 481-9555, fax: (954) 481-9670, www.manchuwok.com

PJ's Coffee & Tea Co. (coffeehouse), 500 N. Hagan Ave., New Orleans, LA 70119, (800) 860-9963, (504) 486-2827, fax: (504) 486-2345, www.pjscoffee.com

Inventory and Supply Sources

Anchor Food Products Inc., appetizers and snack foods: 555 Hickory Farm Ln., P.O. Box 2518, Appleton, WI 54913-2518, (800) POPPERS, fax: (920) 997-7609, www.anchorfoods.com

Daniele Imports Inc., equipment, chocolate, food, beverages, other supplies: 1150 University Ave., Rochester, NY 14607, (800) 298-9410, fax: (716) 461-2234, www.diespresso.com

Great American Stock, food photography: 521 Quantum Rd. NE, Rio Rancho, NM 87124-4507, (800) 624-5834, (505) 892-7747, fax: (505) 892-7713, www.greatamericanstock.com

Insulair Inc., insulated paper cups: 529 Commercial St., #200, San Francisco, CA 94111, (415) 989-CUPS, fax: 415-781-CUPS, info@insulair.com, www.insulair.com

Neighbors Coffee, specialty coffees, gourmet hot chocolate, instant cappuccino mixes, gourmet teas: P.O. Box 54527, Oklahoma City, OK 73154, (800) 299-9016, (405) 236-3932, fax: (405) 232-3729, www.neighborscoffee.com

Rich Products Corp., food products, including meats, desserts, toppings, breads, and rolls: 1150 Niagara St., Buffalo, NY 14213, (800) 356-7094, www.richs.com

Stockpot, fresh refrigerated soups, sauces, entrees, gravies, and side dishes: 18211 NE 68th St., Bldg. E-120, Redmond, WA 98052, (800) 468-1611, (425) 885-0779, fax: (425) 867-5150, www.stockpot.com

Sweet Street Desserts, frozen gourmet desserts: 722 Hiesters Ln., Reading, PA 19605, (800) SWEET-97, www.sweetstreet.com

SYSCO Corp., national distributor of food-service products: 1390 Enclave Pkwy., Houston, TX 77077-2099, (281) 584-1390, fax: (281) 584-4070, www.sysco.com

Magazines, Books, and Publications

Atlantic Publishing, books, videos, training materials, tools, and software for the food-service and hospitality industries: P.O. Box 2075, Ocala, FL 34478-2075, orders:

(800) 541-1336, fax: (352) 622-5836, customer service: (800) 555-4037, atlpub@atlantic-publishing.com, www.atlantic-publishing.com

Bakery Production and Marketing, 1350 E. Touhy Ave., Box 5080, Des Plaines, IL 60017-5080, (847) 635-8800, fax: (847) 390-2445

Beverage World, 226 W. 26th St., 10th Fl., New York, NY 10001, (212) 822-5930

Bread and Butter, National Restaurant Association, 1200 17th St. NW, Washington, DC 20036, (202) 331-5900, www.restaurant.org

Cooking for Profit, CP Publishing Inc., 104 S. Main St., 7th Fl, Fond du Lac, WI 54935, (414) 923-3700

Cornell Hotel & Restaurant Administration Quarterly, 185 Statler Hall, Cornell University, Ithaca, NY 14853, (888) 437-4636, (212) 633-3730, www.sha.cornell.edu/pubs

Fresh Cup magazine, P.O. Box 82817, Portland, OR 97282-0817, (503) 224-8544

Menu Pricing (Restaurant Manager's Pocket Handbook Series) by David V. Pavesic, Lebhar-Friedman Books, 1999

Menu Pricing & Strategy by Jack E. Miller, John Wiley & Sons, 1997

Nation's Restaurant News, Lebhar-Friedman Inc., 425 Park Ave., New York, NY 10022, (800) 944-4676, (800) 447-7133, www.lf.com

Pasta Journal, 2101 Wilson Blvd., #920, Arlington, VA 22201, (703) 841-0818

Pizza Today, P.O. Box 1347, New Albany, IN 47151, (812) 949-0909, www.pizzatoday.com

QSR: the Magazine of Quick Service Restaurant Success, 4905 Pine Cone Dr., #2, Durham, NC 27727, (800) 662-4834, (919) 489-1916

Restaurant Business, 355 Park Ave South, New York, NY 10010, (212) 592-6264, fax: (212) 592-6499, scouture@billcom.com, www.restaurantbiz.com

Restaurants and Institutions, 1350 E. Touhy Ave., Box 5080, Des Plaines, IL 60017-5080, (847) 635-8800, fax: (847) 390-2080, www.rimag.com

Restaurant Economic Trends, National Restaurant Association, Research Department, 1200 17th St. NW, Washington, DC 20036, (202) 331-5900, www.restaurant.org

Restaurant Hospitality, Penton Publications, 1100 Superior Ave., Cleveland, OH 44114, (216) 696-7000, www.penton.com

Restaurants USA, National Restaurant Association, 1200 17th St. NW, Washington, DC 20036, (202) 331-5900, www.restaurant.org

Special Events Magazine, 23815 Stuart Ranch Rd., Malibu, CA 90265, (800) 637-5995, (310) 317-4522, www.specialevents.com

Specialty Retail Report, 293 Washington St., Norwell, MA 02061, (800) 936-6297

Trademark: Legal Care for Your Business and Product Name, by Kate McGrath and Stephen Elias, Nolo Press, (800) 992-6656

Music Licensing Agencies

American Society of Composers, Authors, and Publishers, 2690 Cumberland Pkwy., #490, Atlanta, GA 30339, (800) 505-4052, (770) 661-3470, fax: (770) 805-3410, www.ascap.com

Broadcast Music Inc., 10 Music Sq. East, Nashville, TN 37203, (800) 925-8451, fax: (615) 401-2265, www.bmi.com

SESAC Inc., 421 W. 54th St., New York, NY 10019, (800) 826-9996, (212) 586-3450, fax: (212) 489-5699, www.seasac.com

Successful Food-Service Business Owners

Borealis Breads, Jim Amaral, founder, Portland Public Market, Portland, ME 04101, (207) 228-2038

Cuisine Unlimited, Maxine Turner, 4041 S. 700 East, Salt Lake City, UT 84107, (801) 268-2332, fax: (801) 268-2992

Key Lime, Inc., Kenny Burts, P. O. Box 2002, Smyrna, GA 30081, (707) 333-0043, fax: (770) 436-4280

Meyerhof's & Cuisine M, Ann Crane, owner, 17805 Sky Park Cir., Ste. A, Irvine, CA 92614, (949) 261-6178, fax: (949) 833-2833, www.meyerhofs.com

River City Billiards, Anthony Allen and Michael Greene, partners, 87 Washington St., Haverhill, MA 01832, (978) 372-6988

RV's Seafood Restaurant, Robert V. Owens, III, owner, P.O. Box 935, Nags Head, NC 27959, (252) 441-4963

Viva La Pasta, Rebecca Swartz, owner, 4100 University, #104, West Des Moines, IA 50266, (515) 222-9444

Glossary

Arabica beans: a kind of coffee bean that produces superior-quality coffees that possess the greatest flavor and aromatic characteristics.

Barista: a master espresso maker; a Barista is an expert in both coffees and brewing.

Bump-out: a term describing the addition of a food-service area to a gas station or convenience store in a configuration that resembles a sunroom or porch on a house.

Corrosion-resistant materials: materials that maintain their original surface characteristics under prolonged influence of the food they're in contact with, the normal use of cleaning compounds and bactericidal solutions, and other conditions of use.

Cupping: professional coffee bean tasters use this process to determine the quality, acidity, and aroma of beans for selection in their blends. The cupping process involves steeping the coffee beans, as with tea leaves, and then smelling and tasting the brew at different temperatures as it cools.

Dayparts: a restaurant-industry term that refers to various meal cycles that occur throughout the day, typically breakfast, lunch, dinner, and early evening.

Dramshop laws: statutes that impose a special liability on those in the business of producing, distributing, and selling or serving alcoholic beverages to the public.

Dual-branding: when two or more brand-name operations are located in the same retail space, working cooperatively; also called *dual-concepting*.

Food-contact surfaces: those surfaces of equipment and utensils with which food normally comes in contact and those surfaces from which food may drain, drip, or splash back onto surfaces normally in contact with food.

Front of the house: the area of a restaurant that the customer visits, including the customer service area, bar, and dining room.

HVAC: an acronym for Heating, Ventilation, and Air Conditioning.

Kitchenware: all multiuse utensils other than tableware.

Meat jobber: a distributor that specializes in portion-controlled meat supplies for restaurants.

Peel: a long-handled, shovellike implement used by bakers in moving bread, pizza, etc., about an oven.

Robusta beans: generally, supermarket-grade coffee beans that can be grown in any tropical or subtropical climate and are cultivated for their ease as opposed to their taste; a specialty coffeehouse should stick to serving premium-grade arabica beans in its blends.

Safe materials: articles manufactured from or composed of materials that may not reasonably be expected to result, directly or indirectly, in their becoming a component or otherwise affecting the characteristics of any food.

Single-service articles: any tableware, carryout utensils, or other items that are designed and constructed for one-time, one-person use.

Tableware: eating, drinking, and serving utensils for table use such as flatware, including forks, knives, spoons, bowls, cups, serving dishes, and plates.

Utensil: any tableware and kitchenware used in the storage, preparation, conveying, or serving of food.

Index